CONVEYANCING

Questions and Answer Series

Series Editors   Margaret Wilkie and Rosalind Malcolm

'A' Level Law
Company Law
Conveyancing
EC Law
Employment Law
Equity and Trusts
Family Law
Jurisprudence
Land Law
Landlord and Tenant
Law of Contract
Law of Evidence
Law of Torts

Other titles in preparation

LAW QUESTIONS & ANSWERS Q&A

CONVEYANCING

ROBERT M. ABBEY
BA, Solicitor, Licensed Conveyancer, Principal Lecturer in Law,
University of Westminster

MARK B. RICHARDS
LLB , Solicitor, Senior Lecturer in Law, University of Westminster

BLACKSTONE
PRESS LIMITED

First published in Great Britain 1995 by Blackstone Press Limited, 9-15 Aldine Street, London W12 8AW. Telephone: 0181-740 1173

© R. M. Abbey and M. B. Richards, 1995

ISBN: 1 85431 407 6

British Library Cataloguing in Publication Data
A CIP catalogue record for this book is available from the British Library

Typeset by Montage Studios Limited, Tonbridge, Kent
Printed by Bell & Bain Limited, Glasgow

Contents

Preface

All too often after a conveyancing exam, a student will say, 'I worked hard, I thought I knew my subject but it just didn't come right in the exam'. This book seeks to address this common difficulty by identifying, and offering guidance on, ways of transferring the knowledge acquired during the conveyancing course into competent examination answers.

We think that part of the problem lies in the fact that conveyancing is an inherently practical subject. As such, a study of it differs in approach from other areas of previously studied substantive law. The technical rules of conveyancing are often complex and intimidating and of course have to be mastered – but that is not enough to succeed. The key to excellence in conveyancing is the ability to apply those rules in a practical context. We hope this book will go some way to achieve this aim.

Our thanks go to the staff of the Practice and Legal Services Division of the Land Registry for their assistance with the specimen registers of title and to Stat-Plus Limited for permission to reproduce its epitome of title form. Crown copyright is reproduced with the permission of the Controller of HMSO. The Law Society standard form of contract and the Standard Conditions of Sale are reproduced for teaching purposes only by kind permission of The Law Society and The Solicitors' Law Stationery Society Limited. We also wish to thank everyone at Blackstone Press, in particular Heather Saward and Will England.

Finally, a special note of thanks to Lesley and Alison for their support and encouragement during the writing of this book, and to Emily (6), Abby (4) and Harriet (1) for sustaining Mark with their fun and laughter.

Mark Richards
Robert Abbey
London
February 1995

To Alison and Lesley

Table of Cases

Table of Statutes

1 Introduction to the Book and its Format

In this chapter we will consider the following:

(a) Conveyancing, the subject: an overview in the context of assessment.

(b) Examination technique generally.

(c) Conveyancing and examinations in particular.

(d) Conveyancing and assessed coursework.

(e) Lastly, a few concluding words of wisdom which if nothing else you should commit to memory.

CONVEYANCING, THE SUBJECT: AN OVERVIEW IN THE CONTEXT OF ASSESSMENT

Conveyancing is the transfer of legal title to property – but of course by now this will be well known to you. You now need to apply your conveyancing knowledge to questions that you may encounter in your examinations. This book is here to help you in your endeavour. It is likely that you will benefit from a reminder of the foundations upon which conveyancing has been built. In a way, conveyancing is like Shakespeare's character of Autolycus in '*The Winter's Tale*', a 'snapper-up of unconsidered trifles'. Like this amiable rogue, conveyancing takes from here, there and everywhere. You should therefore reflect upon how conveyancing rests upon the three stanchions of land law, contract law, and equity and trusts. When you are faced with examinations you will have gone through your course and will perhaps be over-concerned with detail. It is therefore of benefit to just stand back a moment and consider the broader view, to give you the kind of holistic understanding of the subject that will help with your examination answers. Remember also that conveyancing concerns itself with several other areas of the law such as company and partnership law, succession, planning law and especially several parts of revenue law. It is this diversity that makes conveyancing a difficult subject to grasp. However, a brief look at the three main supports will help you grip the full perspective of this broad subject.

As you might expect, a strong understanding of land law is critical for success in conveyancing. If you are still unsure of some fundamentals of land law you will surely have trouble with conveyancing. If you are still in doubt about such matters as easements or restrictive covenants then we firmly suggest that you go back to your land law notes and refresh your memory of the salient points. We also suggest you look again at a suitable textbook, and recommend *A Practical Approach to Land Law* by Mackenzie and Phillips, 5th edn, 1994 (Blackstone Press) as a clear and direct guide to the fundamentals of this important buttress to conveyancing.

In the context of assessment, a clear understanding of land law is a fundamental prerequisite of conveyancing. Indeed, this is specifically stated by the Law Society in the standards for the Legal Practice Course. The precise guidance is that the course is based on the assumption that students will have prior knowledge and understanding of the nature of legal estates and interests, equitable interests, easements, covenants and mortgages, joint ownership and unregistered and registered title (including the registration of charges). Accordingly you will appreciate that there will inevitably be questions in examinations that will test not just your knowledge of the conveyancing process but also these foundations from land law on which conveyancing is built.

You will have seen from the Law Society's guidance that contract law is considered to be just as important for students of conveyancing as land law. It is assumed that students will have prior knowledge and understanding of formation of contract, formalities of written contracts, misrepresentation, and remedies for breach of contract. When you consider that conveyancing is about the transfer of title and that these transfers are in the main made by contract, then you will readily appreciate why contract law plays such an important part. Should you end up being a conveyancing practitioner, you will do well actively to maintain your knowledge of the fundamentals of contract law as you will regularly encounter transactions concerned with it. As you now know, each conveyance on sale will involve the actual preparation of a written contract. Indeed your land law will tell you that without a written contract containing all the terms of the agreement there is no deal! (Please look again at the Law of Property (Miscellaneous Provisions) Act 1989.) So, in these circumstances it is not difficult to anticipate questions in conveyancing that will examine your understanding of contract law as well as its application in conveyancing. However, it goes further than just the formation of valid contracts. You will also need to know about misrepresentation, and in particular remedies for breach of contract. It is clear that these areas are of particular interest to examiners and a thorough grounding in both topics is advised if you wish to do well in your conveyancing exam.

Then there is the translucent support subject of equity and trusts. This important stanchion to conveyancing is not so obviously relevant as land law and contract law, but it is nevertheless a pervasive element in conveyancing and certainly as far as assessment is concerned. Why is this? Frankly, it is because this complex area provides challenging questions that are just ripe for a conveyancing examination. For example, the whole topic of third-party rights is a fertile and attractive location for your examiner to find questions that will concern equity and trusts in the context of the conveyancing process. Co-ownership, especially, is the topic for the kind of challenging question beloved of examiners. You will therefore need to be absolutely clear on the law relating to trusts, and in particular trusts for sale. You will need to understand the differences between tenants in common and joint tenants and their relevance to joint ownership in conveyancing. Lastly, you will need to remind yourself about the equitable remedies that are available. It is one thing to understand their availability in theory, but it is another actually to apply them to a practical situation. Conveyancing will in practice be an area that will give rise to the application of those equitable remedies. This being the case, they will inevitably end up in conveyancing examination questions. You have been warned!

So, the key to understanding the nature of conveyancing in the context of assessment is to appreciate how it calls upon these various areas of the law. In doing so it brings together other parts of the law that you should have encountered and which you will now need to apply on a practical basis. You will need to be able to integrate these other areas into your knowledge and understanding of conveyancing. It means that you must abandon a discrete approach to learning and applying the law. Conveyancing requires you to blend your knowledge, and this will need to be displayed in your answers.

EXAMINATION TECHNIQUE GENERALLY

Now that you understand what is expected of you in a conveyancing examination it is appropriate to consider how you should approach the whole process. We will therefore consider the medium by which you are required to show your abilities, namely the examination. To help we set out below some hints and tips to enhance and improve your examination technique:

(a)   First of all, remember the mnemonic P.A.T. – Pause And Think. It is our experience that too often students see a question that triggers off a line of thought, and immediately they are away and writing! Always give yourself time to think about the answer required. Sometimes examiners will make questions look deceptively simple when in fact they are really quite demanding. Another examiner's trick is to set a question that is apparently about a particular topic when really a good answer requires you to consider more than one area. Therefore, never rush ahead without careful reflection. If it means writing less, then so be it. Students are sometimes misled into thinking that the length of their answer will earn them more marks. This is simply not so, and could militate against you when an examiner has to hunt through a lot of superfluous information to find what is actually relevant.

(b)   Know your tutor. Wherever possible, it is always a good move to try to detect the areas of interest shown by the tutors who will be responsible for your examination paper. Clearly, for some this will be almost impossible as some professional examinations are, of course, prepared by external examiners. This predicament will be considered subsequently. For those who can identify their tutor's areas of interest, they would be well advised to reflect upon the likelihood of just those areas appearing as a topic for the exam. If, as mentioned above, there is an external examiner setting the questions then really all you can do in those circumstances is try to assess the frequency of the appearance of certain topics to assist in your strategic approach to the examination.

(c)   What is topical? By this we mean, has there been a change in the law during the time of your conveyancing course? If so, this could very well end up as a topic for a question in your examination. Imagine for a moment that you are your tutor who is about to write your examination paper. You have had this responsibility for the last six years, and have in that time had to write at least 12 such papers when resits are taken into account. Each time you must produce something different and yet sufficiently demanding so as to be a satisfactory test of your students' knowledge and their ability to apply it to the question. Accordingly, if the law has changed it is one way in which you can come up with a novel question arising from a virgin topic that is going to really test your students' knowledge. It will also show whether or not they were paying attention in class as of course the change in the law will have been declared by you and will be so new as to be missing from all the textbooks. A recent example is the changes caused by the Law of Property (Miscellaneous Provisions) Act 1989. Questions set after that looked as if they were asking about the old law, while of course the examiner wanted to see if students were aware of the dramatic changes caused by the statute.

(d)   Matters for you to consider before the actual exam. Be sure you know when and where the examination is to be held. It is awful to see candidates arriving late, all flustered and confused simply because they did not check on the time and place for the examination. Go to revision classes. Do not miss the opportunity of asking your tutor to explain again any area that you are really not quite sure about. Remember to claim your entitlements. Many institutions will give extra time to students with special needs. If you are so entitled please note that this extra time will be granted only on request, so do ask. Seek help when necessary. Many students experience pre-exam nerves. This is an expected response to the stress of the impending examination, but if it becomes so strong that it interferes with your revision, seek help. Many institutions have support services that can help and that will get you back to the task in hand. Your other student colleagues will not as a matter of student honour ever admit to actually doing any revision, or indeed any work at all! Of course it is all bravado and bluster. You will have a revision plan and you must stick with it right up to your examination. Lastly, bear in mind what was last taught on the course. It is the case that the topic that was last taught can often form the basis for a question in the examination. The preparation of the examination paper could coincide with the preparation of the materials for the topic, and as a result it could subsequently appear in a question.

(e)   Know your examination type. Not all examinations are the same. The current vogue is for open book exams, but what exactly do your tutors mean by 'open'? Before getting anywhere near the time for the exam, make sure that you know exactly what you can and what you cannot take in with you. Also, exercise some discretion about what you choose to accompany you into the examination room. You have only a finite amount of time to write the exam, so you do not want to be shuffling through too many textbooks for your own good. A core text plus your own notes should in most circumstances be sufficient; a wheelbarrow full of the practitioner texts will only delay and confuse you. If you can take in books, please be aware that this does not mean you can relax on acquiring your own memory store of knowledge. You will not have the time continually to look up the answer to the question. Examiners will be aware that the books are available and will adjust the style of the question to take this fact into account. Use your textbook, and indeed your notes, to confirm your knowledge when you may be a little unsure. The book and notes should serve as a source of confirmation of your knowledge and not as the basis of it.

(f)   Appreciate the importance of good timing. All examinations are finite and will contain questions or parts of questions that have to be dealt with separately during the examination. This being the case, if you know the number of questions to be answered, always work out in advance the time you can allow for each. This may sound simple, but it is of critical importance. You may be tempted to go on writing on one question when you should really be concluding your effort so that you can devote sufficient time to all the questions. Some exams have extra reading time, some do not. Always allow for reading time if there is none allotted.

(g)   What to do on sitting down at your examination desk. As *The Hitchhiker's Guide to the Galaxy* rightly advises, Don't Panic! If you have completed your preparation properly you should be quietly confident, but if not, now is too late and panicking will not help. Remember P.A.T., and when confronted with the examination paper give yourself time to consider all aspects of the several points concerned. Look to see if there are marks shown for the various sections of the paper. If there are, this is a great help to you in deciding which parts require greater effort than others earning fewer marks. The marks apportionment should therefore reflect the time apportionment wherever possible. Read the preliminary instructions on the examination paper twice. This way you should take in some of the most important information, all of which is there for a reason. For example, a part or parts of the examination maybe compulsory; you should take note and complete your work accordingly. Always read these instructions before launching yourself into the body of the paper. As to the questions, read all of the paper from start to finish, so that you can then decide where your preferences lie. Lastly, remember to read all the accompanying documents with the examination paper. Conveyancing exams will typically rely upon specimen deeds and documents, all of which must be closely reviewed by you so that you can appreciate how they relate to the question concerned.

(h)   Answer style. It is probably the case that in most of your previous exams an essay would have been the appropriate way of answering almost all the questions encountered. Well, this is where that practice ends. Examiners will in many cases have a marking scheme that will include style marks for your answer. You should therefore understand that if the question is in the style of, say, an office memorandum, your answer must follow the same format. Similarly, if the question asks you for a note of your advice, somehow your answer must be constructed to provide exactly that. Style marks are very easy to pick up if you just use P.A.T. to allow you to prepare your answer in the format sought by the examiner. Do not resort to mere essay answers for all your questions as you will lose easy marks by doing so. One last hint in this section – remember that this is a practical subject where answers may need to be seen to replicate office procedures. In the office, time is money and so if you are recording, say, a meeting with the client, put in an estimated time record at the end. This will show the examiner that you understand how an office functions and the marker should be suitably impressed.

(i) Answer structure. What is an answer? Answer – something with a beginning, a middle, and an end. This may seem trite, but if you can noticeably structure your answers in this way the examiner will begin to note and appreciate your approach. The last thing an examiner will want to encounter is a long and indeterminate, rambling answer. When a well-structured answer is encountered it is a refreshing experience for the marker, who will respond positively to your effort. Get the marker on your side with this important element in your examination technique. This tripartite structure can be considered further:

(i) The beginning. This perhaps is the fundamental part of your answer. It is where you should grab the marker's attention by a tight, yet logical, introduction to the answer. Try at the very outset to show to your marker that you know what is expected of you and that you will be answering the question in full in the body of your answer. Try to indicate the nature of your answer by signposts, just as we did at the start of this chapter.

(ii) The middle. This must be where you demonstrate your knowledge and your application of it to the facts of the question. Elements of this process will be considered subsequently.

(iii) The ending is almost as important as the beginning. Try to leave your marker with a final impression of structure by ending with a paragraph, or at least a sentence, summing up and concluding the flow of your answer. Do not leave your marker with the impression that you stopped where you did simply because you ran out of time or things to say!

(j)   When dealing with conveyancing questions it is clear that, in the main, problem-type questions based on a transaction for a client will be the norm. This being so, when using the structure outlined above you could extend that approach in your answer by opening with a clear identification of the area of law involved followed by a more detailed statement of that area. You should then apply the law to the particular circumstances of the question and complete your answer with a conclusion that sums up your advice to the client.

(k)   Things to remember when in 'the middle' (see above). Always cite your authorities. In conveyancing, statute plays an increasingly pre-eminent role. Cases will always be relevant, but you will need to be aware of the major statutes involved. You should all be aware at least of s. 1 of the Law of Property Act 1925! Recent changes can arise from recent decisions. For this reason, always keep an eye on reported cases in the press. However, there is another reason for keeping up to date on recent decisions, and that is because they can form the basis of questions in your examination. As has been noted before, examiners will need to find new and original scenarios for their questions. This being the case, a recent decision is a heaven-sent opportunity for your examiner to adopt those facts for your question. Remember, if you cannot recall the name of a case do not ignore it, simply refer to it as 'in a reported case', or 'in a recent case' if you know it to be novel. Your time in the exam is limited and you may need to repeat long and awkward statute names in your answer. Try writing the Leasehold Reform and Housing and Urban Development Act 1993 a few times and you will understand the problem! To limit the time wasted in this way, if you know you will have to repeat the title after the first instance, insert a short form thus '(the LRHUDA)' and use it subsequently.

(l)   Check dates. In many cases dates are in a question for a significant reason. Has a time limit expired, is the application out of time, or has a priority period any time remaining? Always consider the chronology of the answer carefully as it may be the key element of the whole question. This is particularly the case for searches and the submission of registration applications to the Land Registry. Dates are also of importance in abstracts of title in unregistered land. Is the root of title at least 15 years old? Accordingly, never overlook the importance of dates in the question.

(m)   Write clearly. There is nothing more annoying to a marker than to have to spend too much time on a script trying to read an answer, let alone understand it. Leave lines between sections; it highlights the structure of your answer. Underline headings for the same reason. Start each answer on a fresh page and remember to number your answers. It all helps to get the marker on your side.

(n)   Lastly, if there are special circumstances that may have adversely affected your performance, make sure the institution has some evidence to explain your difficulties. If you were unwell a doctor's certificate is vital. Indeed, if you are aware of the circumstances before the exam make sure the institution knows as well. Always supply reliable evidence to back up your assertions. Simply your statement that you had a head cold will not do; third party support with written evidence is required.

CONVEYANCING AND EXAMINATIONS IN PARTICULAR

We have tried to show you good examination practice throughout the above section, and where necessary we have highlighted this about certain elements from within conveyancing. In this section we want to reinforce this with one or two further comments relevant specifically to conveyancing.

You will now appreciate from your own course how broad a subject conveyancing is, and how widespread the potential is for the content of the likely questions in your examination. Your first problem is therefore to make sure you remain relevant at all times during the writing of your answer. Keep focused on the problem and the requirements of a structured answer. It could be of use, if you can exercise this form of self-discipline, to just look again at the question halfway through your answer to make sure that you are keeping to wholly relevant material. Always bear in mind that you need to answer the question set by the examiner and not the question you had hoped might come up and for which you strategically revised. Furthermore, it is worth repeating that markers are not impressed by length; they are impressed by relevance and organisation.

Make sure you adopt a modern approach to the subject. The Law Society's National Conveyancing Protocol has, for good or ill, been around now long enough for it to appear in all your textbooks. Accordingly, be aware of the nature of the beast and how it differs from the traditional system. Little things can count a lot towards showing your grasp of the material, and this is just as true for the Protocol. Use 'buyer' in place of 'purchaser' and 'seller' for 'vendor', even if some of your older tutors still find it difficult to adopt the modern idiom. (No doubt there will be instances of this in this volume for which we readily apologise!) Adopt the vocabulary of the Protocol wherever possible and use it in your answers. Of course, that is not to say you should blandly accept the Protocol as a system without flaws; be ready to criticise the system, with examples and explanations, for in many ways it deserves that criticism. Lastly, in relation to modernity in conveyancing it is now probably stretching the case to refer to the system of registered land conveyancing as 'new' – after all, the main statute is the Land Registration Act 1925.

Remember that many of your tutors will teach across several subjects, and that in consequence you should expect questions that mix several topics. Co-ownership is a classic example of this, where a question will arise in conveyancing but where there will be valid information from family law, land law, and indeed equity and trusts. Combine all your knowledge and use it in the context of the conveyancing answer. Obviously you will not earn many marks by dwelling too long on the family law aspects, or on other aspects not seen as directly involved as conveyancing. Therefore your task is to balance the information from other topics to show sufficient understanding of the need sometimes to integrate your knowledge, while still being able to show clearly to the examiner your conveyancing proficiency. The point is that, in practice, your client will not turn up with a simple conveyancing problem all neatly placed in its own compartment. The client is far more likely to present to you a set of facts that could well stretch across several parts of the law, all of which could well lead to litigation and advocacy!

Specifically, what kind of question can you expect in a conveyancing exam? Well of course you will know that the subject itself is an intensely practical one. It will therefore come as no surprise that many questions you will encounter are going to be transactional. This means that you must solve theoretical but practical problems for a 'client' by using your own conveyancing knowledge. However, there will still be the opportunity for those of you who are die-hard essayists to reply to essay-style, theory and law questions. This is of course because many examiners will still include an example of just such a problem. To help you in your preparation for both types of question, you will find throughout the book examples of both, although the majority will be, like most modern examinations, of the transactional type.

CONVEYANCING AND ASSESSED COURSEWORK

If open book examinations are currently popular then the same must be true of assessment by coursework. It may not be the case that the whole of your course will be assessed by coursework, but at many institutions a good percentage of the final marks emanate from really quite demanding assessed coursework. If you are required to submit a piece of conveyancing assessed coursework, do bear in mind the need for a deeper approach to the answer than might otherwise be expected from an examination answer on the same topic. To facilitate this deeper consideration of the subject you should of course refer to further cases, other books on the subject and journal articles. It may well be the case that your instructions for your coursework include a word limit. If they do, stick to that limit. While you may not actually lose marks for going over the top, it will be taken by the marker as a probable indication of your inability to organise your material properly. The clear moral is, keep to word limits if only to display to the marker that you have carefully planned your coursework and that all your material has been organised concisely and within the constraints laid down in the assessment instructions. Coursework is set, *inter alia*, to see if you can self-manage your time. It requires you to set your own agenda for the completion of the set task. You must decide on how much time to devote to the coursework and the direction it must take. One thing is clear, however, you should always submit your effort in word-processed or typewritten form. The medium is the message. If it looks good the contents will be good, or at least that is the theory. List all your sources at the end of your paper and make sure your bibliography properly reflects the full extent of your researches. For that is the nature of the exercise; you must make your own research stand out in your answer and highlight to the marker that you have not simply read the suggested textbook for the course. Good marks can be obtained only if you have read around the subject and found further texts and articles on the particular subject area concerned.

LASTLY, A FEW CONCLUDING WORDS OF WISDOM WHICH IF NOTHING ELSE YOU SHOULD COMMIT TO MEMORY

First of all, remember that the answers we have provided are not model answers but are our attempts to provide suggestions of what we consider to be commendation or distinction level answers. If you feel that you could have presented the material in a more efficient manner for any particular question, have the courage of your convictions and write the answer in your own style.

P.A.T. (Pause And Think) remains our key piece of advice for all of your time in the examination room. Remember, a moment or two of careful reflection can be all that is necessary to allow you to integrate all the random thoughts and recollections running around in your mind that will come together as your answer. Give yourself the time to put together a coherent and structured answer – it will make all the difference to your performance generally.

Try to emulate our start to this chapter by listing at the beginning of your answer the bare bones of your structure. It grabs the attention of your marker immediately and, on the assumption that you are on the right lines, he or she will be on your side for the rest of the marking session. The use of these early signposts will be a refreshing change and will help your attempt to stand out from all the others in the marker's looming tower of scripts.

Be aware of the importance of time management. If marks are shown on the paper for each section of it, work out immediately the amount of time you need to devote to each section in the same proportions as the marks are allocated. If marks are mentioned, allocate the time in proportion to the number of questions on the paper. Stick closely to your timetable and try not to overshoot your time limits. Remember, the next answer you write may turn out to be a rich source of marks for you, but if you run out of time you will be limiting the possibility of further marks.

Lastly, good luck with all your examinations; but, frankly, if you prepare properly luck will not be an important factor in your success.

2 Registered and Unregistered Land: Taking Instructions

INTRODUCTION

The two land systems, registered and unregistered, will of course be familiar to you from your land law studies. They are, however, of such fundamental importance to an understanding of conveyancing that you will inevitably review them again at the start of your conveyancing course. You will reconsider in particular the principles of land registration, and you should expect to receive examination questions that test your core knowledge in this area. Question 2 below is just such an example.

Third party rights and their means of protection feature prominently in this part of the conveyancing syllabus and are popular with examiners. They crop up time and time again in examination questions, and in different contexts at that. Consider, for example, Question 4 in this chapter and Question 1 in Chapter 3 dealing with the draft contract. Overriding interests are a particular favourite when it comes to problems concerning registered land. The possibility of unlawful occupiers and the necessity for vacant possession on completion are of constant concern to the conveyancer, and there is much case law on the subject.

Whereas third party rights appeal to the examiner, the topic 'Taking instructions' is normally well-liked by you, the conveyancing student. This could be because it is your first contact with a 'client', and on a vocational course like the Legal Practice Course, the initial mock-interview may well be the first time you have actually *felt* like a solicitor advising a client. Most students seem to enjoy the experience ('learning by doing') and usually say they learn a lot from it. If this applies to you, the opportunity of tackling a question on this topic could be just up your street. If you see a question and like the look of it, why not answer it first and get some early marks under your belt?

Do remember that taking instructions is not just a fact-gathering exercise. Of course, you should be seeking to obtain as much information as possible to carry out the whole transaction, but your client will also need advice and help with important decisions, whether they be financial or otherwise. For example, the client may want guidance on the types of survey available, or the different methods of co-ownership. Some students (and practitioners!) find it beneficial to prepare and learn a check-list of all the key points which might be discussed at the initial interview; note the word 'may' though – your advice must always be relevant.

The client's initial instructions may reveal professional conduct matters, and you should be ready for them. If the examiner wants to test your knowledge and understanding of the rules about client care or acting for more than one party, then a taking instructions type question is the perfect vehicle. You will note that these issues are discussed in the answers below. Other topics of a pervasive nature will also feature at the taking instructions stage, for example, the Financial Services Act 1986, mortgage interest relief in relation to mortgage advice, and the possibility of the proceeds of sale attracting capital gains tax (CGT).

QUESTION 1

Emily Douglas has recently instructed you to act for her on the sale of Appletree Cottage, a detached property with grounds of just under one hectare. The conveyancing partner in your firm acted for her when she purchased the property in 1989, and remembers that she was quite fortunate at the time to secure such a large mortgage with the Cornshire Building Society.

Emily is a senior travel guide and spends much of the year 'on the road' conducting guided tours of Great Britain and Ireland. She owns another house in London.

Emily has told the conveyancing partner that Appletree Cottage is in fairly poor condition and there are signs of dry rot in the study. She had some woodworm and damp treatment carried out a few years ago and believes there may be some guarantees somewhere.

Emily borrowed about £3,000 from her bank last year to finance the installation of central heating at Appletree Cottage. She thinks the bank may have a second charge.

The purchaser is Abby Ward, whose father is an established client of the firm. Abby would like you to act for her as well as Emily in order to speed things along and also, it is hoped, to save on costs.

Emily has an appointment to see you tomorrow. What further information will you require from Emily and what advice will you give her?

Commentary

There are two distinct parts to this question: the first relates to information, the second to advice; and the preferred answering approach would be to deal with each part separately.

The first part of the question is essentially a fact-gathering exercise. It appears on the face of it to be quite straightforward, but to gain high marks you will have to pay close attention to the detail of the question. If you request irrelevant information (e.g. a plan) you are likely to be penalised by the marker.

As far as the second part is concerned, relevance again is the key to a successful answer. There are obvious areas of advice which must be covered – such as the professional conduct rule against acting for both parties – but other more tactical issues should not be overlooked. For instance, given the slump in house prices in the early 1990s, the possibility of Emily finding herself with 'negative equity' should be contemplated, and this is explained in the suggested answer below.

You will notice the reference to 'hectare' in the first paragraph, and this should immediately alert you to the probable inclusion of a CGT point. Why else would it be mentioned?

Suggested Answer

Before advising Emily on her sale we would seek from her as much relevant information as possible. This will prevent us from overlooking important matters, and should enable us to give full and proper advice at an early stage.

The following information will be required from Emily:

(a)   Full names and address of Emily, together with home and work telephone numbers.

(b)   The agreed price.

(c)   Confirmation of the full address of the property and whether it is freehold or leasehold. If leasehold, ask Emily for the last receipt for payment of rent and buildings insurance details (if arranged by the landlord).

(d)   Details of the mortgage with Cornshire Building Society, including the address of the branch and the mortgage account number. These details may be apparent from the firm's old file relating to Emily's purchase of Appletree Cottage. We shall need to request the deeds on loan from the Society and request a note of the outstanding balance.

(e)   Details of the mortgage to the bank (if any). An inspection of the title will establish for certain whether a legal charge has been registered by the bank.

(f)   Whether anyone else, apart from Emily, is living in the property and, if so, whether that person has made any financial contribution towards its purchase or any subsequent improvement. It may be necessary for us to procure that person's consent to the sale proceeding.

(g) Details of any estate agents who may have arranged the sale, and the buyer's solicitors (if known).

(h) Whether Abby has paid a preliminary deposit to the estate agents. If so, this must be taken into account by us in our completion statement.

(i) Details of any chattels to be included in the sale and whether Abby will pay extra for these.

(j) Whether Emily intends to take with her any fixtures. If so, they must be specifically excluded in the contract of sale, otherwise they will be deemed to be included. We could ask Emily to complete the fixtures, fittings and contents form.

(k) Does Emily have a completion date in mind? Has this been discussed with Abby?

(l) Have any other terms been agreed between Emily and Abby?

(m) Whether Emily is intending to buy another property and if so, is it dependent on the sale of Appletree Cottage? If there is no related purchase, what are Emily's instructions regarding the net proceeds of sale on completion?

(n) Is there a chain of transactions? If the National Protocol is being used we shall require Emily's authority to disclose information about the chain to Abby's solicitors.

We would advise Emily generally as follows:

We are told that Emily purchased Appletree Cottage in 1989 with the aid of a large mortgage. There also appears to be a second charge secured in favour of a bank. Given the fall in house prices at the beginning of the 1990s, she should be alerted to the fact that the price at which the house is now being sold could be less than the total amount owing on the mortgage or mortgages to which the property is subject. This situation is known as 'negative equity'. It may be the case that Emily has agreed a lower price than she would have liked because of the cottage's poor condition. The buyer's solicitors will on completion require an undertaking from our firm that the existing mortgage(s) will be discharged on completion, and clearly we would be unable to do this if a negative equity situation has arisen.

We can ascertain from the old purchase file the amount of the loan from Cornshire in 1989 (or perhaps Emily can tell us), but we shall need an up-to-date redemption figure from the Society itself before we can assess the true position. We should warn Emily that if she has negative equity, the cottage cannot be sold unless funds are available from elsewhere to repay the total indebtedness secured on the property.

Emily has indicated that the buyer would like our firm to act for her as well. Rule 6 of the Solicitors' Practice Rules 1990 prohibits a solicitor from acting for more than one party in a conveyancing transaction at arm's length, subject to certain exceptions. Abby's father is an established client of the firm (one of the exceptions), but we are not told that Abby is an established client. Even if she were, we must bear in mind that the exceptions would not apply where there is a conflict of interest. We would therefore advise that Abby must instruct another firm of solicitors to act for her.

As far as the poor condition of the property is concerned, we would advise Emily that this is a matter for the buyer under the maxim *caveat emptor*. Emily is under no duty to disclose physical defects, but she must be careful not to deliberately conceal a defect (e.g. the dry rot), otherwise this could amount to a fraudulent misrepresentation on her part that the property is not defective (see *Gordon* v *Selico Co. Ltd* [1986] 1 EGLR 71). We would ask her to locate the woodworm and damp guarantees because copies should be sent to Abby's solicitors with the seller's Property Information Form (or, if the National Protocol is not being used, with replies to preliminary enquiries).

Emily must be advised of the possible liability to CGT as a consequence of the sale. The Taxation of Chargeable Gains Act 1992 provides for CGT on any gain made on the disposal of a chargeable asset. The gain is exempt, however, where the sale is of a person's principal private dwellinghouse ('PPD'), including grounds of up to half a hectare. Prima facie, CGT will be payable on Emily's land in excess of half a hectare unless she can show that such land is necessary for the reasonable enjoyment of the dwellinghouse. Any chargeable gain can be reduced or eradicated entirely by setting against it her personal annual exemption for CGT.

It should be noted that the PPD exemption will apply only if the property has been Emily's only or main residence throughout her period of ownership. However, various periods of absence can be disregarded for this purpose and, from the given facts, Emily's time away on business would not appear to disqualify her from the PPD exemption.

She owns another property in London and we must advise her that the PPD exemption can apply to only one property. Accordingly, she must make an election as to which house the exemption will apply. It may of course be the case that Emily is selling the property for less than she paid for it, in which case there is no gain and no possibility of CGT!

The Law Society has issued Written Professional Standards on the question of the information on costs which solicitors should give to their clients. These standards are not mandatory but represent a safe and preferred method of practice. Accordingly, we would give Emily the best information possible about the likely costs of the sale, including VAT and all disbursements.

We must also have regard to r. 15 of the Solicitors' Practice Rules 1990, which deals with client care. Emily should be told who is to have the day-to-day conduct of the file, the name of the partner responsible for overall supervision and the name of the person in the firm whom she should contact if she has a problem with the service provided.

Other aspects of client care of which Emily should be advised are the future action to be taken to progress the matter, the likely timescale of the transaction and when we will next contact Emily. We should offer her a brief explanation of the conveyancing procedures and estimate how long before exchange of contracts and completion. It is a requirement that the costs and client care information should be confirmed to the client in writing.

QUESTION 2

(a) Outline the main differences between the registered and unregistered land systems. (6 Marks)

(b) Explain the nature and effect of registration of title. (15 Marks)

(c) Describe the form of a registered title. (6 Marks)

Commentary

Those of you who have acquired a sound and thorough knowledge of the land registration system and how it operates should relish this question and see it as an opportunity for good marks. Those of you whose feel for the subject is unsure should try to avoid it (although you may be in crisis if all questions are compulsory!). If you attempt it, you must remember to answer the questions as written, not the questions you wished had been written. Resist the temptation to write everything you know about registered land.

The subject matter is fundamental to a proper understanding of conveyancing practice in England and Wales, and consequently this type of question will crop up frequently. If you learn the relevant material thoroughly and structure your answer carefully, we can assure you it will pay dividends.

The question is in three sections and you will note that more marks are given for part (b), so naturally you should apportion your time to allow longer for this part.

Suggested Answer

(a)   The present system of land registration was introduced by the Land Registration Act 1925 in order to simplify conveyancing. The detailed rules of the system are to be found in the Land Registration Rules 1925 as amended.

The general aim of the system is to record details of the ownership and enjoyment of land (other than those discoverable on physical inspection of the land) on a central Land Register. A prospective purchaser of the land is then able to discover from an examination of the Register the nature of the existing interests affecting the land to be acquired. The State provides a guarantee as to the accuracy of the registered title and indemnifies those prejudiced by the operation of the system.

By contrast, title to unregistered land is not entered in a central register, but is contained in the title deeds of the land in question. These are held by the owner (or mortgagee if the land is mortgaged). A separate investigation of the title by the buyer's conveyancer is therefore required upon each occasion the land is purchased. The seller must supply the buyer with an abstract or epitome of the title which shows that the estate has been correctly conveyed during at least the last 15 years (s. 23 of the Law of Property Act 1969).

In unregistered conveyancing, the legal estate passes to the buyer when the deeds are handed over on completion. In registered conveyancing, the legal estate passes to the buyer upon completion of the post-completion registration of the buyer as registered proprietor.

(b)   Strictly speaking, it is not the land that is registered but the estate in the land, so there may be more than one title registered in respect of the same piece of land. For example, a freehold, a headlease and a sublease.

The titles capable of substantive registration in their own right are 'estates capable of subsisting as legal estates' (s. 2(1) of the Land Registration Act 1925). In practical terms this will be either a freehold estate of a fee simple absolute in possession, or a leasehold estate of a term of years absolute. It should be noted, however, that the following leasehold estates are not capable of substantive registration:

(i)   a lease with 21 years or less to run;

(ii)   a lease demised by way of mortgage with a subsisting right of redemption.

Unregistered titles are required to be substantively registered ('first registration') if the land in question falls within an area of compulsory registration. Since 1 December 1990, the whole of England and Wales has been an area of compulsory registration. Accordingly, certain transactions must within two months of completion be followed by an application for first registration. This is known as 'compulsory registration'. The transactions inducing first registration are:

(i)   a conveyance on sale of freehold land;

(ii)   a grant of a lease for a term of more than 21 years; and

(iii)   the assignment on sale of a lease having more than 21 years unexpired from the date of the assignment.

As well as compulsory registration, it is possible for an owner of registered land to apply for voluntary first registration. This is often done by developers of unregistered land wishing to sell each plot as registered land, or by owners of particularly complex unregistered titles who wish to simplify the job of proving title when they come to sell.

Upon receiving the application for first registration the Land Registry will investigate the unregistered title and allocate one of the following classes of title:

(i)   *Absolute*. This is recognised as being the most reliable and marketable title that exists. The only matters to which the proprietor is subject are those entered on the register of title (e.g. restrictive covenants, registered charges), overriding interests, if not beneficially entitled to the land personally, any minor interests of which the proprietor has notice and, if the estate is leasehold, all express or implied covenants and obligations in the lease.

(ii) *Possessory*. This class of title will be registered where the Land Registry are not satisfied with the documentary proof of ownership, and consequently the proprietor will be subject to any adverse interests in existence at the date of first registration. Typically, a possessory title is granted where the title deeds have been lost or the applicant's title is based on adverse possession.

(iii) *Qualified*. This is very rare. It has the same effect as registration with absolute title, save that the State guarantee does not apply to some specified defect.

(iv) *Good leasehold*. This has the same effect as absolute title, save that the proprietor is subject to any estate right or interest affecting the right of the landlord to grant the lease. Thus, unlike absolute leasehold title, the State guarantee does not extend to the freehold and any superior leasehold titles. Typically, this class of title will be granted where the Land Registry has not investigated and approved all superior titles.

There is provision in the Land Registration Act 1925 (as amended by the Land Registration Act 1986) for possessory, qualified and good leasehold titles to be upgraded in certain circumstances. Examples of these are the conversion of good leasehold to absolute where the superior titles are approved by the Land Registry, and possessory to absolute where the proprietor has been registered with possessory title for 12 years and is still in possession.

(c) The registered proprietor is issued with a Land Certificate by the relevant District Land Registry containing a copy of the Register. If the title is subject to a registered mortgage the Land Certificate is retained by the Land Registry and a Charge Certificate is issued to the mortgagee.

Each title is allocated a title number. The Register is divided into three parts:

(i) *Property Register*. This indicates whether the title is freehold or leasehold and, if the latter, it will give brief lease details. It also gives a short verbal description and refers to the Registry's filed plan. This plan is prepared by the Land Registry (based on the Ordnance Survey map) for use with the title in question. The land within the title is edged red and matters peculiar to the title may also be shown, e.g. blue tinting for a right of way.

(ii)   *Proprietorship Register.* This records the class of title (e.g. absolute) and the name and address of the registered proprietor. It may also contain entries protecting third party rights and restricting the power of the owner to deal with the land (e.g. a caution or restriction).

(iii)   *Charges Register.* This sets out all encumbrances subsisting at the date of first registration (sometimes by reference to a later schedule) together with all subsequent charges or encumbrances. Examples of these would be restrictive covenants, mortgages and leases.

QUESTION 3

RICHARDS ABBEY AND PARTNERS, SOLICITORS

INTERNAL MEMORANDUM

To   The Trainee Solicitor

From   The Conveyancing Partner

I have received instructions from Mr Justin Dean and Miss Sarah Caswell who wish to buy 10 Eldon Place, a Victorian terraced cottage, for £62,000. The price includes some furniture and fixtures and fittings, the value of which the clients believe to be about £2,000.

Justin and Sarah are first time buyers and are presently living in rented accommodation.

Sarah has £15,000 on deposit at her building society. The balance of the purchase price will have to be borrowed and the clients will want some guidance on this. They have agreed to share the mortgage outgoings and the costs of purchase equally.

Justin would like to work from home and is thinking of converting part of the property into an office.

My secretary has arranged an appointment for them to see you tomorrow. Please prepare a note of the advice you intend to give Justin and Sarah when you see them.

Commentary

This question is in the form of a memorandum from a partner, so the appropriate way to respond would be by reply memorandum in note form. An essay answer would be likely to lose you marks for inappropriate style.

The question is very specific when it asks what 'advice you intend to give ...'. It does not (as does Question 1) ask you to detail the information you will be seeking from the client (e.g. addresses, telephone numbers etc.). Accordingly, you should follow your principal's instructions and note only your intended advice.

There is a fair amount to cover so you cannot afford to go into too much detail in any one area, but allow yourself enough time to cover all the important points. For instance, do not spend too long on the finer distinctions of joint tenancies and tenancies in common at the expense of missing something as crucial as the survey.

Be relevant. Your advice should be tailored to meet the facts and you will lose marks for advice which is beside the point, because that will demonstrate an inability to differentiate according to your clients' circumstances. For example, you might decide to advise at length on the different categories of survey, but if you stop and think, there is really little point in going into great detail about a survey you will not be recommending!

Be practical. It is easy to overlook obvious matters like explaining how long the conveyancing process will take. First time buyers will always want to know when they can move in. How often does one hear the complaint, 'Our solicitor never told us it would take this long'? You will also note the practical matter concerning the giving of notice of withdrawal to the building society.

Two final points. First, notice the three 'pervasive' subjects mentioned in the suggested answer: professional conduct, financial services, and taxation. Never overlook the importance of these. Secondly, note the overlap between different parts of the conveyancing syllabus (e.g. inspection of the property is covered under searches) and other areas of the law as well (e.g. suggesting the clients should make wills).

Suggested Answer

RICHARDS ABBEY AND PARTNERS, SOLICITORS

INTERNAL MEMORANDUM

To   The Conveyancing Partner

From   The Trainee Solicitor

The clients require guidance as to the type of mortgage they will require, but we cannot be sure that they will even be successful in getting one. Obviously, we must advise the clients not to enter into a binding contract until their financial arrangements are in order, and any mortgage offer must be in writing and approved by the clients and ourselves.

In giving mortgage advice we must have regard to the provisions of the Financial Services Act 1986 which regulates the conduct of investment business. Generic advice as to the type of mortgage (e.g. pension mortgage as opposed to endowment mortgage) will not be caught by the Act, but advice that a particular lender should be used may fall within the definition of investment business if the mortgage is linked to an endowment policy. In such a case we must be authorised to conduct investment business (normally given by the Law Society) and comply with the Solicitors' Investment Business Rules 1990.

We must advise the clients on appropriate sources of finance such as banks, building societies or insurance companies. If the firm has an arrangement with a lender for the introduction of clients, this must comply with the Solicitors' Introduction and Referral Code 1990.

We must consider how much the clients need to borrow. The purchase price is £62,000. Sarah is contributing £15,000 so, assuming the clients have funds available to cover costs and disbursements (which we must check), the amount of the loan will be roughly £47,000. If the property is worth £60,000, the loan would be roughly equivalent to 78% of market value. In this event the clients should be advised that the lender is likely to require the additional security of a mortgage indemnity guarantee. This will cover the mortgagee's potential loss in the event of it failing to recover the full amount of the loan on a re-sale. The indemnity policy will incur a single one-off premium (normally several hundred pounds) which will be borne by the buyers through a reduction in the mortgage advance.

In addition, an institutional lender will usually only lend a maximum of three times the main bread-winner's salary plus once the other's salary. We must check that our clients' earnings meet this criterion, because if they do not, the purchase probably cannot proceed without a further injection of capital on their part.

What type of mortgage should the clients have? We would discuss those currently available and explain how they work, in particular the three most popular ones – repayment, endowment and pension – and work out the most suitable for our clients. The factors we would consider are the relative cheapness of the repayment mortgage, the availability of tax relief on a pension mortgage and, on an endowment mortgage, the risk that the policy proceeds may be insufficient to discharge the capital loan. Our clients have no dependants, so a mortgage linked to an endowment life policy is probably not appropriate. If either of them is self-employed or not part of a company pension scheme they should consider a pension mortgage. Otherwise, their best option would appear to be the ordinary repayment method which is generally the least expensive.

We would advise them on the availability of tax relief on mortgages used to assist in the purchase of a buyer's only or main residence. The rate of relief for the year ending April 1995 is 20%, but this will be reduced to 15% for the year ending April 1996. Where the lender is a major institution, the relief is normally dealt with under the Mortgage Interest Relief at Source scheme known as MIRAS. The borrower makes mortgage repayments net of tax and the lender recoups the balance direct from the Inland Revenue. The maximum principal sum on which mortgage relief can be claimed is £30,000, so it would not cover the entirety of the clients' loan.

Lastly, the clients must be advised that their home is at risk if they fail to comply with the terms and conditions of the mortgage. Accordingly, it would be sensible to ensure that the anticipated monthly repayments are not unrealistically high in proportion to the clients' income. We must also advise that the conditions of the mortgage offer will almost certainly preclude any business use at the property. This would thwart Justin's plans to work from home, although this would depend very much on their nature and extent. If in any doubt, Justin should be advised to seek an assurance in writing from the proposed mortgagee that his plans would not contravene the mortgage conditions.

There are two further points on the question of Justin's plans to work from home. He should be advised that any material change of use or alteration to the structure of the house may require planning permission. In addition, if part of the house is used *exclusively* for business purposes, he will lose his principal private dwelling exemption from CGT in respect of the part so used.

We would advise Justin and Sarah of the *caveat emptor* rule ('let the buyer beware'), which is particularly important here because the clients are buying a very old property. We would explain to them briefly the nature and effect of the three types of survey generally available: the ordinary valuation, the house buyer's report and valuation, and the full structural survey. In this case, given the age of the property, we would recommend, notwithstanding the additional cost, a full structural survey. The clients' mortgagee will want an ordinary valuation, so rather than incur two survey fees, the clients could ask the mortgagee to arrange the structural survey upon which they can then both rely (provided the mortgagee's surveyor is reputable!).

In view of the property's age the surveyor may recommend some remedial work, and the clients should be warned that the mortgagee might make a retention from the mortgage advance until the works have been carried out.

A prudent solicitor would always advise a buyer to have a survey, but Justin and Sarah should also be advised to undertake their own physical inspection of the property and its neighbourhood. Although we would raise pre-contract enquiries of the seller's solicitors, if does no harm for the buyers themselves to be on the look-out for potential problems like non-owning occupiers or undisclosed rights of way across the land.

The clients should be advised of the two ways in which the beneficial interest in the property can be held, namely either as joint tenants, where on the death of one the deceased's interest accrues to the other by survivorship; or as tenants in common, where either party's interest is capable of being disposed of *inter vivos*, or by will or intestacy.

A presumption of a tenancy in common will arise here because the parties are contributing to the purchase price in unequal shares. However, we should still advise the clients to record expressly in a separate trust deed (i) that they will hold as tenants in common, and (ii) what proportion of the beneficial interest is held by each of them. This should help to prevent any later disputes. You mentioned Sarah's capital injection of £15,000 and that both clients will share the costs of the purchase and mortgage outgoings equally, so I calculate their respective beneficial entitlements to be Sarah: 62.5% and Justin: 37.5%.

As the clients' shares can be given by will or pass on intestacy, we should strongly advise them to make wills.

They should appreciate that a deposit of 10% (sometimes less) of the purchase price will be payable on exchange of contracts. Presumably this can be provided by Sarah from her deposit account, but if the money is on long-term deposit she will need to give notice of withdrawal immediately if she is to avoid, or at least save on, interest penalties.

You mentioned that the clients are in rented accommodation. They will have to give notice to their landlord to terminate the tenancy and they should check the terms of their tenancy agreement. We should advise them not to give notice of termination, however, until they have a binding contract to purchase 10 Eldon Place; otherwise they could find themselves homeless.

A stamp duty saving may be possible if the purchase price is apportioned between the price for the house and the price for the chattels. *Ad valorem* stamp duty of 1% of the purchase price is payable where the price of the land exceeds £60,000, but no duty is payable where the price does not exceed £60,000. Moreover, no stamp duty is payable on the sale of chattels at all. You say the clients believe the value of the chattels to be £2,000. Provided this is a true valuation an apportionment can properly be made to bring the price of the house down to £60,000. Care must be taken, however, for if £2,000 represents an overvaluation of the chattels, the avoidance of stamp duty would amount to a fraud on the Inland Revenue both by the clients and ourselves. In this event the contract for the sale of the land would be construed as a contract to defraud the Inland Revenue and as such would be unenforceable by action (*Saunders* v *Edwards* [1987] 2 All ER 651).

Any reduction in the purchase price of the property should normally be reported to and first approved by the clients' prospective mortgagee. We should check the conditions of the mortgage offer carefully in this respect.

Lastly, we must give our clients appropriate advice regarding the likely costs and expenses of the transaction, including stamp duty, search fees and Land Registry fees. In addition, client care and complaints procedures should be adhered to, pursuant to r. 15 of the Solicitors' Practice Rules 1990.

Trainee Solicitor: time engaged 40 minutes.

QUESTION 4

Your firm has recently been instructed to act for Stuart Rush and his wife Harriet Rush in the sale of 'Saxifrage' and the related purchase of 'Bentley Lodge'. Your principal has passed you the two files from which you note the following:

(i) The sale price of Saxifrage is £175,000.

(ii) The purchase price of Bentley Lodge is £185,000.

(iii) the clients have an endowment mortgage on Saxifrage securing a loan of £120,000.

(iv) The clients have received a mortgage offer on Bentley Lodge of £130,000. There is a retention of £30,000 on the mortgage advance until essential repairs have been carried out to the roof and chimney stacks.

(v) The clients wish to complete the purchase before the sale as Harriet's mother lives with them and they wish to carry out the repairs before they all move.

(vi) The clients' bank has offered them a bridging loan of £30,000 to enable them to complete the purchase before the sale.

(vii) The bank will release the bridging loan only upon receipt of a solicitor's undertaking to pay the net sale proceeds of Saxifrage to the bank.

(viii) The estate agents' particulars relating to Saxifrage have arrived in this morning's post.

(a) What advice will you give your clients in respect of their proposed financial arrangements, and what factors should you consider before you give any undertaking to the bank?   (10 marks)

(b) Explain briefly whether Harriet's mother has an overriding interest within the meaning of s. 70(1)(g) of the Land Registration Act 1925, and what effect, if any, this may have on the sale.   (6 marks)

Commentary

The first part is an example of a conveyancing question that involves a simple calculation of figures (calculator not essential!), and it will assist you and the marker if you jot down a brief financial statement in your answer book before you start.

Conveyancing clients often arrive in the office armed with an inaccurate financial plan, and it is essential that you check their figures carefully. The obvious point must be made that every conveyancer should at the stage of taking instructions check that the client has sufficient funds available not only to complete but also to cover all costs and expenses. You will notice the question states that estate agents are involved, so their commission will obviously be payable on the sale.

The clients are selling and buying and the two transactions are dependent upon each other, so, even though the proposed completion dates are different, it is essential to synchronise exchange of contracts. If you hint in your answer at an exchange on one property before the other, the examiner will think you have misunderstood your clients' needs.

The question of the undertaking introduces another professional conduct issue, and one of critical importance to conveyancers. You should be aware that professional undertakings turn up time and time again in conveyancing exams, so be prepared for them.

The second part of the question is more academic in nature. There are only seven marks allocated so it is important to be concise in your answer.

Suggested Answer

(a) Before considering our advice, it may be helpful to prepare a brief financial statement:

	Sale price	175,000
less	mortgage redemption	120,000
	sale proceeds	55,000
	Purchase price	185,000
less	net mortgage advance	100,000
		85,000
	Sale proceeds	55,000
add	bridging loan	30,000
		85,000

At first glance the calculations appear to be correct, but a careful analysis of the clients' instructions will reveal that they have overlooked the following matters:

(i)   The amount required to redeem the Saxifrage mortgage will not be exactly £120,000. This is the initial loan and does not take into account any outstanding interest charges, administration fees or redemption penalties. We must obtain from the mortgagee an up-to-date redemption figure. (As the mortgage is an endowment rather than a repayment, the principal sum will not have been reduced.)

(ii)   We are told there are estate agents on the sale so the clients will be liable to pay their commission + VAT.

(iii)   The clients must pay 1% stamp duty on the purchase (£1,850).

(iv)   The clients must pay legal fees on the sale and purchase, plus VAT and disbursements (e.g. Land Registry and search fees). They must also pay their surveyor's fee.

(v)   The bridging loan will incur interest charges and probably an arrangement fee.

In the light of the above, the clients should be advised that the net sale proceeds of Saxifrage will be insufficient to repay the bridging loan. We cannot advise them to proceed unless they can increase their bridging loan or find additional funds. An alternative solution would be to negotiate a reduction in the purchase price of Bentley Lodge.

We would advise the clients that they will need to fund the 10% deposit on the purchase, payable on exchange of contracts. We could seek to utilise the deposit we receive on the sale (the sale contract would have to allow us to hold it as agent for the seller), but this would still leave a shortfall of £1,000. The clients would have to find the shortfall from their own resources or seek a further bridging loan. Alternatively, the owners of Bentley Lodge could be asked to accept a reduced deposit.

Saxifrage appears to be the clients' principal private dwellinghouse, but if this is not the case then they must be advised of their potential liability to CGT.

Lastly, we would advise the clients of their entitlement to tax relief on the interest element of their mortgage repayments. The maximum principal sum on which mortgage relief can be claimed is £30,000, and if the new lender operates Mortgage Interest Relief At Source (the MIRAS system) the clients will make their monthly repayments net of basic rate tax. A bridging loan is eligible for tax relief on the interest element of the loan (provided it is taken through a personal loan account and not by way of overdraft on a current account), but the point is of academic interest only as the mortgage is in excess of £30,000.

In the event of the bridging loan proceeding we must consider several matters before giving an undertaking to the bank. Breach of a solicitor's undertaking is professional misconduct and will result in disciplinary action.

    (i)   Can we trust the clients and are they creditworthy?

    (ii)   The clients must give us an express and irrevocable authority in writing to give the undertaking.

    (iii)   Our undertaking should be in writing and signed by a partner.

    (iv)   We must be sure that we can comply absolutely with the terms of the undertaking. To this end, the wording must be clear, unambiguous and wholly capable of performance by our firm.

    (v)   Are we satisfied that the anticipated net sale proceeds will be sufficient to discharge the bridging finance plus interest?

    (vi)   In our undertaking we would state the sale price and itemise the anticipated deductions (e.g. mortgage redemption, agent's commission, legal fees etc.) to calculate the approximate net proceeds of sale.

    (vii)   As the undertaking is one to pay money, we would make it clear in the wording that payment by us of the net sale proceeds of Saxifrage will be made only if and when the sale proceeds are received by our firm. This safeguards against the possibility of us never receiving the proceeds of sale (e.g. because of client bankruptcy), but still being obliged to repay the bank.

    (viii)   Ideally, the undertaking should not be given until after exchange of contracts. However, as the clients will require a synchronised exchange we would in practice give it shortly before the point of exchange provided there are no unresolved problems.

(b)   Overriding interests are interests which bind a transferee of registered land notwithstanding that (i) they are not recorded on the Register, and (ii) the transferee may have no actual knowledge of their existence.

The categories of overriding interest are laid down in the Land Registration Act 1925, s. 70(1), and paragraph (g) is relevant here. It encompasses, 'the rights of every person in actual occupation of the land or in receipt of the rents and profits thereof, save where enquiry is made of such person and the rights are not disclosed'.

Harriet's mother is clearly 'in actual occupation', but it should be noted that paragraph (g) does not apply to purely personal rights in the land, only proprietary interests which are capable of being overriding (see *Strand Securities Ltd* v *Caswell* [1965] Ch 958). Thus if Harriet's mother has contributed towards the purchase price of Saxifrage (or any subsequent improvement), she would have acquired a beneficial interest under a trust (a proprietary interest) which would be capable of protection as an overriding interest (see *Williams & Glyn's Bank Ltd* v *Boland* [1981] AC 487, where a wife contributed to the purchase price and became a beneficiary under a resulting trust of the land). If Harriet's mother has not acquired a proprietary interest in the property then, notwithstanding her occupation, she will not have an overriding interest.

Even if Harriet's mother has an overriding interest, it will be noted from a reading of paragraph (g) that her interest will be defeated if the proposed transferee/buyer of Saxifrage asks her what rights she has and she fails to disclose them. In order for this to occur the buyer must enquire directly of her. It is not sufficient merely for the buyer to raise an enquiry with the registered proprietors (see *Hodgson* v *Marks* [1971] Ch 892, *per* Russell LJ).

The mother's interest (if any) may also be defeated in another way, stemming from the fact that the property is held on trust for sale by two trustees. The house is registered in the joint names of her daughter and son-in-law, and so a sale by them as trustees would overreach any equitable interest she may have acquired, and in this event her right of occupation would cease (see *City of London Building Society* v *Flegg* [1988] AC 54).

Lastly, it should be noted that overriding interests do not apply to unregistered land, and so if Saxifrage has an unregistered title Harriet's mother is incapable of having an overriding interest under s. 70(1)(g). However, in this event, any equitable interest she may have acquired may still be protected if the buyer fails to inspect the property and is thus deemed to have constructive notice (see the rule in *Hunt* v *Luck* [1902] 1 Ch 428).

3 The Draft Contract

INTRODUCTION

The draft contract is an enduring favourite with conveyancing examiners and you can virtually guarantee a question on it in some shape or form. The classic approach is for the examiner to reproduce a defective draft and ask the student to amend and explain; Question 1 follows this line. Another popular technique is to present a set of facts, similar to those in Question 2, and ask the student to actually draft the contract. Standard forms of contract will normally be provided, but often you will be asked just to draft the Special Conditions.

Since the introduction of the National Protocol, the form of contract most commonly used is the Law Society standard form incorporating the Standard Conditions of Sale (2nd edition) (this is reproduced in Appendix 3); indeed this form must be utilised by the seller and buyer where the Protocol is adopted. Accordingly you would do well to familiarise yourself with the contents of the form, including the Standard Conditions. Fortunately these days it is unlikely that you will be expected to recite the Standard Conditions parrot-fashion, but it is vital that you at least know your way around them and understand the points they cover. This will help you not only on the topic of the draft contract but throughout the conveyancing course. The following Standard Conditions are of particular importance: 2.2 (the deposit); 3.3 (retained land on sales of part); 4.2 (proof of title); 4.5 (the transfer); 5.1 (responsibility for property pending completion), and 6 (completion).

A contract for the sale of part of land is more complex than a contract for the sale of whole, and an example of the type of question you might encounter is set out in Question 4. It is good practice to prepare and learn a check-list of the essential matters that may be relevant on a sale of part. Ask yourself the following questions: How will I describe the part being sold (a plan is nearly always essential)? What new grant of easements will the buyer need? What new reservation of easements will the seller need? What new covenants should be imposed? Will the seller's mortgagee consent to the sale?

Most universities and other teaching institutions are now adopting a more practical approach to their teaching of conveyancing. This is to be welcomed in a subject that is acutely practical in nature and which is normally studied after the substantive law subjects of contract, land law, and equity and trusts. Nevertheless, academic questions do play their part from time to time, and we have included an example in Question 3. Here you will need to exhibit an understanding of the relevant case law and present your answer in the style of an essay.

QUESTION 1

You act for Sandra Ince and Martin Robson, both of 24 Lady Jane Court, Blakey, Cornshire. They wish to buy with vacant possession a freehold house known as 19 Minster Yard, Blakey. They have agreed with the seller a price of £190,500 subject to contract. The price includes carpets, curtains and some items of furniture. You are also acting for your clients in their related sale of 24 Lady Jane Court.

The seller of 19 Minster Yard is the Reverend Giggs, rector of Blakey. He shares the house with his aged aunt, Connie Flowers.

19 Minster Yard is registered at HM Land Registry with absolute title under title number CL 58372. The registered proprietors are stated as the Reverend Julian Giggs and his wife Mildred Giggs. Up-to-date office copy entries do not reveal any restrictions in the proprietorship register and the charges register is blank.

Reverend Giggs has instructed Shark & Co. solicitors who offer the cheapest conveyancing service in town. They have sent you the attached draft contract (refer to Appendix 1).

List and explain fully any amendments you would make to the draft contract.

Commentary

This question is more difficult than it seems on first reading. A sound knowledge of conveyancing practice is required, not only in relation to the drafting of the contract, but also in other areas such as completion and the implied covenants for title. As we mentioned in the introduction, you will also need to know your way around the Standard Conditions of Sale. Moreover, good practical skills and a mastery of detail are essential if high marks are to be obtained. Notwithstanding all this, the question will suit many of you, especially those who thrive on attention to detail and adopt a methodical approach to their work. It will appeal also to those students who have already had some practical experience of conveyancing.

We cannot emphasise enough the importance of a careful reading of the question. You will see from the suggested answer that almost every fact in the question is relevant in some way or another. Notice that the purchase is with vacant possession. Notice the significance of the dependent sale transaction in relation to the special condition dealing with the time for completion. Notice that there are no restrictions in the proprietorship register, which tells you that Mr and Mrs Giggs hold the property as joint tenants not tenants in common. This is crucial because if you discuss tenancy in common considerations the examiner will know that, from an inspection of a registered title, you cannot distinguish one from the other.

Similarly, a weak answer might suggest that a plan should be attached to the contract as referred to in the property description. The reference to a plan is a red herring because the filed plan at the Land Registry is definitive and on the sale of whole of registered land a verbal description referring to the title number will be quite sufficient.

Mrs Giggs is shown in the office copies as a joint registered proprietor, so it is unlikely that she has transferred her interest in the property to her husband. You would not be penalised, though, for posing the question whether such a transfer is in the course of registration. However, if you do, you would also mention that such an application would have been revealed by the office copies, and the question is silent on this point.

Suggested Answer

(a)   There are some typographical errors. The buyer's name is Robson not Dobson, and the seller's address is 19 Minster Yard not 19 Minster Lane. The balance of the purchase price has been incorrectly calculated and should read £171,450.

(b)   The seller's full name as stated on the title register should be stated, not 'Reverend Giggs'.

(c)   Mildred Giggs is a joint registered proprietor, and on the face of it her name should be added as joint seller with her husband. As there is no restriction on the proprietorship register this indicates that Mr and Mrs Giggs hold (or held) the property as joint tenants rather than tenants in common. If Mrs Giggs has died then a copy of her death certificate will be required as evidence of Reverend Giggs's entitlement to her interest by survivorship.

(d)   Enquiry should be made of the aunt to establish whether she has any interest in the property, perhaps by a contribution towards the purchase price. As she is in actual occupation and the land is registered she may have an overriding interest by virtue of the Land Registration Act 1925, s. 70(1)(g). She should be asked formally to release any rights and confirm that she will vacate the property on completion. The following is a suggested form of wording:

> In consideration of your today entering into a contract with Julian Giggs for the purchase of the property known as 19 Minster Yard Blakey, I Constance Flowers agree to release any equitable interest I may have in the property, such interest, if any, being transferred to the proceeds of sale of the property. I also agree to vacate the property on or before completion.

If it transpires that Mrs Giggs is joined with her husband as co-seller then a sale to them as trustees would overreach any equitable interest Aunt Connie might have (*City of London Building Society* v *Flegg* [1988] AC 54). However, this case does not guarantee that the aunt will vacate! As a matter of good practice a release in the terms above should be sought.

(e)   The description is wrong. The alternative of leasehold should be deleted because we are told that the land is freehold. There is no need to refer to a plan (and it is unnecessary to attach one). The property description should read simply:

All that land known as 19 Minster Yard Blakey registered at HM Land Registry with title absolute.

(f)   The title number CL 58372 should be written in place of the words 'Conveyance on sale' and the alternative 'Root of title' should be deleted as the land is registered not unregistered.

(g)   Mr Giggs should sell in the capacity of 'Beneficial owner' not 'Legal owner'. If Mr and Mrs Giggs are to be joint sellers they would be described as 'Trustees' (although they could sell as beneficial owners if they both owned the whole of the beneficial estate). The importance of the seller's capacity is that, once incorporated into the purchase deed, it will determine the covenants for title that will be implied by virtue of s. 76 of the Law of Property Act 1925.

(h)   The completion date is not introduced until contracts are exchanged, when a specific date is inserted.

(i)   The contract rate of interest is unreasonably high because the Law Society interest rate is normally set at 4% above the base rate of one of the clearing banks. The effect of this clause is to put the rate at 8% above base! A fairer suggestion would be the Law Society interest rate for the time being in force (this can be achieved by leaving the clause blank – see Standard Condition 1.1.1(g)) or, say, 4% above the base rate of one of the clearing banks.

(j)   We are told that the price includes some carpets, curtains and items of furniture, and these should be itemised on an attached list (see Special Condition 3). The Law of Property (Miscellaneous Provisions) Act 1989, s. 2, requires all agreed terms to be incorporated into the contract, failing which the contract is rendered invalid. The buyer may also wish to consider an apportionment of the purchase price between the price for the land and the price for the chattels. This will bring about a small stamp duty saving because stamp duty is not payable on the cost of chattels.

(k)   Delete the second alternative in Special Condition 4 as the property is being sold with vacant possession.

(l)   In Special Condition 5 the latest time for completion is far too early where, as is the case here, the clients' purchase is being financed by the monies they are receiving on their sale. We are unlikely to receive the completion monies on the sale in time to pay over the completion monies on the purchase by 12 noon. Our clients would thus be in breach of contract and liable to pay Reverend Giggs interest on the balance of the purchase monies at the contract rate. Unless the clients' purchaser's solicitors can be persuaded to agree in the related sale contract a completion time of earlier than 12 o'clock (which is unlikely), we should insist on the deletion of Special Condition 5 so that the position is governed by Standard Condition 6.1.2. This provides for a latest completion time of 2 p.m. Alternatively, we could compromise at, say, 1.30 p.m. provided we ensure that the stipulated time in our related sale contract is earlier.

(m)   Delete Special Condition 6 and state that the deposit shall be held by the seller's solicitors as stakeholder. This is safer for the buyer because a stakeholder deposit must remain in the seller's solicitor's bank account until completion. It should thus be easily recoverable if the seller defaults.

If the deposit is held by the solicitor as agent for the seller then the agent is entitled to hand over the money to the seller before completion. In this event, if the seller defaults the buyer may have difficulty in recovering the deposit.

Alternatively, Special Condition 6 could be deleted and not replaced with anything, in which case Standard Condition 2.2.3 would govern the position. This provides for the deposit to be held as stakeholder unless the seller intends to use it as a deposit on a related purchase of a residence in England or Wales. The various options should be explained to the clients and their instructions sought.

(n)   Delete the final special condition, or at least qualify it. As drafted, the clause prohibits the buyer from relying on *any* representations, even replies to solicitors' pre-contract enquiries. A reasonable qualification to the clause would be the addition of the words, 'other than the written replies of the seller's solicitors to the pre-contract enquiries of the buyer's solicitors'. This is acceptable to most conveyancers.

(o)   Lastly, details of the parties' solicitors should be entered at the foot of the last page.

QUESTION 2

RICHARDS ABBEY AND PARTNERS, SOLICITORS

INTERNAL MEMORANDUM

To   The Trainee Solicitor

From   The Conveyancing Partner

Re our client Angela Dawkins: sale of 13 Augustine Way, Kerwick
I have acted for the above client for many years. Sadly her husband Paul died last month. Paul's will leaves everything he owns equally between his wife Angela and Paul's brother, Kevin, and we have been instructed to wind up the estate. My probate partner is dealing with this aspect.

Angela has decided to sell 13 Augustine Way and buy a two-bedroomed flat in Kerwick. The owners of the flat have secured a property to buy and the chain above them is complete.

A prospective buyer for 13 Augustine Way has been found. He is Andrew Peach of 25 Woodlands Road, Kerwick. His solicitors are Messrs Young & Price of 1A High Street, Kerwick (Miss P. Knight acting). The agreed price is £70,000 subject to contract, plus £500 for carpets and curtains. I have told Miss Knight that we intend to use the National Protocol although I have not yet confirmed this in writing.

The deeds to 13 Augustine Way are of course held by Angela's mortgagee.

I attach a photocopy of the title entries that I made after Mr and Mrs Dawkins bought the property back in 1990 (refer to Appendix 2).

As you know, I am away on holiday from tomorrow so please progress matters in my absence.

(a)   Explain the matters you would consider and what action you would take before drafting the contract.   (15 Marks)

(b)   Draft the contract using the Law Society Agreement for Sale.
                                                                        (10 Marks)

(c)   Draft a letter to the buyer's solicitors enclosing the draft contract and any other enclosures. Include in your letter any information or enquiries that you consider to be relevant.   (10 Marks)

Commentary

First of all, it is important to note the allocation of marks and apportion your time accordingly when answering the question. Secondly, the question takes the form of a memo from a partner in the firm and so the answer should also take the form of a memo.

The partner has told you that the National Protocol is being used, and this is a clear pointer to the matters you should be considering in answering parts (a) and (c). There is no substitute for actually reading and digesting the *current* edition of the Protocol. The word 'current' is stressed because various changes have been made since the inception of the Protocol. In particular, the original philosophy of the seller carrying out searches on behalf of the buyer has been reversed, and this shows how important it is to keep up-to-date with changes in conveyancing practice. Do not rely on out of date textbooks!

There is no restriction in the proprietorship register stating that the survivor of joint proprietors cannot deal with the property, so you should appreciate that Mr and Mrs Dawkins held as joint tenants and that Angela takes her late husband's share in the property by survivorship. The terms of his will are therefore not relevant.

Parts (b) and (c) require you to demonstrate good drafting skills, and remember that marks will be awarded for style as well as content. The drafting of the contract should be relatively straightforward provided attention is paid to the details of the transaction that you have been given. You will be provided with a blank form of contract to complete. The letter to the buyer's solicitor should be easy enough for those who have practised their letter writing skills, and for those of you on the Legal Practice Course, letter writing will have been covered on the compulsory skills part of the course.

Suggested Answer

RICHARDS ABBEY AND PARTNERS, SOLICITORS

INTERNAL MEMORANDUM

To   The Conveyancing Partner

From   The Trainee Solicitor

Re our client Angela Dawkins: sale of 13 Augustine Way, Kerwick

I refer to your memo regarding the above and respond as follows:

(a)   Having regard to the requirements of The National Protocol we should consider the following:

(i)   Write to mortgagee and obtain deeds
The first thing we should do is write to the mortgagee, Weyford Building Society, for loan of the Charge Certificate and other deeds and documents. Our firm is likely to be on their panel of solicitors, in which case they will instruct us to act for them on the discharge of the mortgage. In our letter we should undertake to hold the deeds to the order of the Society pending repayment of the loan. If, unusually, we are not instructed by the Society, we would write to the Society's solicitors asking for the deeds (or copies of them).

Obviously, it is intended that the mortgage in favour of Weyford Building Society will be discharged on completion, and thus the property will not be sold subject to it. In our letter to the Society we should request confirmation of the amount required to discharge the mortgage. We must ensure that Angela is not in a negative equity situation, and we should therefore check that there will be sufficient sale proceeds to repay the Building Society loan in full.

(ii)   Apply for office copy entries of title
The Protocol requires the seller's solicitors to supply the buyer's solicitors with up-to-date office copies of the title and filed plan which are not more than 12

months old. We cannot use the 1990 copy entries that are on file. Accordingly we must make an application for office copies on Land Registry Form 109.

(iii)   Incumbrances on the title

The covenants created in 1924 are listed in Entry 1 of the Charges Register, but the buyer will also require full details of the restrictive covenants contained in the Transfer dated 29 July 1990 (see Entry No. 3 in the Charges Register). Upon receipt of the deeds from the mortgagee we should send the buyer's solicitors a copy of the Transfer which is sewn into the Charge Certificate (see the note in Entry No. 3 of the Charges Register – *'Copy in Certificate'*). Alternatively, we could apply to the Land Registry for an office copy of the Transfer on Land Registry Form 110.

(iv)   Property Information Form

We should ask Angela to complete the Property Information Form (PIF), part I, and the Fixtures, Fittings and Contents Form. Where the latter is provided it will form part of the contract. We should ask Angela about any target date she may have for completion. We would also ask her for any of the following in her possession: original guarantees with any accompanying specification, planning decisions and building regulation approvals. Once we have inspected the deeds and checked her answers in PIF part I for any discrepancies, we would complete PIF part II.

(v)   Occupiers

We would have to be sure that we can sell the property free from any third party interests and with vacant possession. Accordingly we must ask Angela for the identity of all people aged 18 and over living in the house. We must ask about any financial contribution they or anyone else may have made towards its purchase or subsequent improvement. All persons identified in this way should be asked to confirm their consent to the sale proceeding.

(vi)   Draft contract and send package to buyer's solicitors

We would draft the contract as below and submit it in duplicate for approval to the buyer's solicitors accompanied by the other items in our package recommended by the Protocol (see letter below). We should bear in mind that if it becomes necessary to depart from Protocol procedures then we must give notice to the buyer's solicitors.

If and to the extent that Angela consents to the disclosure, we would supply the buyer's solicitors with information about her own purchase and the other transactions in the chain above.

(b) The suggested form of draft contract is set out in Appendix 3.

(c) The suggested draft letter to the buyer's solicitors is as follows:

RICHARDS ABBEY AND PARTNERS, SOLICITORS

4 Red Lion Square London WC1

Partners
M.B.Richards
R.M.Abbey

Messrs Young & Price
Solicitors
1A High Street
Kerwick
Maradon
Cornshire

For the attention Miss P. Knight

Our ref: MR/TS/PP

[Date]

Dear Sirs

13 Augustine Way Kerwick

We refer to Miss Knight's recent telephone conversation with our Mr Richards and confirm that we act for the intended seller of the above property, Angela Dawkins, to your client Andrew Peach for £70,000 plus £500 for carpets and curtains.

We confirm that the National Protocol will be used in this transaction and accordingly enclose the following documents for your consideration:

1. Draft contract in duplicate,
2. Office copy entries of title and filed plan,
3. Seller's Property Information Form duly completed with supporting documents,
4. Fixtures Fittings and Contents Form duly completed.

Our client has a related purchase which is in its early stages and the chain above this is complete. Our client has in mind a completion date of six weeks from today. Please let us know whether this date is convenient for your client and also your client's position on any related sale. Please confirm that you will be paying a 10% deposit on exchange.

In our Mr Richards's absence on holiday [name of trainee] will be dealing with this matter.

Yours faithfully

RICHARDS ABBEY AND PARTNERS

QUESTION 3

Analyse critically the impact on conveyancing of s. 2 of the Law of Property (Miscellaneous Provisions) Act 1989.

Commentary

This question should be approached from an academic perspective and will require an essay-style answer. You are more likely to come across it in a degree-level examination than you are in the Legal Practice Course, but in any event a sound knowledge of the 1989 Law of Property Act should be a prerequisite for all conveyancing students.

A good start would be to demonstrate that you know (i) what s. 2 is all about, and (ii) what it replaces, i.e. s. 40 of the Law of Property Act 1925. Do not make the mistake of spending too long on s. 40, though – the question does not ask you to analyse that section, and the examiner will certainly not expect a lengthy exposition on matters such as 'part performance'.

You could follow this opening by a discussion of s. 2 in more detail and a review of some of the relevant cases. Remember to mention some practical effects, such as dispensing with 'subject to contract' on solicitors' letters (although it is still customary to use this).

As with most academic essay questions, some critical analysis will be necessary if you are looking for high marks, and you will notice the word 'critically' appears in the question. Do not be afraid to criticise judgments if you feel this is justified. Provided you put your argument well, you will not lose marks simply because the examiner happens to disagree with your opinion.

Suggested Answer

Section 2 of the Law of Property (Miscellaneous Provisions) Act 1989 replaced s. 40 of the Law of Property Act 1925.

Section 40 made an oral contract for the sale of an interest in land unenforceable unless it was evidenced in writing or there was part performance of it, although s. 40 did not *per se* render an oral contract void or voidable. The effect of s. 2 of the 1989 Act has been that, on or after 27 September 1989, a contract for the sale of an interest in land must be made in writing otherwise it does not come into existence at all, i.e. it is void. The court has no equitable jurisdiction to allow the enforcement of a 'contract' that does not comply with s. 2.

Section 2 further provides that the written contract must incorporate all the agreed terms, either in one document or by reference to another document, and the written contract must be signed by or on behalf of each party to the contract. Thus where contracts are to be exchanged, both sides need only sign their respective parts, not both parts. In this way the standard exchange of contracts in a conveyancing transaction is unaffected provided both parts of the contract are identical and incorporate all the agreed terms.

The requirement for the incorporation of all agreed terms is significant because it means that if a term is omitted the whole contract becomes invalid. An example would be on the sale of a house where the price is to include chattels. A term to this effect should be included in the contract otherwise the validity of the entire contract is at risk. Similarly, ancillary agreements recorded in correspondence between the parties' solicitors should be expressly incorporated by reference in the contract in order to satisfy s. 2. The practice of using side letters, once common in commercial conveyancing, can now potentially endanger the whole land contract unless the precise terms of the correspondence are properly incorporated in the formal contract.

The impact of s. 2 is also felt where the parties wish to vary the terms of a land contract. No longer can variations simply be chronicled in correspondence; they must recorded in a document that satisfies s. 2. This can be achieved by an exchange of signed documents referring to the original contract and the subsequent variation.

There are few decided cases on s. 2, but it is interesting to note how the courts seem to be finding ways of restricting its scope. In the case of *Record* v *Bell* [1991] 1 WLR 853, the seller's solicitor gave a warranty as to the seller's title, indicating that office copies of the title would show the seller as registered proprietor. The warranty (although correct) was not included in the written contract and the buyer tried to resist an action for specific performance by claiming that s. 2 had not been satisfied. The judge concluded that there had been two contracts, one for the sale of the estate in land and the other constituting a collateral contract for the title warranty. The collateral contract was not subject to s. 2 because it was not a contract for the sale of land.

Although the reasoning in *Record* v *Bell* may have prevented an injustice, the decision has serious ramifications for property lawyers because the situations in which a collateral contract can or cannot arise are by no means clear. Such uncertainty may ultimately increase the number of disputes over contracts for the sale of land, which is something the introduction of s. 2 was designed to prevent. It is submitted that a stricter application of s. 2 in this case would have left legal advisers in no doubt that all agreed terms must be included in the written contract.

Another case where the court construed two separate contracts was *Tootal Clothing Ltd* v *Guinea Properties Management Ltd* [1992] 2 EGLR 80. As part of one bargain the parties agreed two things: first, the grant of a lease by one to the other and, secondly, that the landlord would pay for the tenant's fitting-out works. The lease was completed and the tenant carried out the works, but the landlord refused to pay for them. The landlord argued that because the agreement for the fitting-out works was supplemental to the lease contract, it was invalid for non-compliance with s. 2. The Court of Appeal held that the agreement for the fitting-out works could stand on its own because the completed lease contract was no longer alive. Even though the two agreements were connected, the court construed them as separate contracts and only one of them was a land contract. The other stood on its own and was not in itself covered by s. 2. Again injustice was avoided but, it is submitted, at the expense of certainty. One might ask the question: When is a bargain construed as a division into separate contracts, and when is it construed as a whole? The answer of course will depend on the facts of each case.

In *Spiro* v *Glencrown Properties Ltd* [1991] Ch 537, the court had to consider an option to purchase and whether the notice exercising the option should comply with s. 2. This was a first instance decision where Hoffman J held that the exercise of the option was a unilateral act. He said, 'It would destroy the very purpose of the option if the purchaser had to obtain the vendor's counter-signature to the notice by which it was exercised'. This line of argument adopts a robust, commonsense approach but disregards the line of cases that say the service of an option notice is an acceptance of an offer in the option agreement. If that were right, s. 2 would apply and both parties would need to sign the notice for the option to come into existence.

Before the enactment of s. 2, a mortgagee could create an equitable mortgage by deposit of title deeds. This took effect as an agreement to create a legal mortgage and could be enforced by part performance. Now, a lender in these circumstances cannot claim an equitable mortgage because the absence of a written document means there can be no valid disposition of an interest in land. Consequently, a prudent lender will, since the enactment of s. 2, always insist on a legal charge.

Another effect of s. 2 is that conveyancers can probably now dispense with the words 'subject to contract' on their letters. The phrase was designed to avoid creating a Law of Property Act 1925, s. 40 memorandum of an oral contract that may already have been in existence. As s. 2 has superseded s. 40, there is no danger of this occurring except in very unusual circumstances, although conveyancers still tend to use the words in their pre-exchange correspondence.

Lastly, it should be noted that s. 2 does not apply to the following contracts: a lease granted for a term not exceeding three years taking effect in possession without a fine, a contract made at public auction and a contract regulated under the Financial Services Act 1986.

QUESTION 4

RICHARDS ABBEY AND PARTNERS, SOLICITORS
INTERNAL MEMORANDUM

To   The Trainee Solicitor

From   The Conveyancing Partner

Re land to the rear of 14 Wellington Road
We act for Philip Brown of 14 Wellington Road, Midchester, who has recently obtained planning permission for the building of a dwellinghouse and garage at the rear of his garden. He has decided to sell this building plot to a property developer. The area in question is approximately half a hectare. A price has

been agreed, subject to contract, and he has asked us to progress the sale as soon as possible. 14 Wellington Road is freehold and registered at HM Land Registry with title absolute under title number MB 34857. Mr Brown bought the property back in 1981. I attach a plan that the client has given me (refer to Appendix 4). The proposed boundary between the building plot and the land Mr Brown is retaining is shown by a thick black line. We will use the Law Society form of contract incorporating the Standard Conditions of Sale.

Mr Brown has given me the following specific instructions:

1.   Access to the building plot will be along the client's driveway which runs from Wellington Road along the side of his garden. Mr Brown will share the use of the driveway with the buyer of the plot. The driveway is shown hatched black on the plan.

2.   The buyer of the plot can lay new drains and sewers and connect them into the client's existing drains and sewers ('the existing services'). The existing services in turn connect into the mains drainage and sewage systems in Wellington Road. The run of the existing services is shown by a broken line on the plan. Once the buyer's connection is made, the buyer can share the use of the existing services and come onto Mr Brown's retained land to carry out any necessary maintenance or repairs to the services.

3.   There is a greenhouse on the building plot, the position of which is indicated on the plan. Once the sale is legally binding on the buyer, Mr Brown says he will relocate it in the part of the garden he is keeping.

4.   The client does not want to be overlooked, so the new building must be no more than one storey high – this is very important. Mr Brown will also want to see and approve the plans for the new property before it is built.

5.   The buyer will put up a suitable fence along the boundary between the plot and the land Mr Brown is keeping, and the buyer will maintain the fence.

(a)   We will have to prepare the draft contract for approval by the buyer's solicitors. Please explain the particular matters we should consider when drafting the contract and draft the Special Conditions of sale that you consider will meet the requirements of both our client and the buyer.   (25 Marks)

(b)   In relation to Mr Brown's proposed sale please let me have a note of any tax advice we should give him.   (5 Marks)

Commentary

The crucial point to appreciate in this question is that you are acting on a sale of part, and by its nature it will necessitate a more complex contract than a sale of whole. There is the need in particular to consider a new, accurate description of the part being sold, the grant and reservation of easements and the imposition of new covenants. Consequently it is an area of conveyancing that finds favour with examiners, both for coursework and exams.

On the Legal Practice Course you should expect some drafting questions, because drafting is one of the core skills of the course. Here is one that asks you to exhibit that skill in a conveyancing context – something that may fill some of you with unease!

Ideally you will need time to go away and consult a precedent book (or computer software), and unless the examiner is feeling particularly mean you will not face part (a) in an examination room (although do not bank on it, especially in these days of open book exams!). Generally speaking, you are more likely to find this type of question as part of a coursework assessment, with a return date of, say, two or three weeks ahead.

Before searching for the precedent or precedent clauses, always stop, and ask yourself what the client is trying to achieve. Remember that a precedent is only your guide, and it will have to be adapted to suit the client's specific needs and requirements. If the precedent is in a book, take a photocopy of it and amend it after careful thought. You will rarely satisfy your client's requirements by copying slavishly word for word from a precedent.

Fortunately your instructions here are quite common in a situation where land is sold off for development, and you should have covered a scenario similar to this in class. Remember that part of your job as the seller's conveyancer is to ensure that your client is adequately protected in terms of receiving the benefit of appropriate covenants and the reservation of appropriate easements. A failure to do this on your part could adversely affect your client's ability to offer a good and marketable title to prospective buyers of the retained land. So again, do not slavishly follow your client's instructions – he is not a property lawyer and doubtless will not have thought of everything. Here for example, Mr Brown does not appear to have considered that if the buyer is permitted to share the use of the driveway and existing drains, then he ought at least to share the cost of maintaining them.

As well as the seller's requirements, the question also asks you to consider the needs of the buyer. From your instructions, anticipate the easements a buyer would want and include them as well. This is courteous to the buyer's solicitor and will avoid unnecessary delay. The question also invites you to explain the relevant points, so you must understand what the clauses mean and why they are necessary. Give your explanation before each draft condition – that way it is easier to mark.

Part (b) raises the topic of revenue law, which of course pervades conveyancing and you have already encountered it in the preceding chapter. This problem is straightforward provided you spot that the relevant tax is CGT. Note the significance of the area being sold ('approximately half a hectare') and also the purchase in 1981 (this affects the calculation of the gain). Do not be drawn into a discussion about stamp duty – this is only payable by purchasers – and advising the clients that they will be paying VAT on your costs is astute but really misses the point! Lastly, note the apportionment of marks between parts (a) and (b); the tax advice need only be brief, so stick to general principles.

Suggested Answer

RICHARDS ABBEY AND PARTNERS, SOLICITORS

INTERNAL MEMORANDUM

To   The Conveyancing Partner

From   The Trainee Solicitor

Re land to the rear of Wellington Road

(a)(i)   Description
As this is a sale of part it is important to describe accurately the land being sold. This will be done by adapting the existing description of 14 Wellington Road on the title register and referring to a scale plan annexed to the contract. For example:

All that freehold land shown edged red on the plan annexed hereto ('the Plan') being part of the land known as 14 Wellington Road Midchester registered at HM Land Registry with title absolute under title number MB 34857.

The land being retained by the client should also be described accurately in the contract by reference to blue edging on the plan. It should be defined as 'the Retained Land'.

(ii) Negate implied grant of easements in favour of buyer

On a sale of part the buyer may acquire certain rights over the Retained Land by virtue of the Law of Property Act 1925, s. 62 and the rule in *Wheeldon* v *Burrows* [1879] 12 Ch D 31. As the nature and extent of the implied rights is not always clear, it is prudent to exclude the effect of these rules and set out expressly the rights and reservations required by the parties. If implied rights of light or air were granted to the buyer here, this could hinder any plans Mr Brown may have in the future to build on the Retained Land.

A suggested negation of implied rights clause would be:

> The Transfer to the Buyer shall contain an agreement and declaration that the Buyer shall not by implication or otherwise become entitled to any rights of light or air which would restrict or interfere with the free use of the Retained Land for building or other purposes.

Alternatively, as the contract incorporates the Standard Conditions of Sale, we could rely on Condition 3.3.2, which provides on a sale of part for the exclusion of rights of light or air. The benefit of our express Special Condition however is that the point is less likely to be overlooked when the purchase deed is drafted.

(iii) The grant and reservation of new easements

Standard Condition 3.3.2 also provides for the mutual grant of easements and reservations on a sale of part, but the condition is not exact and should only be relied upon as a 'fallback' if express easements are overlooked. The Special Conditions should therefore deal with these matters expressly.

The creation of a new easement in favour of the buyer is called a 'grant'; the creation of a new easement in favour of the seller is called a 'reservation'. When acting for a seller wishing to *reserve* easements, reliance should never be placed upon s. 62 of the Law of Property Act 1925 or the rule in *Wheeldon* v *Burrows* (1879) 12 Ch D 31, because both of these relate to implied *grants* not implied reservations.

The following Special Condition is suggested to cover our instructions:

The Transfer to the Buyer shall contain the following rights in favour of the Buyer and the Buyer's successors in title:

(a)   A free and uninterrupted right of way at all times and for all purposes with or without vehicles over the accessway shown hatched black on the Plan leading across the Retained Land ('the Accessway') subject to the Buyer paying a fair proportion according to user of the cost of maintaining repairing and renewing the said accessway;

(b)   The right to lay maintain and use for all proper purposes connected with the Property a new drain and sewer ('the new services') to be laid within a period of eighty years from the date hereof under the Retained Land along the route marked with a broken [orange] line on the Plan;

(c)   The right to connect into the Seller's existing drain and sewer ('the existing services') on the Retained Land and to use the existing services in common with the Seller subject to the Buyer paying a fair proportion of the cost of maintaining repairing and renewing the existing services and making good any damage caused to the satisfaction of the Seller;

(d)   The right on giving reasonable notice and at reasonable times (except in the case of emergencies) to enter the Retained Land for the purpose of inspecting, maintaining and repairing the new services and the existing services, the person exercising such right causing as little damage as possible and making good any such damage caused.

The period of 80 years referred to in (b) above is necessary because if new easements are to be created in the future their grant must be limited to the perpetuity period (see the Perpetuities and Accumulations Act 1964).

It should be noted that the Seller has been protected by the provision for the Buyer to make good any damage caused to the Retained Land and for repairs to be carried out only upon prior notice, save in the case of an emergency. The route of the new services has also been specified so as to avoid unnecessary intrusion onto the Retained Land.

From the information you have provided, it appears that the only reservation Mr Brown will require is the right to remove the greenhouse. The following special condition would cover the point:

The Seller reserves the right to remove the greenhouse on the Property provided that the Seller shall exercise this right before completion and shall cause no unnecessary damage to the Property.

If the National Protocol is being used the right to remove the greenhouse could be taken care of by mentioning this on the standard Fixtures Fittings and Contents Form.

(iv)   The imposition of new covenants

Mr Brown has imposed some specific conditions, and each one will be the subject of a new covenant imposed on the buyer. Although not mentioned in our instructions, it would be prudent in addition (a) to restrict the use of the new property to residential only (this is probably a condition of the planning permission anyway), (b) to prohibit the buyer from obstructing the driveway, and (c) to impose a general covenant against causing a nuisance or annoyance to the owners and occupiers of the Retained Land.

Wherever possible when acting for a covenantor, the covenants should be drafted so as to be restrictive (i.e. negative) in nature because the burden of a *positive* covenant will not run with the land (*Tulk v Moxhay* (1848) 2 Ph 774). This will be done here in the case of the new building on the plot. Rather than say 'The buyer will build only a single storey dwelling ...', say 'Not to erect any building save for ...'. This cannot be done in the case of the obligation to build the fence, but, so far as the fence is concerned, we should stipulate a time limit, a minimum height and its type.

The benefit of the covenants should also be expressly annexed to the Retained Land.

The following Special Condition is suggested:

The Buyer shall in the Transfer enter into a covenant with the Seller to the intent that the burden of such covenant shall run with and bind the Property and every part thereof and that the benefit of such covenant shall be annexed to and run with the Retained Land and every part thereof to observe and perform the following:

(a)   Not to erect on the Property any building or other structure other than one bungalow and garage for residential use and occupation by one family in accordance with plans previously approved in writing by the Seller or the Seller's successors in title;

(b)   Within three months from the date of completion to erect and forever thereafter maintain a close-boarded fence not less than six feet in height along the boundary between the Retained Land and the Property between the points marked A and B on the Plan;

(c)   Not to park vehicles on or otherwise obstruct or cause or permit to be obstructed the Accessway;

(d)   Not to do or permit to be done on the Property anything which may be or grow to be a nuisance or annoyance to the owners or occupiers of the Retained Land.

(b)   We should advise Mr Brown of his potential liability to CGT that can arise on the disposal of an interest in land.

It should be noted that if the land he is retaining (14 Wellington Road and part garden) is his principal private dwellinghouse, he will enjoy an exemption from CGT provided the land being sold does not exceed 0.5 hectares. We are told that the area of the land is approximately half a hectare so it will be important to requisition a survey in order to establish the precise area.

If the land exceeds 0.5 hectares the gain will be calculated by taking the sale price and deducting from it the value of the land in 1982, incidental acquisition costs (including legal fees) and incidental disposal costs. The client has an annual exemption which can be set against the chargeable gain. Any gain above the exemption figure will be charged to CGT at the highest rate at which Mr Brown pays income tax.

Trainee Solicitor: time engaged 1 hour 15 minutes.

4 Searches and Enquiries: Town and Country Planning

INTRODUCTION

The topics covered by this chapter seem on the face of it to be straightforward. However, as is usually the case with conveyancing, topics that seem simple generally turn out to be quite complex. The main difficulty is the broad variety of questions that candidates can expect to encounter. These questions can extend from the very wide, touching upon several areas within the topics, to very particular questions focusing on one area. The questions provided are examples of both these extremes. Your difficulties spread further in that other areas will be involved, as will be seen in the second question. Because conveyancing is an ongoing, forward-rolling process you must expect questions to incorporate several subjects not just limited to the chapter headings. This is inherent in the nature of the subject generally.

You should also note the wide diversity of style of questions displayed in these examples. In one the examiner is looking in the answer for a memorandum, in another a file note, and in another a letter of advice. In all your answers you should provide exactly what the examiner wants. It is important for you to realise that this is of crucial importance to your success and that essay answers to all the questions will not suffice. There will be occasions when an essay is appropriate, and the style of question will readily identify when this is so. However, because an essay format is not called for this does not mean that you should abandon the tried and tested examination technique that is the pathway to success. In preparing your answer you should still draw up a plan of how you are going to structure your answer, then make sure you stay with your plan and then make your points in a clear and concise way. Always make sure you give a cogent conclusion so that the examiner can appreciate that there is style, form and content to your answer.

So far as pre-contract enquiries are concerned, they have been greatly affected by changes ushered in by the Law Society's National Conveyancing Protocol. This being the case you should expect questions to arise that are concerned with this area of considerable change to the traditional system. You should acquaint yourself with the contents of the old style pre-printed traditional forms of enquiries before contract as well as with the new Property Information Forms. By doing this you will come to appreciate the ways in which the forms differ and how the system has been streamlined with the adoption of the Protocol approach. Lastly, there is some overlap between enquiries and planning, in that there should always be planning enquiries in most transactions. You ought to be aware of this and be able to demonstrate your knowledge of this possible combination of topics.

QUESTION 1

RICHARDS ABBEY AND PARTNERS, SOLICITORS

INTERNAL MEMORANDUM

To   The Trainee Solicitor

From   The Training Partner

Purchase of Red Lion House

I have had a brief look at this domestic conveyancing file and understand you are familiar with it having assisted Ms Brownlow, your principal, with the matter since our firm was first instructed by the buyer. As you know, the seller's solicitors have produced full title details by deducing title on the basis of an unregistered title, and it would seem that the Law Society's National Conveyancing Protocol is not being used. When I looked at the file I particularly noted that the property is located on the edge of town adjoining open countryside and fields.

In the circumstances, I would like you to let me know what searches should we and/or our clients make before exchange and why? Where should those searches be made?

Please let me have an explanatory note on this before close of business today. If there are any incidental points arising, please let me know.

Commentary

This is a typical question to be found in modern conveyancing examination papers, and on Legal Practice Courses particularly. It is in the form of an Office Memorandum from a Partner to the Trainee Solicitor and is in fact seeking to reproduce just the kind of note a trainee might receive in the office. This should make you realise immediately that the answer must be in the form of a Memorandum in reply. Style marks could be available if you remember to reply in this uncomplicated way. An essay answer is not appropriate; you must direct your answer in the form of a memorandum dealing with the practical problem point by point. By failing to adopt a memorandum answer form you might lose these all-important style marks that are otherwise easily attainable.

The question is deceptively simple in that you might be tempted to consider just the main local authority search. Of course the answer requires you to consider this along with some of the more unusual, but nevertheless important, searches. The question is in two parts; first you are required to suggest appropriate searches and, secondly, you need to show where these searches should be made. To get full marks you should make sure you deal fully with both aspects of the question. Lastly, reference is made to searches which the client may need to make. Clearly this is mentioned in the question for a reason, as the following answer demonstrates.

Suggested Answer

RICHARDS ABBEY AND PARTNERS, SOLICITORS

INTERNAL MEMORANDUM

To   The Training Partner

From   The Trainee Solicitor

Purchase of Red Lion House

I write to reply to your memorandum enquiring about necessary searches to be made in this case and set out below all the searches I consider appropriate to this matter:

1.   Local land charges search and enquiries of local authority.
A local search should be made by every purchaser before exchange of contracts. It will disclose public charges, many of which are not matters of title and so not within the seller's duty of disclosure. These charges will be registered by the local authority whose obligation it is to record the same. Standard condition 3 of the Standard Conditions of Sale (second edition) makes a sale subject to local land charges. Accordingly, the buyer must search to make sure full details are obtained from the council of all relevant information affecting the property concerned. The search is made at the local authority, accompanied by a plan if the land is not easily identifiable from the postal address. The search also directs important enquiries to the local authority concerned with subjects within their control, such as road schemes, notices or planning matters. The search and enquiries are usually sent by post, but if the matter is urgent you can carry out a personal search of the Local Land Charges Register and ask questions of other relevant departments such as highways and

planning. Unfortunately not all councils will answer all the enquiries on a personal basis. If a complete set of answers is not available a personal search should be avoided. The client should also be warned that the results of personal searches will not have the authenticated stamp of the local authority, so if the council gives an incorrect oral answer, it may later be difficult to prove an error on the council's part.

2. Index map search.

This search should always be made when purchasing unregistered land. It will confirm that the land is unregistered, because if by chance the land is registered then the title number (and tenure) will be revealed. It will also reveal any caution against first registration registered at the Land Registry. The search is made at the District Land Registry accompanied by a plan, although the Registry will issue a search result without a plan if the property can be clearly identified from the postal address. The search is in the Index Map and Parcels Index maintained at the Registry for the relevant locality. As this property is at the edge of town I assume a plan will be required. You mentioned in your memorandum that the title to this property is unregistered. You should bear in mind that all of England and Wales is now an area of compulsory registration. Accordingly, if the last conveyance to the seller was for value (and therefore compulsorily registrable), and this was after 1 December 1990, then the seller must rectify this defect by registering the title. In these circumstances the seller must ensure that the property is offered for sale with a proper and fully registered title.

3. A search in the Land Charges Register.

Again this is relevant to unregistered land only. (Although even with registered land it may be prudent to carry out a bankruptcy search to make sure the seller was not an undisclosed bankrupt!) It is recommended that a land charges search should be made before exchange of contracts as well as before completion. A land charge (e.g. D(ii) restrictive covenant) duly registered will be binding on a purchaser for value. A prudent purchaser will therefore want to be aware of it before exchange, notwithstanding any subsequent cause of action he may have against the seller for non-disclosure. It should be noted that a land charges search against the seller will reveal any bankruptcy or class F Matrimonial Homes Act registration. In this way any such problems can be addressed before exchange when there is sufficient time, rather than after when time is limited by the impending contractual completion date. The search is made at the Government land charges department in Plymouth against the names of the estate owners, not the land, and for their periods of ownership.

4.   Commons registration search.

This search should be made in any case where the land to be purchased adjoins a village green or common land, or is in open country. This is irrespective of whether the land has a registered title or not. It is unlikely that Red Lion House was built on common land, but given the property's position, it would be prudent to search as there could be rights concerning the use of common land that affect the property. It should be noted that in the case of *G & K Ladenbau (UK) Ltd* v *Crawley and de Reya (a firm)* [1978] 1 All ER 682, it was held that failure to make a commons search in circumstances where one ought properly to be made could be grounds for an action in negligence against the solicitor. You make the search at the county council accompanied by a plan.

5.   Physical inspection of the property.

This is of the subject property and should be undertaken by the client buyer in all cases. There are three particular reasons for this. First, to check that there are no undisclosed occupants within the property who could claim rights of occupation and thereby delay, or indeed defeat, completion. Secondly, to check that there have been no material changes to the property that might adversely affect it or its value since the buyers put in their offer. Thirdly, if the purchase includes fixtures and fittings it is always sensible to check that those items are still at the property and properly listed on the contract. In this way there can be no doubt as to what is actually being purchased and whether or not it actually exists.

6.   Mining search.

I am not personally acquainted with the locality of the subject property and I am therefore not sure whether it is or has been affected by mining. This kind of search is necessary in an area of coal mining, or in an area that has been so affected in the past. If you are not sure whether the property is so affected, British Coal maintains a detailed list of each and every area that has been concerned with coal mining either presently or in the past. The Law Society issue a 'Coal Mining Directory' to which you can also refer to see if a search is required. The main concern is of course subsidence that might affect the property, and whether or not compensation has been paid, or indeed whether or not there are any relevant claims pending. The search should be sent to British Coal with a plan.

7.   Other uncommon searches.

Should the property be affected by an adjacent river or canal, a search should be directed to the appropriate water authority to check on matters relevant to the water way, such as fishing rights and bank side ownership. The search is made by letter to the relevant water authority. Local mineral extraction searches can also be considered, although they may not be relevant to this particular property as they are very much limited to the localities where the mineral is to be found. The minerals concerned include brine, tin and limestone. As I am not acquainted with the area, could you please decide if any of these are necessary; although if in doubt a search should be made. Where they should be made depends on each type of mineral.

I do hope this explanatory note is of assistance, but if there is anything else I can assist with please let me know.

QUESTION 2

Your principal's secretary has taken a telephone call from Ms Alexandra Temple, a long-established and important client of the firm, who needs some urgent advice. Ms Temple would like someone from the firm to ring her back before 3 p.m. as she is leaving for her summer holiday in Spain this afternoon and wants to resolve matters before going. Your principal is out at a meeting in the City for the rest of the day. It is your responsibility to provide cover for your principal during this afternoon.

The secretary's note of the telephone conversation is as follows:

12.25 p.m. Attending Ms Alexandra Temple on the telephone.
Now that her car restoration business is so successful she is thinking of buying a detached house (apparently about 11 years old) in a small and exclusive residential area. The house is on the edge of the area occupying a good sized corner site. The road running along the side of the residential area is unmade and does not appear to be maintained by the local authority. The side road is very quiet and is used infrequently as it leads down to a private paddock at the rear of the residential area. She especially wants this particular house because the present owner, a Mr Smith, built a large double garage and rear workroom for his own cars five years ago at the bottom of the garden and fronting right onto the side road. For the last four years he has been using the garage for repairing, renovating, respraying and servicing all sorts of vehicles, and Ms Temple has plans to do just the same. When Ms Temple asked about planning permission the owner, Mr Smith, said as far as he was concerned he didn't think it was a problem, and anyway no one so far as he knew had objected. In any event it was only a single storey garage that was entirely in keeping with the general style of buildings in the area. Can someone ring her back as soon as possible to advise her if there are any unforeseen problems?

You duly rang the client after considering all the circumstances. Consider the issues which would have concerned you and prepare an attendance note for the file of the advice you gave the client when you rang her back.

Commentary

This is another searching question that, on the face of it, seems simple. Do not be deceived! There are several difficult areas that need to be considered and analysed. However, your first concern is the format of your answer. You have been asked for an attendance note, and you must adopt this form to ensure that your answer is on the right lines. Conveyancing is a system that relies heavily upon rigorous file management along with the accurate recording of events and details. An attendance note, being a record of a telephone conversation or of a meeting between the client and the solicitor, is a fundamental constituent element of just such a file. The areas of concern should be considered in turn, and especially the planning issue which patently merits careful examination. However, the question is not just about planning; it actually touches upon other important issues highlighted in the following answer. In conveyancing it is common to find that competent answers will require a broad base stretching over several topics. Remember this is a practical matter and in practice you must always record your time. This being the case, end your attendance note with an indication of how long the conversation was. For any solicitor or licensed conveyancer, time is money.

Lastly, do not be rushed by your client into giving hasty advice which may be inaccurate. However much time pressure the client is exerting, always consider the problem carefully before giving a definitive response. If there is not enough time to do this before the client's deadline, advise the client of this and indicate that more time is required to enable you to provide proper and well-researched advice.

Suggested Answer

Suggested telephone attendance note of advice:

Re Alexandra Temple and her proposed residential house purchase with garage

Subsequently telephoning back Ms Temple and advising her as follows:

1. Planning

There are two potential planning difficulties. First, was the garage built with planning consent? Secondly, has there been a material change of use of that garage from a mere garage for the storage of cars conveniently close by the house, into commercial garage premises (s. 55(1) of the Town and Country Planning Act 1990)?

(a)   So far as the building of the garage is concerned, I advised the client that this appeared to be a building that would have required a planning consent from the local planning authority, usually a department within the local authority, prior to erection. However, there is a time limit for enforcement action of four years, and this has passed so no enforcement notice can be served by the local authority requiring the garage's demolition (s. 172(4) of the Town and Country Planning Act 1990).

(b)   I further advised Ms Temple that there has been a material change of use in relation to the garage from residential to business use. This would have required planning permission, which it seems was not granted. There is a 10-year time limit for the service of an enforcement notice by the local authority in these circumstances, and the council could therefore serve an enforcement notice upon the owner of the property at any time requiring the business use to cease (s. 4 of the Planning and Compensation Act 1991). A buyer would buy subject to the breach and the possibility of an enforcement notice affecting her in the future. A local search would reveal the existence or otherwise of an enforcement notice. Failure to comply with an enforcement notice is a criminal offence.

(c)   There is a third difficulty allied to planning, and that is whether or not the seller obtained building regulations approval from the local authority for the garage at the time it was built. Indeed, even assuming the garage did not need a planning consent, it would have had to comply with building regulations that have been issued to ensure that buildings comply with precise and detailed standards of construction. However, there is a time limit of one year from completion of the works during which the local authority can take enforcement proceedings (s. 36 of the Building Act 1984). It should be noted that any breach of these regulations can be a criminal offence. Although this time limit has passed and there is therefore no potential risk of proceedings, the concern must remain that without building regulations approval the premises may have been erected in a sub-standard condition. If this was the case there could be grave potential problems for a purchaser who would be responsible for the maintenance of the structure.

2. Title

The title will need to be checked to establish whether the land is subject to a restrictive covenant prohibiting business use. It is very likely that the developer of the estate would have imposed such a covenant when he sold the house to the first purchaser. He may have created a building scheme so that the covenants are enforceable by the owners of the other houses on the estate. Furthermore, there is the distinct possibility that there was another restrictive covenant imposed at the same time requiring the original developer's permission for the erection of new buildings on the estate, such as the double garage. There is the possibility that a restrictive covenant indemnity policy could be obtained to protect Ms Temple in the light of a claim against her for breach of covenant, although the premium for this could be prohibitively expensive.

3. Side road

A local search of the property will reveal whether the road is a public highway. If not, the deeds must be checked to see if the owner has the right to walk and drive cars along it. Clearly, if there is not such express legal right of way there are very real difficulties for a proposed purchaser who might face the daunting prospect of being lawfully denied access to the garage by the legal owner of the road. If the local authority decides to adopt the road in the future then the cost of making up the road to an adoptable standard will fall on the frontagers, which would include the owner of the property in question.

4. Advice

In the light of the above I advised Ms Temple against making any firm plans to proceed until we were in receipt of further information, and in particular until we knew precisely the position concerning planning issues, building regulations, the ownership of the road and whether or not there were any adverse restrictive covenants affecting the property. She was informed that a local authority search would reveal information about the side road that would influence her decision as to whether or not she should proceed. I went on to say that planning consents relating to the property would be referred to in the search result and that further, more specific enquiries could be directed to the local planning authority. I also indicated that we would check the seller's title deeds carefully to see if there were any such problematic restrictive covenants, but that if there were, there could be the possibility of obtaining a restrictive covenant indemnity policy from an insurance company. It was difficult to be optimistic about the business use question and we would probably advise her not to go ahead if this aspect was crucial to her.

Trainee Solicitor: time engaged 20 minutes.

QUESTION 3

You have been consulted by Mr Ivan Curtess in connection with his proposed sale of his small bachelor flat within a large mansion block of flats in the fashionable area of London called Knightsbridge. He has asked you to provide some preliminary advice with a view to his perhaps instructing your firm in connection with the sale. He has decided to sell because he wants to move to Hampstead and he has contacted your firm because he has been told by his former neighbour, Glennis Gould, what a quick and efficient job you did for her when she recently sold her flat in the same block. On coming to see you Mr Curtess indicated that his previous neighbour had explained to him that the reason for her sale going through so quickly was that a lot of the usual time-wasting questions normally asked by the buyer before exchange of contracts had been avoided by you adopting something called 'The Protocol'. As a consequence, Mr Curtess wants to know more about the Protocol, and in particular how it changes the system of asking questions before exchange of contracts takes place.

Would you please make a written file note of the advice you gave Mr Curtess, summing up the way in which enquiries are dealt with within the context of the Protocol and the manner in which this differs from the traditional approach.

Commentary

This is a very specific question, in that the area concerned is very precise and narrow. Accordingly, you should attempt questions of this type only if you have a comprehensive understanding of the relevant area. In this question you will be required to show a detailed understanding of the way in which preliminary enquiries have been affected and altered by the introduction of the Law Society's National Conveyancing Protocol. Arguably, this has been the most successful element of the whole Protocol and the one most commonly adopted by practitioners throughout England and Wales. It is therefore not surprising to see a question of this very specific nature which seeks to identify the candidate's knowledge not only of Protocol enquiries but also of orthodox preliminary enquiries. The answer required will not comprise a detailed examination of the whole of the Protocol. What is called for is a thorough examination of the area of enquiries only, although a brief introduction to the Protocol is appropriate. A good answer will clearly highlight the differences between the old and the new systems and their strong and weak aspects.

Lastly, on the whole subject of preliminary enquiries we would like to refer you to a letter in the *Law Society's Gazette* of 7 September 1994, in which it was suggested that all enquiries before contract could be reduced to one, namely: 'If we asked the usual silly questions would you give the usual worthless answers?'!

Suggested Answer

RICHARDS ABBEY AND PARTNERS, SOLICITORS

File Note:

Attended upon Mr Ivan Curtess to provide him with some preliminary advice in the hope that he will instruct the firm in connection with his proposed flat sale. He asked about conveyancing in general and preliminary enquiries in particular, with special reference to the National Conveyancing Protocol and how its implementation might speed up the sale of his flat. I advised him in general terms about the process of conveyancing, and in particular about pre-contract enquiries. I pointed out that the buyer will want to find out as much as possible about his flat before contracts are exchanged. I mentioned that in the main *caveat emptor* still applies to a conveyance and that there were therefore compelling reasons for a buyer to raise as many questions as possible. Indeed, I explained that the buyer's solicitor had a duty to make all usual and necessary enquiries, and that if they were not made a solicitor might be liable in negligence.

I went on to mention that in the orthodox style of conveyancing the system of asking questions is normally by standard, pre-printed questionnaires issued by the buyer's solicitor and to be answered by the seller. These standard enquiries will include, amongst others, questions about boundaries, disputes, notices, alterations to the property, and planning matters. These are all material, relevant and important matters that a buyer will want to know about before proceeding with a purchase. I pointed out that solicitors acting for buyers will raise vast numbers of enquiries on the basis that if they do not they might be seen to be acting negligently. It is not unusual to see such enquiries stretching over 20 or more pages and comprising dozens of multi-sectioned questions. Of course a seller can refuse to give answers, but if this happens then any sensible buyer will back out of the proposed transaction immediately on the basis that the seller must have something to hide. I indicated that this system can be particularly time-consuming because the seller must wait for the buyer to raise preliminary enquiries even though they will probably be in a standard, pre-printed format.

I then referred to the modern system of conveyancing ushered in by the Law Society in 1990 in the form of the National Conveyancing Protocol. The intention of the Protocol was to streamline the system of conveyancing; the Law Society wanted to limit the time between the buyer making the offer and contracts being exchanged. To ensure that their intention was fulfilled, the Protocol envisaged the adoption of standardised documentation. In the case of pre-contract enquiries I explained that this meant the introduction of new enquiry forms that were to be used in all Protocol conveyancing cases. These were called by the Law Society 'Property Information Forms'. The critical change, and indeed the novel element brought in by the Protocol, is that these are issued and completed by the seller's solicitor with help from the seller, and then sent off to the buyer with the contract and other supporting documentation such as the title details. In this way a great deal of time is saved by the seller supplying standard enquiries with answers at the very earliest opportunity, and in particular along with the contract and title details. I pointed out that the client would be expected to help in the completion of these forms as they are in two parts, one for the seller to complete and the other for the solicitor. I made it clear that I would of course check his answers and let him peruse mine to make sure that the answers were as accurate as possible. I also noted that because the property he intended to sell was a flat it was most probably leasehold, and that consequently there would be an additional form to complete, the Seller's Leasehold Information Form. This is used to provide extra information applicable to leasehold properties only and calls for the provision of further documents such as the last ground rent receipt.

I went on to explain that because of the provisions of section 5.8 of the Protocol, the buyer's solicitor can only raise extra or additional enquiries that fulfil specific conditions defined by the Law Society. First, they must be necessary to clarify something within the documentation supplied, and/or, secondly, they must be relevant to the nature or location of the property. It is also accepted that questions raised specifically by the buyer can be asked expressly of the seller. However, I made it clear that it is also the case that no enquiry should be made that is about the condition of the property, or which could be answered elsewhere such as from the buyer's own searches, survey or inspection. In this way clearly defined limits have been fixed to the extent of the enquiries that can be required. I pointed out that it should be noted that there is no such limitation in the traditional approach where anything goes, right down to questions about the type of telephones in the house or other matters more properly dealt with elsewhere. I made it clear to Mr Curtess that we would be under no obligation to answer any additional enquiries that did not come within the above parameters, especially if they were pre-printed on standard forms other than those contemplated by the Protocol.

I did have to point out to Mr Curtess that the National Protocol is 'preferred practice' and in some circumstances it may not be adopted – for example, when it is necessary to depart from the Protocol procedures. I summed up by advising Mr Curtess that the Protocol procedure could speed up the process, but he would have to assist by helping with the completion of the relevant forms and by providing all necessary documents. I indicated that the traditional system was open to delay and involved the possibility of unnecessary and irrelevant questions being raised that could delay the progress of the sale. I made it clear that the fact that the Protocol seeks to limit the number and nature of the buyer's enquiries must assist; and I finally pointed out that as we will be issuing the forms with answers at the earliest opportunity it will enable us to control the progress of the sale from the very start of the transaction. Mr Curtess said that he would think about it and would get back to me later this week.

Trainee Solicitor: time engaged 45 minutes.

QUESTION 4

You have been instructed by Ms Benazir Khan in connection with her proposed purchase of a large house on four floors with a basement in West Manchester. She has just come from the estate agents and has told you that she wants to buy the house as quickly as possible, because she considers the price to be considerably under the true market value. The last person to live in the house died at the end of last year and the house is being sold by the deceased's executors. Ms Khan intends to let the building to students in bedsits. However, she has mentioned to you some concerns which she has, being:

(a)   that the house is on a main road which has been widened a few miles further on, and she wants to know about future widening plans;

(b)   that the basement seems to be capable of being lived in but at the moment it is all boarded up, and she wants to use it for bedsits;

(c)   that some of the houses nearby have been pulled down by the local authority to enable it to build some new council accommodation;

(d)   that she thinks the house has been occupied by just one family for many years;

(e)   that she knows that just around the corner the same kind of houses are very expensive and are similar, fine examples of Victorian architecture that the local authority is keen to preserve; and

(f)   that she wants to put in some modern aluminium double glazing and remove the old original sash and stained glass windows.

She has asked you to write to her to let her know how you might check on these points. She is particularly concerned because she does not think that much information will come from the sellers, who are only executors with little or no personal knowledge of the property or the locality.

Commentary

This is another example of a question that is based on a specific and narrow area of the conveyancing process, namely the local authority search and enquiries made of the local authority. The question requires you to have a detailed knowledge of the kind of information that might be disclosed in a search result and how that information might be of use to a client in deciding whether or not to purchase a property. In this particular example the points in the question are all included for several good reasons. Each raises a factor that might affect a client and whether or not a property is suitable. Because the buyer will be bound to the transaction once contracts are exchanged, it is important to emphasise in your answer that you appreciate this by advising the client to resolve all outstanding points on the search before exchange. The answer must be in the form of a letter of advice and needs to highlight what might be disclosed in the search, and should therefore address each point in turn. The client's intentions should be borne in mind at all times, namely the proposed use of the property as bedsits. This is a material change of use, but as the question does not make this clear you will immediately appreciate that the examiner wants you to concentrate part of your efforts on this point. Mention should also be made of the seller's limited duty of disclosure even when the sale is by executors. See the case of *Rignall Developments Ltd* v *Halil* [1988] Ch 190, in which it was made clear that there was a duty of disclosure if the seller was aware of a subsisting local land charge.

Suggested Answer

RICHARDS ABBEY AND PARTNERS, SOLICITORS

4 Red Lion Square London WC1

Partners

M. B. Richards
R. M. Abbey

Dear Ms Khan,

Re Your proposed purchase in West Manchester

I refer to your recent instructions concerning your proposed purchase of the above and write to provide you with the information you require. I note particularly that you intend to use the property for student bedsits and I will refer to this subsequently.

I can confirm that most of, if not all, the concerns you have can be addressed by a local search sent to the appropriate local authority. The local search is actually a local land charge search together with enquiries of the local authority. Section 3 of the Local Land Charges Act 1975 requires local authorities (usually the district, metropolitan or London Borough council) to maintain a local land charges register. The register is a record kept by the local authority of important matters that could affect the property, and in some ways adversely. There are various matters capable of registration, but with particular regard to your concerns it should be noted that the register will contain details of planning charges. The effect of registration is that a buyer is bound by the registrations whether or not a search was made. Accordingly, a search of this kind is an absolute necessity for a prudent buyer. The items capable of registration are limited, and as a consequence other important details can be sought from the local authority by means of pre-printed enquiry forms. There are 16 standard enquiries of which questions are asked about road schemes, outstanding notices, compulsory purchase, areas designated for slum clearance, and planning applications and consents.

Turning to your specific requirements, you are first concerned with road widening schemes in view of the fact that the property abuts a main road that has been widened a few miles further on. Enquiry 4 that the council must answer specifically asks if there are any such schemes which may affect the property. Clearly if there are, then details must be sought before any decision is made to exchange contracts. Apart from road widening, the reply to enquiry 4 will also disclose new road schemes that might similarly affect the property.

You say that you would like to use the basement for bedsits although it is at present boarded up. Indeed, your intention is to change the use of the whole of the property from a single dwelling house in the occupation of one family to multiple occupation in the form of bedsits. Two points arise: first, can you use the house in this way and, secondly, can you use the basement? Having considered the basic terms of planning law, and after consultation with my departmental partner, I am of the view that your proposed use would be a material change of use for planning purposes. Without any planning consent authorising the change, the multiple occupation proposed by you would be a breach of planning law. However, the local authority search and enquiries would, from the answer to enquiry 7, reveal planning applications and consents. If there was a consent for the property to be used in this way then there is no difficulty; otherwise you will need to make a planning application, and consequently you will have to decide whether or not you will want to exchange while awaiting the outcome of the application. The risk is, of course, that your application may be unsuccessful notwithstanding that you may well have already exchanged. You could try to make completion conditional upon the consent being issued, although the sellers are unlikely to agree to this as it will inevitably delay completion.

As to the basement, there is a possibility that due to its condition the council have made a closing order declaring the area to be unfit for human habitation. If this is the case the council search and enquiries will reveal this and you may well want to renegotiate the price or withdraw from the transaction altogether.

You have mentioned that nearby, the council has demolished houses to make way for a new area of council houses, and you are clearly concerned to ensure that your proposed property is not similarly affected. Enquiry 13 asks if the property is subject to a compulsory purchase order and any such orders will be registered as land charges. Similarly, enquiry 14 will disclose if the property is in an area designated for slum clearance. Accordingly, a local search result will indicate if a property is or is likely to be the subject of compulsory acquisition by the council; and if this is the case then of course my advice would be that you should not proceed.

Lastly, you have mentioned that there are similar houses nearby that the council is keen to preserve, and you have also mentioned the fact that you are considering making some external alterations by way of double glazing. I have taken these two items together because in fact they are interrelated so far as my advice and the council search are concerned. If councils want to preserve a neighbourhood they can do so by declaring a conservation area. If the property is so affected this will be seen as a land charge, being a restriction on the use of the land, and will be disclosed in the local land charge search result. Indeed, if the property is covered by a conservation order then there are severe restrictions placed on an owner which include a prohibition on external alterations such as new windows. Accordingly, if the property is in a conservation area you will need to enquire of the council to see if it would allow new aluminium windows, otherwise you would be in breach of planning law if you went ahead with the changes without council consent.

I know you do not think that the sellers will provide much information because they are executors who know little or nothing about the property. However, I can tell you that, notwithstanding their capacity, the sellers are still obliged to disclose a local land charge if they are aware of it. (The court case that decided this is called *Rignall Developments Ltd* v *Halil* (1988) and I can let you have further details of it if it is of interest to you.) If the executors have become aware of a local land charge from the deceased's papers then they will be obliged to provide details, failing which you may be entitled to damages or rescission of the contract.

To sum up, I am of the view that your concerns will be addressed by the result of a local land charge search and from the council's replies to enquiries. I therefore suggest that the search be sent to the local authority as a matter of priority and that I will then let you know the result, which should be available two to three weeks from the date of dispatch.

Yours sincerely,

The Trainee Solicitor.

QUESTION 5

You have been instructed by Ms Jane Foat in connection with her freehold property at 1 Storey View, Dunstable. She recently bought the cottage with the aid of a High Wycombe Equitable Building Society mortgage. It was her first purchase and her mortgage was 90% of the purchase price. She particularly liked the house because of the large line of mature willow trees in the neighbour's garden that afforded her garden a lot of attractive summer shade.

She has now moved in, and to her alarm has noted several cracks along the flank wall of the house. She thinks that she did not notice them when she first saw the house because of the heavy shade from the willow trees and the fact that the seller had put lots of garden things, tools, trellis work and large earthenware pots, against that wall. She did not instruct a surveyor herself, but she has shown you the surveyor's report for the Building Society. She has told you that she paid for that survey, having handed over £150, being the fee requested at the time she made her mortgage application. She was told that the Society always gives its applicants copies of the report. A builder has looked at the cracks and thinks that they have been there some time, that they are probably due to subsidence and that the repairs will require underpinning that could cost not less than £20,000. Having recently purchased the house, she does not have any savings to pay for these repairs. Ms Foat requires some advice. Please explain her situation.

Commentary

This is an example of a question which you might encounter in a conveyancing exam that could be answered as an essay. You will still need to refer in your answer to advice for the client, but it is also the kind of question that requires considerable in-depth academic knowledge of the areas involved. In other words, it is one of the few examples of a question in a conveyancing exam that requires legal debate rather than a knowledge and understanding of conveyancing practice.

The difficulty with this kind of question is that it is necessarily going to involve other areas of your legal knowledge that you might have thought would not be required in conveyancing. However, as we hope you by now appreciate, you should always expect the unexpected in conveyancing exams. In this example you will need to draw upon some of your knowledge of the tort of negligence and how it could affect professionals and might arise from any advice they may have given. (See *Hedley Byrne & Co. Ltd* v *Heller & Partners Ltd* [1964] AC 465.) So, you may ask, how is this relevant to conveyancing? Well of course every buyer should obtain his or her own survey report. However, if he or she does not, what other forms of redress will be available? The question seeks to address this topic. But why is this topic arising in this chapter on searches and enquiries? It is located within the chapter because an inspection of the property before exchange is extremely important, both as a survey and to check that the contract describes or shows the property correctly. If such an inspection is not made and there are boundary changes, this could lead to disputes and claims for adverse possession, matters that a buyer will not want to be concerned with when moving in.

Lastly, remember that if you do answer this question as an essay, you must still show form and structure in your answer. Remember that a rambling and diffuse display of your knowledge will not impress the marker. While you may include in the answer all the relevant information, if the marker cannot see any coherence you will inevitably lose marks.

Suggested Answer

Ms Jane Foat has recently purchased a property in Dunstable and now finds that it is affected by subsidence. She did not have her own survey, but she did pay for a report for her mortgagee. She now wants to know what she can do as it seems that she does not have the money to pay for the repairs. She will need to know who, if anyone, she could sue to seek compensation to enable the repairs to be completed. In these circumstances claims against the following will be considered – the seller, the buyer's solicitor and the Building Society's surveyor. However, it should also be carefully noted that in *Low* v *R J Haddock Ltd* [1985] 2 EGLR 247, it was held that a buyer suing over damage caused by tree roots might be contributorily negligent if that buyer did not arrange a survey at the time of purchase.

Is there a claim that could be advanced against the seller? In her instructions Ms Foat has said that she could not see the flank wall of the house when she looked at the property prior to purchase. It seems that there were various garden items obscuring the wall and thereby covering the cracks. It should be noted that in general a seller is under no obligation to reveal defects in the property. There is no warranty given about the state of the property, and it is of course for this reason that all buyers should obtain their own survey report before exchanging contracts. The common law rule of *caveat emptor* applies. Indeed, the Standard Conditions provide in condition 3.1.3 that the buyer accepts the property in the physical state it is in at the date of the contract (unless the seller is building or converting it). However, if the seller has taken steps actually to obscure a physical defect then this might be deemed to be a fraudulent misrepresentation. The misrepresentation would be that the property is free of that defect, and as a consequence the seller could be liable. The case of *Gordon* v *Selico Co. Ltd* [1986] 1 EGLR 71 may be considered similar to Ms Foat's particular circumstances even though it concerned the grant of a lease. In the *Gordon* case the defendant covered over some dry rot in the premises that were being let, and as such the court held that the defendant was indeed liable. Accordingly, if the court accepts that the seller tried to cover up the subsidence by the strategic placing of the garden items then a claim could succeed against the seller.

Is there a claim against the buyer's solicitor? The immediate need is to consider whether there was a duty of care on the part of the buyer's solicitor. It was clear that the buyer was a first-time purchaser who was clearly naïve and unused to the conveyancing process. In these circumstances it must be the case that a solicitor should advise such a buyer to obtain a full survey. If this was not done then the solicitor might be liable. It was also the case that it was known that there were large trees nearby. The close proximity of large trees is considered to be a factor indicating the desirability of a full survey. However, did the solicitor know about the trees? Could he or she, or should he or she, have known about them? If not then this is likely to limit the liability of the solicitor. To sum up, if the solicitor was dealing with a buyer who should have been advised about the need for a survey and no such advice was given, then there could be a claim against the lawyer. If the solicitor knew about some special circumstances that meant a survey was vital, and if the solicitor then failed to suggest a survey, then a claim could arise. (Please also see *Neighbour* v *Barker* [1992] EGCS 50, CA.)

Is there the possibility of a claim against the Building Society's surveyor? Certainly a surveyor who is neglectful and slack in his preparation of a survey report privately commissioned by the buyer is liable in negligence. (This is reinforced by s. 13 of the Supply of Goods and Services Act 1982, whereby a term is implied that the report will be carried out with reasonable skill and care.) The damages will be the difference between the contracted purchase price and the true market value. (See *Perry* v *Sidney Phillips & Son* [1982] 1 WLR 1297.) Also the surveyor will be under a duty of care, of course, to the lender. (See *London and South of England Building Society* v *Stone* [1983] 1 WLR 1242.) The question that must therefore be asked is whether Ms Foat is entitled to a similar duty. The case of *Yianni* v *Edwin Evans & Sons* [1982] QB 438, clearly shows that the law now is that a surveyor will also owe a duty of care to the proposed borrower as well as to the lender. In this case it was held that if a report for a mortgagee was negligently prepared and as a result the buyer suffered loss, the buyer could sue the surveyor in negligence. Here the buyer did not see the report, but the court was of the view that the surveyor had missed obvious structural defects and owed a duty of care to the buyer. This was further confirmed by the House of Lords in the case of *Smith* v *Eric S Bush (a Firm)* [1990] 1 AC 831. It was held that where a surveyor was instructed by the lender to survey a 'modest' house then the lender's surveyor did indeed have a duty of care owed to the borrower. It had to be understood that the borrower would not be arranging his own survey and would rely on the lender's report. This case also highlighted the court's willingness to strike down exclusion clauses that are unfair and unreasonable and which contravene s. 2 and s. 3 of the Unfair

Contract Terms Act 1977. Thus the report cannot exclude liability by the incorporation of an exclusion clause where a 'modest' house is concerned.

Provided Ms Foat can establish that the surveyor was negligent in the preparation of the report by failing to highlight the cracks caused by subsidence, then it seems that the above cases, and in particular *Yianni* and *Smith*, clearly suggest that a claim will succeed against the lender's surveyor. There would seem to be a strong case for alleging negligence, in that a prudent surveyor should have looked carefully at all the outside walls, especially where they are close to mature trees that are known to cause subsidence to nearby buildings.

To sum up, there could be a claim against the seller if there was an attempt to hide the structural defects. There might be a claim against the buyer's solicitor if the lawyer failed to advise a naïve first-time purchaser of the need to commission a survey, particularly if that solicitor knew of the nearby large trees. However of even more importance is the strong possibility of a successful claim against the lender's surveyor for the negligent preparation of the report that Ms Foat may have relied upon when deciding to proceed with the purchase.

5 Deducing and Investigating Title

INTRODUCTION

This is the part of the conveyancing syllabus that invariably seems to cause law students most pain and anguish, in particular the deduction and investigation of title to *unregistered* land. The statutory and common law rules and procedures can appear, in theory at least, extremely complex, and many students understandably find them difficult to grasp. The position is compounded by the fact that until these rules are put into practice, the explanation on the written page can at times seem almost incomprehensible. That is why this topic more than any other warrants the phrase, albeit hackneyed, 'practice makes perfect'. Indeed, if there is one part of the conveyancing syllabus where practising past questions really pays dividends, this is it. Due to the relative complexity of unregistered title, four out of the five questions that follow relate to unregistered land.

In comparison, the investigation of *registered* title is relatively straightforward, in that the entries on the register will be definitive, and the conveyancer can be guided quite easily by the Land Registration Acts and the accompanying rules. You will appreciate that all areas of England and Wales are now in a compulsory area of registration and so the majority of titles you will encounter in practice will be registered. That at least may be of some comfort to you, but it does not hide the fact that in practice you will have to deal with unregistered titles and, more importantly for you right now, you may have to cope with one in the conveyancing exam. The secret, as always, is to be prepared.

Here are some tips when faced with an unregistered title. Before plunging headlong into the minutiae of each document, pause a moment and take an overall view of the title. Check first that the proposed root of title is 'good'. Remember that to be a 'good' root not only must the document be at least 15 years old, but it must also (i) deal with or show title to the whole legal and equitable estate, (ii) contain an adequate description of the property, and (iii) do nothing to cast doubt on the title.

Secondly, trace the chain of ownership from the root document right down to the present owner and ask yourself some basic questions. Are there any gaps in the chain of title? Are there any missing documents? Have the names of the parties changed? Are the dates in order? Have the land charges searches been made correctly against all the estate owners? Did the individual estate owners have the ability to sell? Should the title have been substantively registered following an earlier disposition?

Thirdly, check whether there has in the past been a sale of part. If there has, look out for obvious defects such as an inadequate property description, no memorandum on the previous conveyance, no acknowledgement for production of earlier deeds and no evidence of copy documents having been examined against originals.

Having taken a global view of the title, you can now begin to consider the detailed provisions of each document. Check for such matters as missing clauses, any failure to stamp, references to earlier deeds, incorrect plans and imperfect execution of deeds.

We suggest that you try this approach for yourself in Question 2. Sometimes the examiner will give you an epitome of title without actually attaching the documents of title and Question 3 follows this format.

QUESTION 1

Your principal has passed you the deeds of 'Tregavean', Ridgewood Close, Seatown. Your firm is acting for the owners, Christopher and Jill Browning, in the sale of the property with vacant possession. The property is freehold and has an unregistered title. Seatown came within an area of compulsory registration on 1 December 1990.

The property is presently mortgaged to the Cornshire Building Society who have forwarded the deeds to your firm to be held to order on the usual terms.

Your principal has asked you to deduce title to the buyer's solicitors. He has handed you the file and the deeds packet. The deeds packet contains several documents, each listed in the schedule below.

Identify with reasons which document or documents would be suitable as the root of title and then deduce title by drafting an epitome. Explain your reasons for including or excluding the following listed documents in your epitome:

SCHEDULE OF DOCUMENTS

1.   A conveyance on sale dated 20 July 1963 from Richard Tyler to Ashley Perryman containing a restrictive covenant ('the 1963 covenant') imposed on Ashley Perryman.

2.   A conveyance on sale dated 3 July 1971 from Ashley Perryman to John Little, stating that the property is sold subject to the 1963 covenant.

3.   A legal mortgage dated 3 July 1971 given by John Little to the Westhampton Building Society, with a receipt endorsed on it dated 5 October 1974.

4.   A lease of part of the property dated 9 July 1971 by John Little to Wendy Webb for a term of 12 years.

5.   A land charges search dated 29 September 1974 against Richard Tyler, Ashley Perryman and John Little, revealing no entries save for a D(ii) entry against Ashley Perryman.

6.   A conveyance on sale dated 5 October 1974 from John Little to Mary Ann Jessop, stating that the property is sold subject to the 1963 covenant and also subject to and with the benefit of the lease dated 9 July 1971.

7.   A legal mortgage dated 5 October 1974 given by Mary Ann Jessop to the Cornshire Building Society with a receipt endorsed on it dated 1 October 1979.

8.   A general power of attorney dated 15 September 1979 given by Guy Budd to Steven Cox.

9.   An examined copy grant of probate of the estate of Mary Ann Jessop deceased dated 23 September 1979 to her executors Guy Budd and Ann Budd.

10.   A land charges search dated 25 November 1979 against Mary Ann Jessop, Guy Budd and Ann Budd revealing no entries save for a C(i) entry against Mary Ann Jessop.

11.   An assent dated 30 November 1979 from Guy Budd (executed on his behalf by his attorney Steven Cox) and Ann Budd to Philip Ross.

12.   A lease of the whole of the property dated 28 February 1985 by Philip Ross to Peter Kay for a term of 25 years.

13.   A copy of a planning permission dated 14 March 1988.

14.   A deed of surrender dated 11 April 1988 of the lease to Peter Kay.

15.   A local land charges search dated 4 May 1990.

16.   A land charges search dated 8 June 1990 against Philip Ross, Peter Kay, Christopher Browning and Jill Browning revealing no entries.

17.   A conveyance on sale dated 12 June 1990 from Philip Ross to Christopher Browning and Jill Browning as joint tenants stating that the property is sold subject to the 1963 covenant.

18.   A legal charge dated 12 June 1990 given by Christopher Browning and Jill Browning to the Cornshire Building Society.

Commentary

This question will exercise your skill in spotting the relevant from the irrelevant, the hallmark of any competent lawyer. Modern questions will endeavour to mirror real life and so, unlike most law degree questions, you will sometimes be given facts or documents which bear no direct relevance to the answer required. This process of sifting for relevant material will be carried out by a solicitor in practice almost on a daily basis.

Those of you who understand the concept of 'root of title' and are proficient in finding your way around unregistered titles should have little trouble in achieving high marks on this question. Conversely, those with thin knowledge are likely to flounder!

A careful reading of the question ('... or excluding ...') should alert you to the fact that not all documents are to be included in the epitome.

Choose your root of title and explain succinctly why you have chosen it. The choice of root may not be straightforward and there may be more than one document which could qualify, so do not be afraid to discuss possible alternatives.

Once you have dealt with the root, run down the list of documents and tick those you intend to include in the epitome while at the same time making a rough note of the reasons why each document should or should not be included. It may be safer to deal with your explanation first before attempting to draft the epitome. That way you will have more time to think through your reasoning fully (and perhaps change your mind to the good without recourse to the correcting fluid!).

You may decide that some documents strictly do not need to be included but that it is courteous and customary to do so. For example, land charges searches are normally abstracted (and indeed must be if the National Protocol is being used). Do not be afraid to make these points in your explanation; it will help the examiner to appreciate your understanding of the question.

Lastly, draft the epitome clearly and legibly. Do not forget to complete the heading and all columns, just as you would in a conveyancing office.

The far righthand column of the epitome form often confuses students. Generally, unless there has been a sale of part or administration of an estate, all original documents will be handed over to the purchaser's solicitor on completion. The grant of probate in this case is not the original (which is probably still held by the executors) but an examined copy. This is sufficient to deduce title and thus the original grant will not be handed over on completion.

Suggested Answer

The suggested draft epitome is set out in Appendix 5.

Explanation of draft epitome

It is first necessary to determine which document will constitute the root of title. The following criteria should be noted:

(a)   It must be at least 15 years old (Law of Property Act 1969, s. 23 amending Law of Property Act 1925, s. 44(1)).

(b)   It must deal with the ownership of the whole legal and equitable estate.

(c)   It must contain a description by which the property can be identified.

(d)   It must show nothing to cast any doubt on the title of the disposing party.

The 1979 assent is the latest document that may be used but it should be checked as it may fail test (c) above. Assents often describe the land transferred by reference to a full description in an earlier deed, e.g. here possibly the 1974 or earlier conveyances. Moreover, it may fail to specify the estate assented to, simply vesting the property for all the estate or interest of the deceased. If the description is inadequate then the 1974 conveyance should be used as the root (assuming this also satisfies the criteria for a good root). There is nothing to prevent any of the earlier conveyances (or even the 1971 mortgage) being used as the root, provided the above criteria are met.

The draft epitome in this answer assumes that the assent is a good root and will be used as such. The 1979 grant of probate is also deduced as proof of the assentors' title to make the assent. A memorandum of the 1979 assent should have been endorsed on the rear of the original grant before this copy was made and examined, so this should be checked.

Having established the root of title it is then necessary to deduce all the links in the chain of the freehold title from the root document to the document by which ownership became vested in the seller, i.e. the 1990 conveyance.

Can the documents created earlier than the root be disregarded and excluded from the epitome? Not without checking whether any of them fall within the

Law of Property Act 1925, s. 45(1), which lists the exceptions to the general rule that precludes a buyer from requiring production of or raising requisitions about the pre-root title.

There are two documents here which do fall within the exceptions. First, the power of attorney of 15 September 1979 granted to Steven Cox under which the abstracted 1979 assent is executed. This exception was confirmed in the case of *Re Copelin's Contract* [1937] 4 All ER 447. Secondly, the 1963 conveyance, although dated pre-root, imposes a restrictive covenant which, as it is protected by registration (see D(ii) entry in Land Charges Search of 29 September 1974), will bind a purchaser of the legal estate for money or money's worth (s. 4(6) of the Land Charges Act 1972). Accordingly, both the power of attorney and the 1963 conveyance should be abstracted by inclusion in the epitome.

The land charges search certificates are also included. Although a seller is generally not obliged to deduce these (because they are not documents of title) it is standard practice and courteous to do so, because it saves the buyer's solicitor from having to repeat them. If the National Protocol is being used then the seller's solicitor *must* provide a certificate of search against 'appropriate' names. The 1974 search certificate is pre-root but it confirms that the 1963 covenant has been protected by registration.

The land charges search against Mary Ann Jessop reveals a C(i) puisne mortgage. Presumably Mary Ann took out a second mortgage after her first mortgage to Cornshire Building Society. This could be a potential problem and we would need to check that the puisne mortgage has been discharged. We could do this by requesting an office copy of the C(i) entry from the Land Charges Registry in Plymouth (which would reveal the name of the mortgagee), and then by writing to the mortgagee requesting confirmation of discharge (it is hoped!). If it is discharged our client would then be entitled to require the mortgagee to remove the C(i) entry.

The property is being sold with vacant possession, so do the leases have to be abstracted? The 1971 lease, although still subsisting post-root, does not have to be abstracted because it has expired by effluxion of time. However, some conveyancers may choose to include it in the epitome on the basis that it is still part of the post-root title. The 1985 lease is no longer subsisting but it has not expired by effluxion of time; it has been surrendered. Consequently, the lease and the surrender will be deduced to enable the buyer to check the validity of the surrender.

The 1988 planning permission and the 1990 local land charges search are not documents of title and have no place on an epitome of title.

The 1990 conveyance to the seller is included to complete the chain of title. The legal charge of the same date is also listed. Although the latter will no doubt be discharged by the seller on completion, it is still a subsisting mortgage affecting title to the property and as such must be deduced.

QUESTION 2

Your client is purchasing The Corner House, Chiltern Road, Pitton. The property has an unregistered title which your principal has asked you to investigate. In the draft contract, the root of title is expressed to be a Conveyance of 13 January 1980 and the seller is stated as Flora Nicholson. The property came within an area of compulsory registration on 1 December 1990.

Investigate the attached Abstract of Title (refer to Appendix 6) and list and explain the requisitions you would raise on the title deduced.

Commentary

You will need no reminding to read the introductory paragraph carefully. It is likely to, and does, contain information which will have a crucial bearing on the requisitions you will raise. Note especially that the title in question is unregistered. Different considerations apply to the investigation of an unregistered as opposed to a registered title.

The question asks you to raise requisitions 'on the title deduced', so it is important that you confine your requisitions exclusively to the title you have been given. Do not be drawn into a discussion of generalities concerning such matters as local searches, standard pre-contract enquiries or requisitions of an administrative nature commonly found on the Completion Information Form (e.g. What are the arrangements for release of keys?).

This is a traditional abstract. It takes the form of a précis of the documents and events which constitute the title. In the interests of brevity an abstract is often abbreviated (which can make it virtually indecipherable to non-conveyancers!), but in this question the text is set out in full. These days the traditional form is not as commonly used in practice as an epitome of title with copy documents attached, but it does crop up from time to time so you must know how to deal with it.

Before putting pen to paper it is vital that you spend enough time familiarising yourself with the abstract. The first thing many students do when faced with an abstract is to start writing before thinking through a logical plan of action. Don't panic! Just read the abstract carefully and jot down on a piece of rough paper the defects and discrepancies which will form the subject matter of your requisitions. For instance, you will note from a careful reading of the January 1994 conveyance that the buyers purchased as tenants in common. If you fail to spot this, you may be drawn into an irrelevant discussion of the Law of Property (Joint Tenants) Act 1964.

Notice that the question says 'list *and explain*'. A buyer's solicitor will raise requisitions by submitting to the seller's solicitor a list of numbered questions, in the same way as enquiries before contract. For this problem, however, you must demonstrate that you understand *why* you are raising the requisitions; that is the reason for having to explain them as well.

The preferred approach is to write the requisition and then follow it with your explanation before moving on to the next requisition, and so on. You should not attempt an essay-style answer, which will be harder to write and take the examiner longer to mark.

We recommend that you familiarise yourself with abstracts and practise this type of question as much as possible before sitting a conveyancing examination. In this way you should become adept at coping with abstracts and will tackle them with confidence.

Suggested Answer

1. 'Please supply a copy of the Conveyance dated 18 January 1975.'

The abstract of title as deduced does not contain an adequate description of the property. It is clear from the contents of the 1980 Conveyance that the property is fully described in the 1975 Conveyance. This Conveyance also creates a right of way and imposes covenants and conditions which, provided they are registered as D(ii) land charges, will bind a purchaser for value. Accordingly we are entitled to examine the 1975 Conveyance, notwithstanding that it is dated prior to the root of title.

2. 'The 1986 land charges search certificate is out of date. Please supply copies of all land charges search certificates in your possession.'

The June 1986 Conveyance was not completed within 15 working days of the April 1986 search certificate and so the latter cannot be relied upon as evidence that there are no subsisting entries against Benjamin Edwards. The seller's solicitors will be asked to see whether the search was renewed, and also to check for other search certificates which, if they exist and are valid, will obviate the need for the buyer's solicitor to carry them out now.

3. 'The Conveyance of 20 June 1986 does not appear to have been stamped. Please clarify and, if necessary, confirm that it will be stamped before completion at the seller's expense.'

The 1986 Conveyance is the only conveyance abstracted which does not indicate a stamp beneath the date in the margin. The conveyance does not contain a certificate for value so it seems likely that the *ad valorem* stamp and particulars delivered (PD) stamp were overlooked. The importance of this requisition is that an improperly stamped document is not admissible in evidence (Stamp Act 1891 s. 14). A buyer is entitled to have every deed forming a link in the chain of title properly stamped (see *Whiting* v *Loomes* (1881) 17 Ch D 10, CA).

4. 'The Mortgage dated 20 June 1986 does not appear to have been discharged. Please confirm that a receipt for all money due under the mortgage, naming Sharon Munro and properly executed by Blakey Bank Ltd, is endorsed on the mortgage deed.'

The buyer's solicitor must ensure that all mortgages revealed by the abstract have been properly discharged. The receipt referred to above is that prescribed by the Law of Property Act 1925, s. 115 for unregistered land. The section also provides that the receipt should name the person making the payment. Here, we should check that the person named in the receipt as making the payment was the then owner of the property (Sharon Munro), otherwise the receipt may not discharge the mortgage but instead operate to transfer ownership of it from the original mortgagee (Blakey Bank Ltd) to the person named as making the payment. (See also *Cumberland Court (Brighton) Ltd* v *Taylor* [1964] Ch 29.)

5. 'Please supply a copy of the Grant of Probate dated 19 January 1991 and confirm that the original or an examined copy will be handed over on completion.'

It is likely that the original Grant has been retained by the personal representatives. However, the Grant is still a document of title and, as such, a subsequent buyer is entitled to receive at least an examined copy of it.

We will need to see a copy of the Grant to be sure that all proving personal representatives named therein duly joined in the subsequent Assent in favour of Elizabeth Campbell. This is a requirement imposed by the Administration of Estates Act 1925, s. 68.

We must also check the Grant for any memoranda endorsed thereon. There should be one endorsement only, namely that of the Assent to Elizabeth Campbell. The absence of such an endorsement would constitute a defect in title as the Assent may theoretically have been defeated by a later sale of the land by the personal representatives to a buyer who took from them a written statement that they had made no previous assent or conveyance of the land (i.e. a statement under the Administration of Estates Act 1925 s. 36(6)).

6. 'Please confirm that the Assent dated 29 July 1991 contains an acknowledgement for production of the Grant of Probate dated 19 January 1991.'

Whenever an original document of title is retained on completion (in this case, the Grant of Probate) the buyer (or in this case the assentee) and successors in title are entitled to an acknowledgement of the right to production of the original (*Cooper* v *Emery* (1884) 1 Ph 388). This is because a subsequent owner of the land may need to inspect the original at a later date. The benefit of the acknowledgement runs with the land.

7. 'Please explain why the title was not registered following completion of the Conveyance dated 14 January 1994 and confirm that the sellers will register the title with Title Absolute at their own expense before completion.'

The question tells us that the land became compulsorily registrable on 1 December 1990. Accordingly, the 1994 Conveyance would have induced compulsory registration and the seller must therefore regularise the position immediately. It is noted that an assent (e.g. the 1991 Assent) does not induce first registration. (Our other requisitions will be rendered superfluous if the seller can achieve registration with Title Absolute but this seems unlikely at present given the apparent defects in title!)

8. 'Why is Alastair Nicholson not selling the property in conjunction with Flora Nicholson? Please deduce devolution of title from them jointly to Flora alone.'

Unless Alastair also joins in the contract there will be a break in the chain of ownership and a consequent defect in title. It is apparent from the Conveyance of 14 January 1994 that Alastair and Flora purchased the property as tenants in common. Accordingly, if Alastair has died we shall need to see evidence of his death (e.g., death certificate) and then a second trustee will need to be appointed to overreach the equitable interests under his will or intestacy. Alternatively, he may have conveyed his interest to Flora (perhaps pursuant to a divorce settlement), in which case a copy of the conveyance to Flora will be required.

9. 'Please confirm that the Mortgage dated 14 January 1994 will be discharged on or before completion.'

It is essential that all subsisting mortgages are discharged on or before completion. Normally, the seller's solicitors give the buyer's solicitors on completion an undertaking in Law Society format to discharge the mortgage from the proceeds of sale. It is therefore prudent to raise this point at the requisitions stage.

QUESTION 3

You act for prospective buyers of the freehold property known as 9 Oak Avenue, Downminster. You have received the epitome of title set out opposite. The seller is Walter, selling as beneficial owner. Explain with reasons the matters which from a perusal of the epitome will concern you. You may assume that the documents are in the correct form, have been properly executed and (where appropriate) are correctly stamped. Downminster became an area of compulsory registration on 1 December 1990.

EPITOME OF TITLE

relating to freehold property 9 Oak Avenue, Downminster

DATE	DOCUMENT/EVENT	WHETHER ORIGINAL TO BE HANDED OVER
31 May 1979	Conveyance on sale by Ian, Greg and Trevor to Greg	Yes
7 February 1982	Power of attorney by Greg to Neil	Yes
10 November 1983	Conveyance on sale by Greg (acting by his attorney Neil) to Jack and Jill as joint tenants in equity	Yes
3 July 1985	Death of Jack	N/A
4 August 1990	Conveyance on sale by Jill to Dennis	Yes
4 April 1994	Death of Dennis	N/A
24 June 1994	Letters of administration of estate of Dennis granted to Walter	No

Commentary

The information provided will be sufficient to answer the question so do not worry that you have not been given copies of the documents. Similarly, you have been told that the documents are all in order so it is important not to waste time raising hypothetical technical points about the form, execution or stamping of the documents.

This question is clearly practical in nature because you have been given a title to consider, but there is scope for academic appraisal as well. You have the opportunity, if you wish, to answer in essay style, and this will clearly suit some students. Others may prefer to answer in point form and would not be penalised for doing so. To add variety to the style of answering in this book our suggested answer takes the form of an essay. You will note that the essay begins by listing the relevant areas of discussion and then goes on to deal with each one in turn. A well-structured approach will naturally appeal to the examiner who will immediately see that you have grasped the important points. Try not to ramble around the issues, but meet them head on, clearly and concisely.

Lastly, a mention about evidencing the death of estate owners (you will notice two deaths in this title). It is our experience that students sometimes fail to appreciate that production of a death certificate as evidence of death is unnecessary where a grant of representation has been obtained to the estate; the grant itself is quite acceptable evidence of the death. One occasion, however, when a request for a death certificate would be appropriate is on the death of a joint tenant in equity, a situation that has arisen here.

Suggested Answer

The areas of concern arising from this question are essentially four-fold and relate to: a conveyance by trustees to one of themselves; an out of date power of attorney; the operation of the Law of Property (Joint Tenants) Act 1964, and the capacity in which a personal representative may sell land. Each area will be considered in turn.

(a)   By the conveyance of 31 May 1979 it appears that the co-owners, Ian, Greg and Trevor, conveyed the property to one of themselves, namely Greg. From the information provided it is unclear in what capacity the three of them held the equitable interest in the property, although they would have held the legal estate as personal representatives or trustees for sale. The Law of Property Act 1925, ss. 34 to 36 impose a statutory trust for sale where land is held by co-owners, and as such Ian, Greg and Trevor were trustees. Consequently, prima facie, the sale by trustees to one of their number is in breach of trust and the conveyance is voidable by the beneficiaries under the trust unless one of the following can be proven:

(i)   proof of a pre-existing contract to purchase, or a right of pre-emption or option to purchase in favour of Greg;

(ii)   proof that all the legally competent beneficiaries consented to the conveyance to Greg;

(iii)   that the conveyance to Greg was made pursuant to a court order;

(iv)   that the conveyance to Greg was sanctioned by the trust instrument;
or

(v)   that Greg was a beneficiary under a will or intestacy.

We should therefore request our seller's solicitor to provide evidence (in the form of one of the above) that the transaction by the trustees to one of their number was not in breach of trust.

(b)   The conveyance by Greg dated 10 November 1983 was executed on his behalf by his attorney, Neil. We may assume from a reading of the question that the power of attorney was in the correct form and the sale was therefore within the attorney's authority. However, it is vital to determine whether the power was revoked before the attorney executed the conveyance of 10 November 1983. The purchasers in that conveyance would have taken good title only if they bought in good faith without knowledge of revocation of the power (s. 5(2) of the Powers of Attorney Act 1971). Our client being a subsequent buyer will obtain the protection of s. 5(4) of the Powers of Attorney Act 1971 if either:

(i)   the transaction between the attorney, Neil, and Jack and Jill took place within 12 months of the grant of the power; or

(ii)   the purchasers Jack and Jill made a statutory declaration within three months of completion of the transaction stating that they had no knowledge of any revocation of the power.

As more than 12 months elapsed between the granting of the power, on 7 February 1982, and the conveyance to Jack and Jill, on 10 November 1983, a statutory declaration must be obtained. If one was not signed at the time this could be a problem as Jack is dead and the whereabouts of Jill may be unknown. However, even if Jill cannot be found, the position may not be irretrievable if the solicitors who acted for Jack and Jill on their purchase can be located. The reason for this is that a certificate of lack of knowledge of revocation given by *that person's solicitor* may be sufficient for Land Registry purposes (see Practice Direction of 26 April 1991).

(c)   The epitome states that Jack and Jill held the property on trust for themselves as joint tenants in equity. Provided the joint tenancy was not severed prior to Jack's death, it appears that the only evidence of Jack's death we shall require is a certified copy of his death certificate. This is because Jill was entitled to Jack's share by survivorship, and on Jack's death Jill became beneficially entitled to the whole legal estate and equitable interest in the land. Once the legal and equitable interests merged and vested in Jill, the trust for sale became extinguished and Jill was able to convey as sole beneficial owner (see s. 7 of the Law of Property (Amendment) Act 1926). In this event, the terms of Jack's will or intestacy are of no relevance to the title, and will not concern us.

However, as the land is unregistered we must check against the possibility of Jack and Jill's joint tenancy having been severed before Jack's death. If this had occurred, Jack's equitable interest would not have passed to Jill by survivorship but would have passed under the terms of Jack's will or intestacy. In this event, the trust for sale would have continued and, unless it could be shown that Jill was entitled to the whole equitable estate anyway (for which we would want to see the grant of representation to Jack's estate and an assent made in favour of Jill), another trustee should have been appointed to sell jointly with Jill (in the conveyance of 4 August 1990). A sale by two trustees would have overreached the equitable interests under Jack's will or intestacy.

A severance of a joint tenancy can occur in several ways. For example, by one joint tenant serving on the other a written notice of severance, or on the bankruptcy of a joint tenant. How can we be sure that Jack and Jill's joint tenancy has not been severed? The answer lies in the Law of Property (Joint Tenants) Act 1964, which offers protection to a purchaser of unregistered land where there has been a sale by a sole surviving joint tenant since 1925 (interestingly the 1964 statute acted retrospectively). The 1964 Act provides that a purchaser in these circumstances may assume that no severance of the joint tenancy has occurred provided:

(i)   no memorandum of severance has been endorsed on or annexed to the conveyance to the joint tenants; and

(ii)   at the time of the conveyance to the joint tenants, no bankruptcy proceedings were registered against either joint tenant; and

(iii)   either the conveyance by the survivor contained a statement (usually in the recitals) that the survivor was solely and beneficially entitled to the property, or that the survivor actually conveyed as beneficial owner.

Points (i) and (iii) above can be checked by examining the conveyance by Jill to Dennis dated 4 August 1990, but point (ii) can only be verified by carrying out a land charges search against both Jack and Jill to ensure there were no bankruptcy proceedings. We could do this ourselves, or ask to see the search made at the time of the 1990 Conveyance on behalf of the purchaser, Dennis.

(d)   Lastly, the question tells us that Walter is purporting to sell as beneficial owner. However, the epitome does not support the contention that the seller is beneficially entitled to the land. Walter is the personal representative of Dennis's estate as evidenced by the grant of letters of administration dated 24 June 1994. As such we cannot accept that Walter sells as beneficial owner unless this is proven. To this end we would ask to see a copy of the assent that Walter should have executed in favour of himself. The point here is that even if Walter is beneficially entitled to the property under Dennis's intestacy, Walter cannot properly sell as beneficial owner unless he first executes an assent in favour of himself (see *Re King's Will Trusts* [1964] Ch 542).

It is noted from the righthand column of the epitome that the original grant of letters of administration is not being handed over to us on completion. Any assent by Walter to himself should therefore contain an acknowledgement for future production of the grant. This acknowledgement will run with the land thus benefiting future estate owners. In addition, a memorandum of any assent by Walter to himself should be endorsed on the Grant, and we should check this.

Instead of selling as beneficial owner Walter could sell to our client in the capacity of personal representative – this would obviate the need for him to execute an assent and would seem the most sensible course to take in the circumstances. However, we must appreciate that the implied covenants for title given by a personal representative are not as extensive as those given by a beneficial owner.

On completion of our client's purchase, the land will become compulsorily registrable and our client will wish to receive an Absolute Title, being the best class of title that can be granted. The title as deduced is defective and the Land Registry would not grant an Absolute Title until all the above points have been resolved. In conclusion therefore, we would want to be satisfied on these matters before we could advise our client to proceed with the intended purchase of the property. We could also consider the possibility of defective title indemnity insurance to be arranged at the seller's cost.

QUESTION 4

RICHARDS ABBEY AND PARTNERS, SOLICITORS

INTERNAL MEMORANDUM

To   The Trainee Solicitor

From   The Senior Partner

Re our clients Sam and Jane Cluanie: purchase of Flat 3, 125 Clothier Street, Kemptville, Cornshire

Sam and Jane are old friends and clients who have put in an offer to buy the above leasehold property from Provincial Finance Ltd, a mortgagee in possession. Our clients are buying with the aid of a mortgage and we are also instructed by their mortgagee. Apparently the owners of the flat are mortgaged up to the hilt. Provincial Finance Ltd is second in a line of three mortgagees and we shall obviously have to make sure that Sam and Jane get good title. It is some time since I acted on a purchase from a mortgagee. Please would you research the following points and let me have your brief report by this evening:

(a)   Do we have to investigate the seller's entitlement to sell?

(b)   As matters stand, how do we ensure that Sam will buy the property free from any of the mortgages?

We shall be using the Law Society contract incorporating the Standard Conditions of Sale. The seller's solicitors have deduced title by sending me a copy of the entries inside their client's Charge Certificate, which I attach (refer to Appendix 7). In your report, please mention any problem regarding the title and the deduction of it. I have to say I am a little concerned about the presence of the restriction and caution – can you reassure me?

Commentary

You have received a memorandum from the senior partner who requires a 'brief report by this evening' so you will need to act quickly! A busy senior partner will not appreciate a long-winded diatribe on the finer points of sales by mortgagee or registered leasehold titles. The partner has told you specifically what is required, so stick to the matters in question and make your memorandum in response short and to the point.

You will need to demonstrate a clear understanding of the principles of overreaching in the context of a sale by a mortgagee. There are a number of entries on the register to consider. You should appreciate that the third mortgage and caution registered after the seller's charge will be overreached by the mortgagee's sale, and so may be ignored. The restriction is also something of a red herring. Although this affects future dispositions by a survivor of one of the registered proprietors, it does not prevent a disposition by a mortgagee under its power of sale.

This is a classic case for P.A.T. (Pause and Think). Unless you think the question through, you run the risk of setting off on the wrong track, for instance by writing at length about the implications of the restriction and caution which is completely uncalled for. You will not want to find, after writing perhaps a page about cautions, that you realise only then that the presence of a caution *on these facts* will be no obstacle to a sale.

You will notice also the reference to the copy (not *office* copy) entries of title and the Standard Conditions of Sale, with the specific query concerning deduction of the title – easy marks should be gained here if you appreciate the fundamentals of deduction of title to registered land.

Lastly, whenever you are given a registered leasehold title in an exam, always check its class – very often it will be good leasehold, thus inviting an appraisal of the deficiencies of this class of title.

Suggested Answer

RICHARDS ABBEY AND PARTNERS, SOLICITORS

INTERNAL MEMORANDUM

To   The Senior Partner

From   The Trainee Solicitor

Re our clients Sam and Jane Cluanie: purchase of Flat 3, 125 Clothier Street, Kemptville, Cornshire

I refer to your memorandum on the above and report as follows:-

Sale by mortgagee

1.   A purchaser from a mortgagee must be satisfied on the following two counts:

(a)   That the mortgagee's power of sale exists.

(b)   That the mortgagee's power of sale has arisen.

2.   A power of sale is implied into every legal mortgage unless expressly excluded in the mortgage deed (s. 101 of the Law of Property Act 1925). We shall need to inspect the second mortgage deed to check this.

3.   We must also check the second mortgage to ensure that the selling mortgagee's power of sale has arisen, i.e. that the principal monies have become due for repayment. This is normally stated to be a date early on in the mortgage term (e.g. one month after the date of the mortgage).

4.   It is not necessary for a purchaser from a mortgagee to check that the power of sale has become exercisable (although the mortgagee must check this, otherwise the mortgagee may be liable in damages to the mortgagor).

5.   A sale by a second mortgagee cannot affect the security of a prior mortgagee. Therefore Mr and Mrs Cluanie will take subject to the first mortgage unless the selling mortgagee discharges the first mortgage from the proceeds of sale. We must obviously insist on this by requiring the seller's solicitors to give an undertaking on completion to discharge the charge in favour of Cornshire Building Society and to send us Form 53 upon receipt from the Society.

6.   The buyers will take free of the seller's registered charge, although on completion, the charge technically is not discharged.

7.   The third mortgage was registered after the registration of the seller's charge and thus will be overreached by the sale. Mr and Mrs Cluanie will therefore take free of it.

The Title

8.   I note that the Standard Conditions are being used. Under Standard Condition 4.2.1 a seller's solicitor must deduce title to registered land by means of office copy entries, so the photocopies we have of the entries inside the Charge Certificate will not be sufficient. Moreover, when we come to do our pre- completion Land Registry search, we must specify a 'search from date' which is less than 12 months old. The search from date is taken from the office copies, so it follows that we cannot do the search unless we have office copies which are less than 12 months old (see the Land Registration (Official Searches) Rules 1993). We must insist that the seller's solicitors deduce title in this way.

9. Entry No. 4 in the Property Register reveals a Deed of Covenant dated 8 March 1984 which is supplemental to the registered lease. The register indicates that a copy of the Deed is filed at the Land Registry. We must ask the seller's solicitors to produce an office copy of it, so that we can establish the nature and extent of the rights and obligations contained in the deed and how they may affect our clients' proposed use and enjoyment of the property.

10. We should be concerned that the leasehold title is registered only with a good leasehold title. This means that the Land Registry are satisfied that the lease itself is good, but they have not approved the superior freehold title (and, if they exist, any intermediate leasehold titles). Consequently the right of the landlord to grant the lease is not guaranteed and our clients, once registered as proprietors, would take subject to any right in derogation of the landlord's title to grant the lease. These days a good leasehold title is unlikely to be acceptable to Mr and Mrs Cluanie's mortgagee, for whom we also act, and we must report the position to them and seek instructions before committing our clients to the purchase. In order for the leasehold title to be become fully good and marketable, it must be upgraded by the Land Registry to an absolute title. Accordingly we should ask the seller's solicitors to deduce the whole title to the freehold (which is presumably unregistered) and any intermediate leasehold titles. Once we are happy with the superior title(s) and are satisfied that the Land Registry will approve the superior title(s) and will upgrade the leasehold title to absolute, then we can accept the leasehold title.

The Restriction
11. This indicates that Margaret Elsie Logsdail and Constance Logsdail hold the property as tenants in common in equity and prevents a disposition by the survivor of them except by order of the registrar or court. However, the restriction will not prevent a sale by the mortgagee under its power of sale (nor indeed any sale by *both* proprietors) so we need not be concerned with it.

The Caution
12. This protects a third party interest in the property (possibly an equitable mortgage) in favour of the cautioner, Stephen Longman (Finance) Ltd. The nature of the interest need be of no concern to us, however, as it will be overreached by the sale by Provincial Finance Ltd, the proprietor of a registered charge.

Trainee Solicitor: time engaged 30 minutes.

QUESTION 5

RICHARDS ABBEY AND PARTNERS, SOLICITORS

INTERNAL MEMORANDUM

To   The Trainee Solicitor

From   The Training Partner

Re our client William McKnight
William McKnight came to see me this morning about a problem he has with
some unregistered land he has inherited. His father, James McKnight, died 10
years ago. His will appointed James McKnight's two brothers to be his
executors and the land in question was left to William. The two brothers duly
obtained probate and executed an assent to vest the land in William.

It has now come to light that the executors, instructing different solicitors,
subsequently and erroneously purported to sell the land to a friend and
neighbour of the deceased, Claire Henderson. She has been to see our client
and is claiming the land is legally hers.

Our client will be sending us the deeds, but in the meantime perhaps you would
prepare a note reminding me of what needs to be checked. I seem to recall the
Administration of Estates Act 1925 may be relevant here.

Last year, William transferred the land into the joint names of himself and his
wife, June, and they now intend to sell the land. William is going abroad on
business shortly. He will be out of the country for several months and wishes
to appoint June as his attorney to enable her to deal with the formalities of the
sale in his absence.

Please also research whether we can give effect to William's wish to appoint
June as his attorney.

Commentary

There are two quite distinct questions here, and each should be answered
separately.

First, the problem over who has good title to the land. Initially this appears to
be quite tricky, but note the help you are given in the question – 'the

Administration of Estates Act 1925 may be relevant here'. Take the hint! It points to the need to consider the position of personal representatives when dealing with unregistered land, and in particular the importance of s. 36(6) of the Administration of Estates Act 1925. Do not be side-tracked into a discussion about personal representatives and registered land; the question says the title is *unregistered.*

The deeds are not yet available so you cannot give a definitive answer to the problem. You will therefore need to consider each possible alternative, e.g. 'if the deeds say this then the position is X, if they say that then the position is Y'.

From a professional conduct point of view, you should appreciate that if a memorandum of the assent has not been endorsed on the grant of probate, this raises the question of whether your firm may have been negligent. It would be appropriate to discuss this aspect of professional conduct in your answer.

The second part of the question raises the topic of powers of attorney, an area of conveyancing normally covered within the context of deducing and investigating title. Notice that the question requires an explanatory answer. It is important to appreciate that William and his wife are trustees for sale because the answer very much hinges on this.

Your answer should take the form of a memorandum in response to the partner's memorandum.

Suggested Answer

RICHARDS ABBEY AND PARTNERS, SOLICITORS

INTERNAL MEMORANDUM

To   The Training Partner

From   The Trainee Solicitor

Re our client William McKnight
I refer to your memo. I have conducted some research and my conclusions are as follows.

   (a)   Title to the land
The executors first executed an assent of the land in favour of William McKnight. The Administration of Estates Act 1925, s. 36(5), enables a person

in whose favour an assent or conveyance of a legal estate is made by a personal representative to have notice thereof endorsed on the grant of representation. Thus a memorandum of this assent should have been endorsed on the grant of probate at the time of completion of the assent. We must check the grant for this endorsement, and if it is present our client will have good title to the land.

If, however, the endorsement is not present our client may have a problem. Under the Administration of Estates Act 1925, s. 36(6), where a conveyance by personal representatives contains a declaration that there has been no previous assent or conveyance, the purchaser (in this case Claire Henderson) is entitled to rely on this statement *even if it is wrong* as sufficient evidence that no assent has been given – unless of course there is an endorsement on the grant. If this is the case here then s. 36(6) will operate to transfer the legal estate to Claire Henderson as if no previous assent had been made to William McKnight.

Thus Claire Henderson's claim will succeed if:

(i)   the conveyance to her contained the above declaration; and

(ii) there is no endorsement of the assent on the grant.

If our firm failed to ensure that a memo was endorsed on the grant at the time of the assent then regrettably this raises the possibility of professional negligence. If this is the case we should immediately advise the client to take independent advice and inform our professional indemnity insurers of the situation.

(b)   Power of attorney

This is a separate issue but must be considered within the framework of the title problem. The point has to be made that if the title vests in Claire Henderson then quite clearly the sale by William and June cannot proceed, and William's query about appointing an attorney becomes immaterial.

Assuming that William and June do have good title:

The house is held in joint names so there is a trust for sale. The Powers of Attorney Act 1971, s. 9 (replacing the former power contained in the Trustee Act 1925, s. 25) enables a trustee by power of attorney to delegate for a period not exceeding 12 months the exercise of all or any of the trustee's powers. However, s. 9(2) of the 1971 Act prohibits the donor of the power from appointing as attorney the donor's only other co-trustee.

On the face of it this would seem to prevent William from appointing June as his attorney. However, he could get around the problem by appointing her under a power created under the Enduring Powers of Attorney Act 1985. Although intended for different circumstances (subsequent mental incapacity), it can be used in the present situation. The restriction upon the choice of attorney that can be made by a trustee would not apply. It should be noted that the form and execution of the power are prescribed by the 1985 Act, and William must be of sound mind at the time of the creation of the power.

Alternatively, William could appoint a trustworthy third party to be his attorney, for example his solicitor.

Trainee Solicitor: time engaged 55 minutes.

6 Exchange of Contracts

INTRODUCTION

Exchange of contracts is recognised as being the most critical stage in the conveyancing process, the moment when the parties become legally bound to proceed. If the conveyancer makes a mistake here the consequences for the client (and the conveyancer) can be very grave indeed.

Many people selling a house or flat will also be buying one, and *vice versa.* In this event, the conveyancer must ensure that exchange of contracts on both transactions is synchronised so that the client does not end up with two properties or none at all. Many students overlook the importance of synchronisation when answering a question on exchange of contracts and get bogged down in the minutiae of the formulae for telephonic exchange. We cannot emphasise enough the importance of this one word – *synchronisation.* You may be able to recite perfectly the formulae for telephonic exchange (and you should be able to), but you will probably fail the question unless you can demonstrate the significance of synchronisation. Look carefully at the suggested answers to Questions 2 and 3 in this chapter.

Naturally, questions on exchange of contracts are not limited to the physical act of exchange itself. You should anticipate questions concerning the requisite conveyancing steps immediately before exchange (such as arrangements for bridging finance) and also the steps you should take following exchange, for example, arranging insurance, and whether the contract should be protected by registration.

Insurance is a common feature in conveyancing examinations and is a topic you would do well to revise thoroughly. Standard Condition 5.1 deals with risk and insurance and has come in for much criticism from the profession; you should be aware of its failings. Question 4 is typical of the type of question you might get on insurance, and you will find another in the very last question in the book.

As you read this chapter, notice how the style of questions differs, thus inviting different ways of answering. You will see how two questions take the form of internal office memoranda, another requires a direct answer in point form, while another is more academic in nature and will require an answer in the form of an essay.

QUESTION 1

Your firm is acting for Charlotte Mathysse on a dependent sale and purchase. The Standard Conditions of Sale (2nd edition) are being adopted in both contracts. The sale price is £50,000, the purchase price is £70,000. The solicitor in your office handling the two transactions is away ill. Charlotte has telephoned to raise two matters upon which she requires your advice:

(a) Charlotte has insufficient funds to finance the deposit on her purchase. What are her options and what advice would you give her?   (12 Marks)

(b) Subject to the deposit problem being resolved, she would like you to exchange contracts immediately. What other matters should you consider before you exchange?   (10 Marks)

Commentary

This question concerns the preparations for exchange, a stage of critical importance for both solicitor and client. Part (a) asks you to consider the client's arrangements for the deposit, so you will need to discuss the 'pros and cons' of bridging finance and the ways of circumventing it. One method commonly adopted to avoid bridging is to utilise the deposit on the related sale (note that the Standard Conditions are being used), but do not overlook the deposit guarantee scheme as well.

There are two more marks for part (a) so you can afford to spend a little longer on it. Part (b) can be dealt with competently by simply listing the points that need checking. As well as the obvious things like the contract being signed and the results of searches being acceptable, do not forget practical points like making sure other people in the chain are ready.

Suggested Answer

(a) Charlotte has several options:

    (i) to agree a reduced deposit on the purchase and utilise her sale deposit;

    (ii) to borrow the deposit (or part of it) by way of bridging loan; or

    (iii) to offer her seller a deposit guarantee instead of cash.

Each option will be considered in turn.

(i) Utilising her sale deposit

The first thing Charlotte should try (through us) is to use the deposit she receives on her sale as the deposit on her purchase. Whether she can do this will depend on the capacity in which we as her solicitors hold the sale deposit. If we hold it as agent for the seller it can be done; but if we hold it as stakeholder, we are obliged to retain the sale deposit in our client account until completion. The simplest way of achieving the 'agent' capacity is to agree a special condition in the sale contract stating that we hold the deposit as agent for the seller. In this way, Charlotte will be free to use the deposit after exchange in any way she chooses. However, this may not be acceptable to Charlotte's buyer who is likely to prefer the security of paying a stakeholder deposit. In this event the Standard Conditions (which we are told are being used) will assist Charlotte. Assuming Charlotte's purchase is in England or Wales and she is buying it as her main residence, Standard Condition 2.2.2 will permit her to utilise her sale deposit towards the deposit on her purchase, provided ultimately the deposit is held by a solicitor as stakeholder.

The amount of the deposit is normally 10% of the purchase price. Although Charlotte will have £5,000 available from the sale deposit, the deposit payable on her purchase is £7,000, and so she still has the problem of finding a further £2,000. The practical answer to this is to negotiate the payment of a reduced deposit on her purchase which is equivalent to the deposit she will receive on her sale (i.e., £5,000). Provided Charlotte can persuade her seller to accept this, and provided Charlotte insists that her own buyer pays a full 10% deposit, the problem of finding the further £2,000 will be overcome.

What should Charlotte do if her seller insists on a full 10% deposit? Where will she find the additional £2,000? She has two clear options: bridging finance or the deposit guarantee scheme.

(ii) Bridging finance

After taking into account the money she has available, Charlotte could borrow the shortfall from her bank (or another lender) on a short-term bridging loan. Most banks will be happy to help their customers in this way, especially where the loan is for only a short period. However, before releasing any funds, the bank will normally require, from their borrower's solicitor, an undertaking to repay the bridging loan from the net proceeds of the related sale.

We should advise Charlotte that her bank will probably charge an arrangement fee for the bridging loan. We should also advise her that the interest charges on the loan will be high and, in the unlikely event of a delay on completion of the sale, the bridging loan could ultimately prove to be expensive. We would advise her that tax relief at 20% (15% from April 1995) may be available on the bridging loan, provided it is arranged through a separate loan account rather than an overdraft facility. The tax relief has to be claimed direct from the Inland Revenue rather than through the MIRAS system.

(iii) <u>Deposit guarantee scheme</u>

Instead of offering her seller a cash deposit, Charlotte could offer a deposit guarantee from an insurance company. If this is agreed then an appropriate provision would be needed in the contract. The scheme operates in the following way. Charlotte would pay a single premium to the insurance company, which in turn would provide a guarantee to Charlotte's seller for the amount of the deposit. If Charlotte were to default under the purchase contract entitling her seller to forfeit the 'deposit', the insurance company would pay the seller the amount of the deposit. The insurance company would then exercise its right of recovery against Charlotte. The scheme is intended for use where a buyer enters into a simultaneous exchange of contracts on a sale, and so would be appropriate in this case. However, Charlotte's seller has of course to agree! Many sellers would prefer to have the security of 'cash' rather than a claim against an insurance company, and it should also be borne in mind that Charlotte's seller may have a dependent purchase, the deposit for which is to be financed from Charlotte's cash deposit.

In conclusion, we would advise Charlotte to pursue the first option of negotiating a reduction in the deposit on her purchase to £5,000 and utilising the sale deposit. If this is not successful, she would have to consider the other alternatives and weigh up the respective costs of each, for example by comparing the cost of bridging against the amount of the deposit guarantee premium. Ultimately the decision could lie in her seller's hands, for if the seller insists on a full 10% cash deposit, Charlotte will be forced to borrow funds.

(b) An exchange of contracts will commit Charlotte to binding and irrevocable legal obligations to buy and sell, and so before exchange it is vital that we check the following matters:

(i) Both sale and purchase contracts should contain all the agreed terms and be signed by the relevant parties. Charlotte should have signed her two parts in readiness for exchange, and these should be on file. Note that we should not sign on Charlotte's behalf without her express authority (*Suleman v Shahisavari* [1989] 2 All ER 460). We would check that any non-owning occupiers who are required to sign the contracts have also done so.

(ii)   The deposit arrangements (including, if necessary, bridging finance and any requirement to give a solicitor's undertaking) would have to be finalised. If we are to draw a cheque for the deposit monies to her seller's solicitor, we would need to be put in cleared funds by the client.

(iii)   If Charlotte requires a mortgage to finance her purchase, she and we must see and approve the written mortgage offer. We should check in particular that the conditions of the intended mortgage are satisfactory. If the mortgage is based upon an endowment policy, have the life policy arrangements been made? We would check generally that Charlotte's financial arrangements are in order.

(iv)   If she has a mortgage on her existing property, we would make sure that there is a redemption figure on file from her mortgagee, and that the sale proceeds will be sufficient to discharge it.

(v)   We would ensure that the local authority search and all other relevant searches have been made, and that the results are satisfactory and do not reveal anything adverse.

(vi)   We would check that we have on file satisfactory replies to all relevant pre-contract enquiries, and that there are no adverse replies.

(vii)   We must be satisfied that the client is happy with the result of her surveyor's report and her own inspection of the property.

(viii)   It is vital that the title to the purchase property is good and marketable and free from any onerous or unusual incumbrances. If the title is registered, there should be up-to-date office copy entries in the file which we would inspect. If the title is unregistered we would consider the abstract or epitome. If the solicitor who has the conduct of the file has raised any requisitions on the title, we should check that these have been satisfactorily answered.

(ix)   Following on from the above, we would as a matter of good practice always read the entire correspondence files to verify that there are no unresolved issues between the solicitors and that we are entirely happy.

(x)   We would check the files and make sure that our firm has reported fully to Charlotte on the results of our pre-contract searches and investigations, and the terms of the contracts. Preferably the report should have been written, in which case there should be a copy on file. If the report was delivered orally, e.g. at a meeting with the client, then an attendance note of the meeting should have been placed on the correspondence file.

(xi)   If we have any doubts at all, we should not exchange but refer the matter to a partner. In the event of uncertainty it may be necessary to contact our colleague in his sick bed!

(xii)   Even if we are happy that everything is in order, we obviously cannot exchange until Charlotte's buyer and seller are also ready to exchange. Charlotte's sale and purchase are dependent upon each other and so the exchange of contracts and completion dates for each property must be synchronised. We shall therefore have to contact the other solicitors by telephone to discuss exchange and any proposed completion dates.

QUESTION 2

RICHARDS ABBEY AND PARTNERS, SOLICITORS

INTERNAL MEMORANDUM

To   The Trainee Solicitor

From   The Training Partner

Re Jack Brinicombe
Our firm has acted for Jack and Mabel Brinicombe for many years. Our first dealing with them was more than 30 years ago when they bought Green Willows, a four-bedroomed victorian freehold house. Sadly, last year Mabel died, and since then Jack has realised that Green Willows is really far too much for him on his own.

He came to see me a few weeks ago to say that he had found a small freehold bungalow he wanted to buy. The address is 15 Lingfield Avenue and it has a registered title. The owners have retired to the coast and moved out already so the bungalow is unoccupied, and Jack is very keen to move in as soon as possible. There is no chain above Jack's seller.

Fortunately Jack has also secured a buyer for Green Willows. The buyer does not have a place to sell so both Jack's sale and purchase have proceeded quickly. The pre- contract conveyancing work on both properties has been done to my satisfaction.

I attach the files for each property. Green Willows is being sold for £100,000. The price for 15 Lingfield Avenue is £70,000. You will note that Green Willows is not mortgaged and Jack does not require a loan to finance his purchase. The second edition of the Standard Conditions of Sale is incorporated into both contracts, save that in the purchase contract Standard Condition 5.1 is excluded. The National Protocol is being used in both transactions.

We are ready to exchange contracts. We have received from Jack's purchaser's solicitors their client's signed part of the contract and cheque for the 10% deposit. We hold on file Jack's sale and purchase contracts duly signed by him. Jack will be out of the country for a couple of months and so has instructed me to exchange immediately for completion 10 weeks today.

Please advise me, on these facts:

(a)   how you will effect a telephonic exchange of contracts today; and

(b)   what action you will take (if any) immediately following exchange.

Commentary

The question tells us that you are ready to exchange so there will be no marks for discussing whether pre-contract matters have been attended to, for example searches, enquiries etc. The question requires you to demonstrate how you will effect a telephonic exchange, so stick to that – and a telephonic exchange at that, not any other kind.

When a sale and purchase are inter-dependent, as they are here, then unless otherwise agreed, the client will expect to move out of one property and into the other on the same day. So, the completion dates must be the same, i.e. synchronised. Moreover, the physical act of exchange must be synchronised so that the two moments of binding legal obligation are as close together as possible. Remember that until exchange occurs either party is free to withdraw, and consequently, unless synchronisation is achieved the client is in danger of ending up with two properties or none at all.

The post-exchange action, including possible registration of the contract, should be a source of easy marks for most students, but read the facts carefully – note the significance of the proposed 10-week completion and the fact that 15 Lingfield Avenue is registered land.

Suggested Answer

RICHARDS ABBEY AND PARTNERS, SOLICITORS

INTERNAL MEMORANDUM

To   The Training Partner

From   The Trainee Solicitor

Re Jack Brinicombe
I refer to your memo regarding our above client's sale and purchase, and report as follows.

(a)   Procedure to effect exchange of contracts today

First, we will telephone the firm of solicitors acting for Jack's seller and the firm acting for his buyer to verify that they are both ready to exchange today. A convenient completion date for all parties will also have to be agreed. The suggested 10-week completion is an unusually long time between exchange and completion and the client should appreciate that this may not be acceptable to both his buyer and seller. I appreciate that the client is going abroad but it may be necessary to take his instructions on an earlier completion date. He may also need to consider granting a power of attorney to allow documents to be signed on his behalf.

Once a completion date has been agreed in principle, we must check that the solicitor acting on the sale of 15 Lingfield Avenue has in his possession a signed contract in identical form to the part signed by our client. We will advise the solicitor that we have a signed contract and deposit for 10% of the purchase price. The Standard Conditions of Sale permit our client to use the sale deposit for the deposit on his related purchase provided it is held ultimately by a solicitor as stakeholder (Standard Condition 2.2.2). Accordingly, we must check that there is no special condition in the 15 Lingfield Avenue contract providing for the deposit to be held as agent for the seller.

Once we are satisfied on this point, we will ask the seller's solicitor to release the seller's part of the contract to us until a time later in the day. The effect of this will be that the seller's solicitor undertakes to exchange if, by an agreed time later that day, we ring back to request an exchange. This will allow us time to exchange on our client's related sale and subsequently to telephone the seller's solicitor again to exchange. The 'release' is important to aid synchronisation, which is essential where, as in this case, there is a dependent sale and purchase.

Following the 'release' of the 15 Lingfield Avenue contract, we will telephone the solicitor acting on the purchase of Green Willows to effect a telephonic exchange under Law Society *formula A*. This is the appropriate formula where one solicitor (our firm) holds both signed parts of the contract. We will advise the buyer's solicitor that our client's signed contract is identical to the buyer's part. We will then formally agree the exchange and, as a result, undertake to send to the solicitor that day (by first class post, document exchange or hand delivery) our client's signed part of the contract.

We will then ring back immediately the solicitor acting on the sale of 15 Lingfield Avenue to effect a *formula B* exchange. This is the appropriate formula where each solicitor holds his own client's signed part of the contract. Each solicitor will undertake to send their respective client's signed contract to each other that night. In addition, we will send the other side our firm's client account cheque for the deposit of £7,000. The remaining £3,000, being the balance of the Green Willows deposit, must remain in our client account because we hold it as stakeholder under the Standard Conditions of Sale (2.2.2). Our client will be entitled to receive interest on the stakeholder monies.

(b) Action immediately following exchange

We should draft a memorandum on each of the sale and purchase files noting the following: names of those who agreed the exchange; date and time of exchange; amount of deposit; completion date; the Law Society formula used.

We should telephone Jack to inform him that exchange has occurred and further advise him to insure the property from exchange. Standard Condition 5.1 has been excluded from the 15 Lingfield Avenue contract so the open contract position prevails, which is that the risk in the property passes to the buyer from exchange. Normally a buyer's mortgagee would insure, but it is noted that Jack does not require a mortgage. We could offer to help him arrange the insurance. We should confirm our advice in writing.

We should inform the estate agents (if any) of the exchange of contracts and the completion date and ask them to send us their commission account.

We should enter the completion date in our diary so that it is not overlooked.

We should consider whether the purchase contract requires protection by registration. This is not normally done in practice unless the circumstances are unusual. If a 10-week completion is agreed, this would be unusual enough to contemplate registration. As the title is registered, our client's interest under the contract will be a minor interest which would be protected by the entry of a caution in the Proprietorship Register or, if the seller's solicitors agree to lodge the Land Certificate at the Land Registry, a notice in the Charges Register.

We should also consider registration of the contract if we believe the seller to be untrustworthy, or if a dispute arises between the seller and our client.

Trainee Solicitor: time engaged 25 minutes.

QUESTION 3

What is the legal position if, between exchange of contracts and completion, a dwellinghouse suffers damage by fire as a result of faulty electrical wiring?

Commentary

This question appears deceptively easy but is in fact very wide-ranging and requires you to demonstrate a broad academic knowledge. The sparsity of factual information leaves all kinds of possibilities, and a very competent answer would consider each of these in turn. For example, is it an open contract or are the Standard Conditions being used? Is the property freehold or leasehold? Is the house occupied or vacant?

If you have revised the topic of insurance thoroughly and appreciate and understand the recent criticisms of Standard Condition 5.1, this is definitely the question for you and you should score high marks. Those of you who prefer to answer questions of a more practical nature would do well to leave this one alone (provided you have the choice!).

Your answer will take the form of an academic essay.

Suggested Answer

The question does not indicate the tenure of the property or whether the house is occupied. We do not know whether the contract incorporates any general conditions (e.g. the Standard Conditions of Sale), or whether it is governed by statute and common law (i.e. an 'open' contract). In order to answer the question fully, we must consider in the alternative (a) if the contract is an open contract, and (b) if the Standard Conditions are included. The problem of double insurance will also be considered, as will the position if the property is leasehold.

(a) The open contract position

The position under an open contract is that the beneficial ownership in the property passes to the buyer on exchange of contracts, and consequently the risk in the property passes to the buyer at the same time. The onus is on the buyer to insure the property from exchange because, even if the property is damaged by fire, as is the case here, the buyer will still be contractually bound to complete.

If the property is damaged by fire after exchange and the buyer has failed to insure, the buyer may be able to recover his loss in certain circumstances, which are as follows:

First, where the buyer's loss is due to a lack of proper care on the part of the seller. Between exchange and completion, the seller holds the legal estate as qualified trustee for the buyer and as such owes a duty of care to look after the property. If the seller breaches that duty and loss is caused as a result, the seller will be liable to the buyer in damages (*Clarke* v *Ramuz* [1891] 2 QB 456). This would apply in the present case if the wiring had become faulty as a result of the seller's neglect. If the seller happens to have moved out and the house is empty, the seller is not released from this responsibility (*London & Cheshire Insurance Co. Ltd* v *Laplagrene Property Co. Ltd* [1971] Ch 499). Similarly, if the buyer has moved in before completion, the seller's duty to take care is unaffected (unless the parties expressly agree otherwise, e.g. as part of a licence to occupy).

Secondly, there is s. 47 of the Law of Property Act 1925. This section enables a buyer to claim loss from the seller's insurance policy, if one exists. It provides that insurance money payable to the seller after the date of the contract in respect of loss or damage to the property shall be paid to the buyer on completion (or upon receipt, if later) as long as:

(i)   the contract does not exclude s. 47;

(ii)   the buyer pays a proportionate part of the insurance premium; and

(iii) the insurance company gives its consent.

Thirdly there is s. 83 of the Fires Prevention (Metropolis) Act 1774. Under this Act, if there is damage to a property by fire, a 'person interested' in the property can compel the insurance company to apply the insurance proceeds towards the reinstatement of the property. There is some doubt as to whether a buyer under a contract for sale would constitute an interested person for the purposes of the Act. In *Rayner* v *Preston* (1881) 18 Ch 1, there are *obiter dicta* indicating that a buyer of land would be included within the definition. The operation of the Act is not confined solely to the metropolis of London (*Ex parte Gorely* (1864) 4 De GJ & S 477).

Lastly, the buyer may have recourse against his solicitor in negligence, under the principles enunciated in *Hedley Byrne & Co. Ltd* v *Heller & Partners Ltd* [1964] AC 465, if the solicitor failed properly to advise the buyer to insure on exchange of contracts.

(b)   The position under the Standard Conditions of Sale

Standard Condition 5.1 reverses the open contract position and provides that the seller retains the risk until completion. It also excludes s. 47 of the Law of Property Act 1925.

Standard Condition 5.1.2 provides that if at any time before completion the physical state of the property makes it unusable for its purpose at the date of the contract then the buyer may rescind. The seller may also rescind if it is damage against which the seller could not reasonably have insured, or damage which it is not legally possible for the seller to make good. In the present circumstances (damage by fire to a residential property), the seller is unlikely to be entitled to rescind, but there is every possibility that the buyer could rescind if the fire damage is severe.

Under Standard Condition 5.1.1, the seller must transfer the property in the same physical state as it was at the date of the contract (except for fair wear and tear), but interestingly Standard Condition 5.1.3 states that the seller is under no obligation to insure the property. In the present situation, the buyer could sue the seller for damages for breach of contract, but this is no guarantee for the buyer that he will recover his loss if in fact the property is not insured for its full reinstatement value. Accordingly, if the buyer has been well advised, the contract may well include a special condition varying Standard Condition 5.1.3 so that the seller is obliged to insure to the full reinstatement value.

Another option for the buyer is to exclude Standard Condition 5.1 altogether and revert to the open contract rule, where the risk will pass to the buyer on exchange. In this way the buyer (or if the buyer requires mortgage finance, the buyer's mortgagee) controls the insurance arrangements and does not have to rely on a claim against the seller. The special conditions of the contract should therefore be read to establish whether Standard Condition 5.1, or any part thereof, has been amended or deleted.

If the buyer has moved into occupation between exchange and completion, the terms of the occupation are set out in Standard Condition 5.2.2. The buyer is required, *inter alia*, to insure the property in a sum not less than the purchase price against all risks in respect of which comparable premises are normally insured. Unlike the open contract position when a buyer occupies before completion, Standard Condition 5.2.3 provides that Standard Condition 5.1 ceases to apply and the buyer assumes the risk until completion.

(c)   Double insurance

There is also the potential problem of double insurance. If the parties agree to adopt the open contract position, the buyer should be advised to insure from exchange. The seller will also be advised to keep his existing policy on foot until completion in case the buyer defaults and the sale does not complete. In this event, whose insurance company will meet the claim? Each company may say that the other should meet it, and, in any event, they will not pay out twice for the same damage. This could result in the unhappy situation of the buyer and seller receiving only part of the whole claim.

The dilemma of double insurance can be circumvented by the parties agreeing a special condition whereby, in the event of damage, the buyer will complete but receive an abatement in the price. This abatement would be equivalent to the amount by which the buyer's insurance proceeds are reduced by reason of the existence of the seller's insurance policy.

(d)   Leasehold property

Lastly, one must consider the position if the property is leasehold. Invariably the lease will stipulate whether it is the landlord or the tenant who insures. If the tenant insures, the same issues apply as above, with the additional consideration that, if the Standard Conditions are being used, Standard Condition 8.1.3 provides that the tenant/seller must comply with any lease provisions requiring the tenant to insure. The landlord normally has to approve the policy first, and it is usually simpler for the buyer/assignee to take over the seller/assignor's policy, rather than take out a new one. If the landlord insures, a claim will be made under the landlord's policy. If the fire was the tenant's fault, and as a result the landlord's insurance is invalidated, the tenant may, depending on the terms of the lease, be in breach of covenant under the lease.

QUESTION 4

RICHARDS ABBEY AND PARTNERS, SOLICITORS

INTERNAL MEMORANDUM

To   The Trainee Solicitor

From   The Training Partner

We act for Tom Hayward who is selling 'Wickets', The Hyde, Eastminster to a first time buyer. Tom has a related purchase: he is buying (with the aid of a mortgage) Peartree Cottage, Hailey Lane, Great Amwell, a town some 40 miles away from our office. The seller of Peartree Cottage has instructed a firm of solicitors in Great Amwell. The sale and purchase are part of a large chain of transactions, of which 'Wickets' is at the bottom.

Each solicitor in the chain holds his or her client's signed part of the contract and – save obviously for the seller's solicitor at the top of the chain – deposit cheque. All parties are ready to exchange today although a completion date has yet to be finalised. Both Tom's contracts incorporate the Standard Conditions of Sale and the National Protocol is being used. Tom has asked whether he can complete his sale and purchase at the end of this week.

(a)   Please advise me of the methods by which an exchange of contracts could be achieved and the moment at which the contract would become binding in each case. Explain which method would be most suitable and why other methods may not be suitable.   (15 Marks)

(b)   What matters should we consider before answering Tom's question about the completion date?   (5 Marks)

Commentary

This question will appeal to those students who have had some practical experience of conveyancing, and indeed some readers may have carried out several 'real-life' exchanges. To score high marks it is important to answer the question according to how exchange ought *properly* to be carried out. Bear in mind that the prescribed methods of exchange (in particular the telephone formulae) do not always correspond with general practice!

Those students who rush into their answer may fail to appreciate that the question does not ask you to appraise the different formulae for telephone exchange. It asks you to discuss the various *methods* of exchange, i.e. personal, postal or telephone. Notwithstanding that you can show your expertise on the Law Society formulae for telephonic exchange, you will regrettably fail the question if you discuss only the telephone method.

As well as covering the relevant ground, you must give your opinion as to the suitability or otherwise of each method as they apply to the facts, and indicate the time at which the contract under each method will become binding. The fact that the Standard Conditions of Sale and Protocol are being used is relevant.

Part (b) also raises practical issues concerning the considerations a solicitor should have before agreeing a completion date on exchange of contracts. Those students who have had practical experience of conveyancing should find this straightforward, but others may experience difficulty. Do try to keep focused on the facts of the case which inevitably will offer clues. For example, here note the existence of a long chain and the fact that the client needs a mortgage.

Lastly, as always, note the allocation of marks and apportion your time accordingly.

Suggested Answer

RICHARDS ABBEY AND PARTNERS, SOLICITORS

INTERNAL MEMORANDUM

To   The Training Partner

From   The Trainee Solicitor

(a)   There are three methods of exchanging contracts:

(i)   in person;

(ii)   by post (or document exchange); or

(iii)   by telephone.

(i)   In person

Both parties' solicitors meet at the office of the seller's solicitors. Each have their own clients' signed contracts, and the buyer's solicitor holds a cheque for the deposit. The solicitors check that the two contracts are identical, and that the seller's contract has been signed by the seller and the buyer's contract signed by the buyer. When both solicitors are ready to proceed, the contracts are physically exchanged – the buyer's solicitor receives the seller's signed part and *vice versa*. The buyer's solicitor also hands over the deposit cheque. It is at this moment of physical exchange that the contract becomes legally binding.

A personal exchange is recognised as being the safest method because it is an instant exchange and both parties can check there and then that the contracts are identical. However, in Tom's case there is a chain and he must synchronise his sale and purchase. An exchange in person will not therefore be suitable. We must also bear in mind that Tom's seller's solicitor's office is 40 miles away, making a personal exchange on Peartree Cottage impracticable.

(ii)   By post or document exchange

The buyer's solicitor sends to the seller's solicitor, by post or document exchange, the buyer's signed part of the contract and cheque for the deposit. Upon receipt, the seller's solicitor inserts the agreed completion date on both signed contracts and dates them. To effect the exchange, the seller's signed part is posted or sent in the document exchange to the buyer's solicitor.

As the contract incorporates the Standard Conditions of Sale, Condition 2.1.1 provides that the contract will come into existence when the seller's part is actually posted or deposited at the document exchange. An exchange by this method will not be suitable in Tom's situation (where there is a chain), because there is a danger that Tom's buyer may withdraw between the time when Tom's seller's contract is posted and the time we receive it. This would leave Tom with two houses.

(iii) By telephone

This is the most popular method of exchange and was given judicial acknowledgment by the Court of Appeal in *Domb* v *Isoz* [1980] Ch 548. It will nearly always be appropriate where there is a chain of transactions, and will be the most suitable method for us to use in Tom's sale and purchase. The contract will become binding as soon as the parties' solicitors agree over the telephone that exchange has taken place.

The National Protocol is being used so if we decide to exchange by telephone we must adopt one of the three telephone exchange formulae introduced by the Law Society to avoid uncertainty. They are as follows:

(1) *Formula A* The seller's solicitor holds both signed parts of the contract and the buyer's deposit. In the telephone conversation the seller's solicitor confirms to the buyer's solicitor that both parts of the contract are identical. The solicitors agree a completion date which the seller's solicitor inserts in the contracts. The solicitors then effect the exchange and, by doing so, the seller's solicitor undertakes from that moment to hold the seller's signed part to the buyer's order, and to send to the buyer's solicitor that day by first class post, document exchange or hand delivery, the seller's signed contract. Formula A can also work in reverse where the buyer's solicitor holds both parts, but this is less common.

(2) *Formula B* This is where each solicitor holds his or her own client's signed contract. In the telephone conversation they confirm that the respective parts are identical and insert the agreed completion date. They then effect the exchange, and by doing so undertake to hold the contract in their possession to the other's order and to send it to the other that day by first class post, document exchange or hand delivery. The buyer's solicitor must also send the deposit cheque. Formula B is the most commonly used formula.

Following exchange under Formula A or B the solicitors must record on file the following: names of the persons who agreed the exchange; date and time of exchange; completion date; the formula used and any agreed variations; amount of deposit.

(3) *Formula C* This is designed for use where there is a long chain of transactions and would be suitable in our case. As with Formula B, both solicitors hold their own client's signed contracts but, to aid synchronisation along the chain, the formula is in two parts. First, the buyer's solicitor undertakes to exchange by an agreed time later in the day, if the seller's solicitor so requests in a call back (the client's authority should be obtained before the undertaking is given). Each solicitor makes a detailed written note of the conversation. The seller's solicitor then activates the same procedure in the next link up the chain, and so on, to the top.

The second part of the formula occurs when, starting at the top and working down, the respective seller's solicitors ring back their respective buyer's solicitors by the appointed time to effect the exchange. The contracts are then sent out that day as with the other formulae. The parties may agree (on specified terms) that the buyer's deposit is sent direct to a solicitor further up the chain. Following exchange, the solicitors should make a second note, recording the actual exchange.

In conclusion I recommend that we exchange by using one of the telephone formulae.

(b)   The traditional period between exchange of contracts and completion is 28 days, but in modern times the parties normally agree a much shorter period. As Tom's contract incorporates the Standard Conditions of Sale, Condition 6.1.1 stipulates that the completion date shall be 20 working days after the date of the contract. It is more usual, however, for the parties to agree a specific date which is then written into the contract and overrides Condition 6.1.1. If Tom requires a quick completion this is the procedure we must adopt.

Tom is asking for completion within a matter of days. Although it is possible to agree such a short period (in some cases exchange and completion can take place on the same day), it is unlikely to be feasible in Tom's situation. The reasons for this are as follows:

(i)   The long chain of dependent transactions. Unless Tom is willing to incur the expense of bridging finance (which we would not recommend in the present circumstances), every person in the chain would have to agree the short completion. As the chain is very long, I doubt whether unanimity could be achieved (bearing in mind also that the other conveyancers would be considering points (ii) and (iii) below), but to help Tom we could at least ask the rest of the chain to consider it.

(ii)   We must allow ourselves sufficient time to carry out the post-contract conveyancing work, for example, the preparation, approval and execution of the purchase deed and mortgage deed. We will also have to carry out pre-completion searches, the results of which must be received before completion and, although there are telephone, fax and computer terminal search facilities available, we may not achieve this by the end of the week.

(iii)   Lastly, and most crucially, Tom needs a mortgage to assist in his purchase. I note that we are ready to exchange today, so Tom will have received and we will have approved his mortgage offer. However, we will also have to report on title to the mortgagee and request drawdown of the mortgage advance. Most mortgagees require three or four days or longer notice to release funds. This would have to be checked immediately with the mortgagee.

We should inform Tom of our reservations about the short completion and perhaps, in the circumstances, he should consider a slightly later date which is mutually convenient to everyone in the chain.

Trainee Solicitor: time engaged 45 minutes.

7 The Purchase Deed: Mortgages

INTRODUCTION

The purchase deed tends to be a fairly popular topic with students. This may have something to do with the fact that question spotting in this area can be reasonably straightforward. As the questions in this chapter will demonstrate, very often the examiner will simply present a set of facts and ask you what form the purchase deed should take, and invite you to explain (or draft!) its contents. Accordingly, if you can really master the form and content of the different purchase deeds, you should do well when a question like this comes up.

Remember that all land in England and Wales is now in an area of compulsory registration, so a conveyance on sale will induce first registration and the Land Registry will accept a transfer under r. 72 in lieu of a traditional conveyance. Having said that, do not disregard the contents of conveyances, because many questions specifically require a knowledge and understanding of them. You should be aware that some practitioners still prefer to draft a conveyance in preference to a r. 72 transfer, especially where the purchase deed is not straightforward, and in such cases the drafting of a conveyance can sometimes be easier than the drafting of a transfer.

Another reason for mastering the contents of a conveyance is that it will help you to understand some of the complexities of another topic, investigation of unregistered title, where of course conveyances will have to be read and their essential ingredients (or lack of them!) understood.

Whereas students normally enjoy getting to grips with the purchase deed, the related topic of mortgages is a different matter altogether, and many students make the mistake of paying too little attention to it. Remember that a conveyancer acting for a mortgagee will be just as concerned to ensure that the property in question has a good and marketable title, in the same way as a conveyancer would if acting for the buyer; the mortgagee will, after all, want the comfort of knowing that the property is good security for the loan and that if it becomes necessary to exercise its power of sale, there is no technical impediment to prevent it from doing so.

The question of whether there should be separate representation for mortgagee and mortgagor is presently the subject of some lively legal debate, so do not be surprised if a question on conflict (or potential conflict) of interest and/or client confidentiality crops up in your exam. Matters of professional conduct are very important for conveyancers, and problems and queries occur frequently in practice. If you are taking a vocational course, such as the Legal Practice Course, you will need no reminding that professional conduct is a pervasive topic and ripe for inclusion in conveyancing problems. You will note that professional conduct considerations play a part in the suggested answer to Question 5.

The questions on mortgages may well overlap with other conveyancing topics, such as taking instructions and completion, and you will find frequent reference to mortgages throughout this book.

QUESTION 1

Your firm acts for David Hobbs and Stephen Ingles in their purchase as tenants in common of land to the rear of 10 Ellesmere Close for £20,000. The land they are buying forms part of a registered title number KM 74859 comprising the whole of 10 Ellesmere Close which is mortgaged to the Cornshire Building Society. The seller is Ingrid Smits. Contracts were exchanged last week for completion three weeks today. The contract provides for the grant of easements to your clients and corresponding reservations in favour of Ms Smits. It also provides for the buyers to enter into restrictive covenants with the seller. The contract incorporates the latest edition of the Standard Conditions of Sale. Your principal has asked you to deal with the post-contract conveyancing work and has passed you the file.

(a) Having regard to the Standard Conditions and other matters, explain what factors are relevant so far as the submission, approval and execution of the purchase deed are concerned. (5 Marks)

(b) List and explain the contents of the purchase deed which would be acceptable to both buyer and seller. (15 Marks)

Commentary

This question appears quite straightforward but you must read the facts carefully. You should always consider the terms of the contract as these will govern the contents of the purchase deed. Moreover, a competent answer to part (a) will be impossible unless you grasp the significance of the reference to the Standard Conditions of Sale.

Once you have recognised that the transaction involves a sale of part of registered land, part (b) at least should be plain sailing. Note that part (b) is worth three times as many marks as part (a), so do not get carried away on part (a). Leave yourself enough time to give part (b) the attention it deserves.

Many students get confused as to when an acknowledgement for production and undertaking for safe custody of deeds is required in a purchase deed. Such a clause is normally only appropriate on a sale of *part* of *un*registered land, or on a sale by personal representatives (PRs) of *un*registered land (whole or part) where the grant of representation is being retained by the PRs. As PRs are fiduciary owners, they can give only the acknowledgement, not the undertaking.

An acknowledgement and undertaking is not required on the transfer of part of registered land. This is because the transferor will not retain the Land (or Charge) Certificate relating to the whole title, but will instead place it on deposit at the Land Registry to facilitate the creation of the transferee's new title. Accordingly, it is not necessary to include an acknowledgement and undertaking clause in the purchase deed under discussion in this question.

Suggested Answer

(a) The contractual completion date is three weeks today. As the contract incorporates the Standard Conditions of Sale, regard must be had to Standard Condition 4.1.2. Where the period between exchange and completion is 15 working days or more (see Standard Condition 4.1.4), as is the case here, the draft transfer should be sent to the seller at least 12 working days before the completion date. The seller then has four working days after delivery to approve or revise the draft, and either return it or retain it for use as the engrossment. If the draft is returned, the buyer must send an engrossment to the seller at least five working days before the completion date.

The transferor must execute the deed in order to transfer the legal estate. Execution by both transferees is also necessary in this case because the transfer imposes fresh restrictive covenants and other obligations on the transferees. The transfer plan must be signed by the transferor personally, and also by the transferees or someone on their behalf, for example their solicitor (see Land Registration (Execution) Rules 1990).

When the transfer has been approved and the engrossment is ready for signature, the transferees should execute the transfer first. This is because the transferor will not wish to complete before the transferees have executed it, bearing in mind that they are entering into new obligations. After execution by the transferees, the transfer deed will be delivered to the transferor in escrow (i.e. conditional upon the transferor also executing it) for execution by the transferor in readiness for completion.

(b) The Law of Property Act 1925, s. 52 provides that in order to transfer the legal estate to the buyer the transfer document must be in the form of a deed. This deed must implement the terms of the contract and will mirror those terms.

As 10 Ellesmere Close has a registered title the relevant purchase deed is a Land Registry transfer, the form of which is prescribed by the rules made under the Land Registration Act 1925. The clients are buying part of the land within the title of 10 Ellesmere Close and the contract provides for new restrictive covenants to be imposed. The appropriate form of transfer is therefore a Transfer of Part imposing fresh restrictive covenants and Land Registry Form 43 may be used.

The transfer deed will commence with the usual Land Registry heading setting out the county and district, title number and short description of 10 Ellesmere Close. When the transfer is registered the Land Registry will issue a new title number for the land transferred. Next comes the consideration and receipt clause, the full name, address and occupation of the transferor and the capacity of the transferor (e.g. beneficial owner). Following that the full name, address and occupation of the transferees will be stated.

A clear description of the land being sold (including the words 'part of title number KM 74859') is then inserted with reference to a plan which is annexed to the transfer. The description of the land given in the contract should be adequate for this purpose. The plan should be securely bound in the engrossed transfer. The land retained by the seller should also be defined and identified on the plan.

The contract provides for the mutual grant and reservation of easements and these must be expressly repeated in the transfer. The same applies to the new restrictive covenants. If the easements and covenants are lengthy the best practice is to make only short reference to them in the main body of the deed and to set out the detailed provisions in numbered schedules near the end of the deed, before the attestation clauses.

The contract incorporates the Standard Conditions of Sale. Standard Condition 3.3 provides that where the seller is retaining land near the property, the buyer will have no right of light or air over the retained land. As this applies here, the transfer should include a declaration by the parties in these terms.

Mr Hobbs and Mr Ingles are purchasing as tenants in common. The transfer will thus contain a declaration by them that the survivor cannot give a valid receipt for capital money arising on a subsequent disposition of the land.

As the price is below the stamp duty threshold of £60,000 a certificate of value will be required. This will be the final clause in the main body of the deed.

The schedules will then follow, itemising the easements and covenants referred to above, following which the transfer concludes with the attestation provisions, providing for execution by all parties in the presence of a witness. The attestation will read 'signed as a deed' to make it clear on the face of the document that it is a deed (s. 1(2) of the Law of Property (Miscellaneous Provisions) Act 1989).

The Cornshire Building Society must release its mortgage over that part of the property being sold to Mr Hobbs and Mr Ingles. The Society could do this in the transfer, in which case it would be added as a party to the deed. More usually, however, the mortgagee will, following receipt of funds on completion, simply execute a Land Registry discharge of part. This is called Form 53 of part.

QUESTION 2

You will recall in Chapter 5, Question 2, that you were acting for the buyers of The Corner House and were asked to raise requisitions on the abstract of the unregistered title.

Assume that contracts have been exchanged and you are required to draft the purchase deed. Your clients are Trevor Clarke and his wife Kathleen Clarke, both currently residing at 9 Churchacre, Fordington, Cornshire. They are purchasing as joint tenants in equity and the price they are paying for the property is £90,000. The contract incorporates the current edition of the Standard Conditions of Sale.

Consider the Abstract of The Corner House again (refer to Appendix 6). Draft the document that will vest the title in Mr and Mrs Clarke and explain fully its contents.

Commentary

The Law Society places much emphasis on the need for law students to acquire vital legal skills before they start their training contracts. The skill of drafting is an essential part of any conveyancer's armoury, and you should therefore expect a drafting question to feature periodically in conveyancing examinations.

As a drafting exercise, this question is very straightforward, especially if you choose the simpler form of purchase deed in unregistered conveyancing, the r. 72 transfer, instead of the more traditional conveyance. A r. 72 transfer is entirely acceptable and appropriate in a situation where the whole of an unregistered title is being sold, as is the case here. You should appreciate, however, that the r. 72 transfer does not necessarily lead to any greater simplicity in drafting where the transaction involves a sale of part and new easements and covenants are being created.

In this question you would not lose marks for electing to draft a conveyance, but this would necessarily involve you in a lengthier drafting exercise and could leave you short of time for the other questions in the exam.

Obviously there is more to the question than simply drafting a purchase deed. You have to explain *fully* its contents as well. Do not fall into the trap of making your explanation too general. You have been given specific information and are referred to a lengthy abstract of title, which you must read and assimilate before you begin your answer. In this way you can determine whether, for instance, a buyer's indemnity covenant is required, or whether a certificate of value for stamp duty purposes is needed.

Suggested Answer

The suggested form of draft transfer is set out in Appendix 8.

Explanation

The freehold title to the property is unregistered. Since 1 December 1990 the whole of England and Wales has been in a compulsory registration area. Consequently, the title to the property is compulsorily registrable following the sale to Mr and Mrs Clarke.

The document that will vest the title in Mr and Mrs Clarke is known as the purchase deed. Although it is customary to use a traditional conveyance as the purchase deed for unregistered titles, r. 72 of the Land Registration Rules 1925 provides that where the transaction, as here, gives rise to first registration, the deed may take the alternative form of a Land Registry transfer.

It is submitted that a r. 72 transfer is the appropriate deed to vest the title in Mr and Mrs Clarke because it is shorter and simpler to prepare than a conveyance. For example, in a transfer deed there is no requirement for recitals.

The contents of the r. 72 transfer in this transaction are explained as follows:

1. The usual Land Registry heading comprising the county and district in which the property is situated and a brief description of the property. There is then room for the date which is inserted on completion.

2. Consideration (in this case £90,000) and receipt clause. The Stamp Act 1891, s. 5, requires that all facts and circumstances affecting the liability of any instrument to stamp duty must be fully set out and thus a statement of consideration on the face of the deed is essential. The receipt clause, although not conclusive evidence of payment, acts as a sufficient discharge to the buyer (s. 67 of the Law of Property Act 1925) and it also acts as authority to the buyer to pay the purchase money to the seller's solicitor (s. 69 of the Law of Property Act 1925).

3. The seller's full name, postal address, occupation and the capacity – here beneficial owner – in which the seller is expressed to transfer the land. The capacity implies the appropriate covenants for title by the seller.

4. The operative words then follow: 'transfer to'. These show the seller's intention to pass the legal estate to the buyers.

5. The buyers' names, addresses and occupations for entry on the Register. The correct address for the transfer is The Corner House address (where they will reside following completion) rather than their current one, 9 Churchacre. These details are then often followed by a statement of their beneficial interest in the property – here, 'as beneficial joint tenants'. Alternatively or in addition, the parties can make the declaration in paragraph 9 below, although such a declaration on its own is not conclusive of the holding of the beneficial interest.

The parties are referred to again later in the document, so for clarity of drafting they are defined as 'the Transferor' and 'the Transferees' respectively.

6. Description of the property. The full extent of the land transferred should be precisely described. If a verbal description is not possible, a detailed plan must be attached to the transfer, or be identified by referring to the plan on a prior deed which forms part of the title deduced. In this case, reference should be made to the plan in the conveyance of 18 January 1975 made between (1) Mark Ellins and (2) Charles Lane. As this conveyance is also later mentioned, it too is defined for the sake of clarity as 'the Conveyance'.

It is not necessary to refer to the right of way granted by the 1975 conveyance as this will pass automatically by virtue of the Law of Property Act 1925, s. 62.

However, in practice it is often customary to mention existing easements introduced by the words 'Together with . . .'. so that they are not overlooked by the Land Registry on first registration.

7.   There follows immediately a statement of any existing incumbrances – in this case the covenants and conditions in the 1975 conveyance – introduced by the words 'subject to . . .'.

8.   An indemnity covenant should given by Mr and Mrs Clarke to the seller in respect of any future breach of the covenants and the conditions contained in the 1975 conveyance. An examination of the title reveals that a chain of indemnity covenants has been built up by successive owners right the way through to the seller. As the contract incorporates the Standard Conditions of Sale, Standard Condition 4.5.3 obliges the buyer to enter into an indemnity covenant if the seller will remain bound by any obligation affecting the property. Clearly the seller, Flora Nicholson, remains bound by her own indemnity covenant given to Elizabeth Campbell in the conveyance of 14 January 1994.

9.   As mentioned in paragraph 5 above, the buyers can at this stage in the deed make a separate declaration that the survivor of them can give a valid receipt for capital money arising on a disposition of the land. For Land Registry purposes this is sufficient to indicate that they hold as beneficial joint tenants and thus the Land Registry will not enter a Restriction on the Proprietorship register.

10.   A clause enlarging the trustees' (i.e. buyers') powers is not necessary if Mr and Mrs Clarke are also the persons absolutely and beneficially entitled to the land. This is because in this event they are free to deal with the property as they wish.

11.   As the consideration exceeds the stamp duty threshold of £60,000, a certificate of value in the purchase deed is not appropriate.

12.   A testimonium (i.e. 'In witness etc.') is not required in Land Registry transfers but the deed must contain proper attestation provisions. The Law of Property (Miscellaneous Provisions) Act 1989, s. 1(2), provides that an instrument shall not be a deed unless it makes it clear on its face that it is intended to be a deed. The attestation will therefore read, 'Signed as a deed by...'. The seller will execute the deed to transfer the legal estate, and the buyers will also execute as they are entering into an indemnity covenant and a declaration.

QUESTION 3

You are acting for Roseanna Russell-Wilks who has exchanged contracts to buy some grazing land to the rear of Badger's Bottom, Tadchester, owned by her uncle, James Turnbull, who lives in Badger's Bottom.

Mr Turnbull is known for his eccentricity. He wants to give the land to Roseanna but believes that 'no-one should get something for nothing'. The contract therefore provides that Roseanna will pay a nominal consideration of £5 for the land.

In the contract (which incorporates the Standard Conditions of Sale (2nd edition) Roseanna has agreed to enter into a new covenant to erect and maintain a stock-proof fence along the boundary between Badger's Bottom and the land she is buying. Her uncle James has agreed in the contract to grant Roseanna a right of way across his garden to enable her to reach the land.

The whole of the land owned by Mr Turnbull is unregistered and is included within one title. Tadchester came within an area of compulsory registration on 1 December 1990. From your investigation of the title you note the following:

(a)   There are just two documents of title: a conveyance of 14 September 1978 made between Hugh Meyers and Dale Clarkson (which is the root of title) and a conveyance dated 30 November 1989 between Dale Clarkson and James Turnbull.

(b)   The only incumbrances affecting the title are restrictive covenants created in the 1978 conveyance.

(c)   The 1989 conveyance contains a covenant of indemnity by James Turnbull to observe and perform the covenants in the 1978 conveyance.

Your principal has asked you to consider the terms of the purchase deed. Without actually drafting the deed, explain the form it will take and describe its contents.

Commentary

Unlike the previous question, this one does not ask you to draft the purchase deed; and it is probably a good job because a conveyance of part is much longer and more complex than a transfer of whole! If you make the mistake of drafting instead of explaining, you will surely run out of time, as well as lose marks for failing to answer the question correctly.

From a careful reading of the question you will appreciate that the consideration for the conveyance is only five pounds, and this is a clear invitation for you to discuss s. 123 of the Land Registration Act 1925 and whether or not the transaction would constitute a conveyance 'on sale' and thus be compulsorily registrable. It will obviously be satisfying to get this part right, but do not worry about failing the second part of the question if you miss the point. The examiner will give you credit for demonstrating a proper understanding of a r. 72 transfer of part.

Suggested Answer

On completion of the purchase of this land, the question is whether the title to it will become compulsorily registrable by virtue of the Land Registration Act 1925, s. 123. If it does, the buyer's solicitor has a choice: the purchase deed may take the form either of a conveyance, or of a transfer under r. 72 of the Land Registration Rules. If the transaction does not fall within s. 123, the land will remain unregistered after completion (although the buyer may if she wishes apply for voluntary registration) and the correct form of purchase deed will be a conveyance.

Section 123 of the Land Registration Act 1925 lists those transactions which give rise to compulsory registration, and one such transaction is a conveyance on sale of freehold land. On the facts of this case, does a conveyance of land in consideration of five pounds constitute a conveyance 'on sale', or is it effectively a gift of the land which would not trigger compulsory registration? The answer is that the Land Registry will generally take the view that a conveyance at a substantial undervalue will be regarded as a gift, and accordingly it is submitted that the appropriate form of purchase deed in this case is a conveyance.

The point can also be made that even in an unregistered 'on sale' situation, if *part* of land is being sold off where new easements and covenants are being created and other specific clauses are required, the draughtsman will often prefer to use a traditional form of conveyance on the basis that a transfer of part does not necessarily make the draughtsman's job any easier.

The contents of the draft conveyance in question will be as follows:

1.   Commencement, date (left blank until completion) and full names and addresses of the parties.

2.   Recitals. These commence with the word 'WHEREAS...' and state the seller's title to make the conveyance and the price at which the property is agreed to be sold.

3.   Testatum. This introduces the operative part of the deed with the words, 'NOW THIS DEED WITNESSETH...'

4.   Consideration and receipt clause. The price is stated and the receipt of it acknowledged by the seller.

5.   Capacity of the seller. Assuming that Roseanna's uncle is legally and beneficially entitled to the land, his capacity will be 'Beneficial owner'.

6.   The words of grant, 'HEREBY CONVEYS...'.

7.   The parcels clause introduced by the words, 'ALL THAT...' set out the physical description of the land being conveyed. This is very important on a sale of part. The description must be accurate and should be made ideally by reference to a scale plan which is attached to the conveyance showing for instance, 'the land more particularly described thereon edged red'.

8.   The grant of the new right for Roseanna to pass over the land being retained by uncle James subject to her contributing towards the cost of maintenance and repair. The grant is introduced by the words, 'TOGETHER WITH...'. The 'retained land' should be accurately defined. This is normally achieved by reference to blue edging on the conveyance plan.

9.   Habendum (this describes the estate to be vested in the buyer) and statement of existing incumbrances. Here: 'TO HOLD unto the buyer in fee simple SUBJECT TO the restrictive covenants contained in a conveyance dated 14 September 1978 made between (1) Hugh Meyers and (2) Dale Clarkson'. Some draughtsmen may also add the words, 'so far as the same affect the property hereby conveyed and are still subsisting and capable of being enforced'.

10. A declaration negating any implied grant of easement of light or air over the retained land. This is relevant on a sale of part and follows the contractual provision contained in Standard Condition 3.3.2.

11.   An Indemnity covenant given by Roseanna to her uncle in respect of any future breach of the covenants created in the 1978 conveyance. Her uncle has a continuing liability under his own indemnity covenant which he gave to Dale Clarkson in the conveyance to him of 30 November 1989 and, as such, the effect of Standard Condition 4.5.3 is to require Roseanna to continue the chain of indemnity.

12.   A clause imposing the new fencing covenant on Roseanna. This could begin with the words, 'The buyer hereby covenants with the seller...'.

13.   Acknowledgement and undertaking. As this is the sale of part of unregistered land, the uncle will on completion keep the original deeds of Badgers Bottom in order to prove title to it at a later date. Roseanna will receive examined copies only but is entitled contractually by virtue of Standard Condition 4.5.4 (see also s. 64 of the Law of Property Act 1925) to an acknowledgement for the future production of the originals. If the uncle is selling in the capacity of beneficial owner, then Roseanna will also be entitled to an undertaking from him for safe custody of the original deeds. The deeds which will be the subject of the acknowledgement and undertaking are the 1978 conveyance and the 1989 conveyance.

14.   Certificate of value. This is necessary because the consideration for the land is less than the stamp duty threshold, presently at £60,000.

15.   Testimonium. This will say, 'IN WITNESS whereof the parties hereto have set their hands to this deed the day and year first before written'. The inclusion of the words 'this deed' makes it clear that the conveyance is intended to be a deed and thus satisfies s. 1(2) of the Law of Property (Miscellaneous Provisions) Act 1989.

16.   Attestation. The appropriate words are, 'SIGNED AS A DEED AND DELIVERED'. Because Roseanna is entering into an indemnity covenant and a declaration (negating implied grants of easement), she will execute the conveyance as well as her uncle, who of course must do so in order to convey the legal estate.

QUESTION 4

You are acting for Mr and Mrs Irving in their purchase of Coronation House, Hursey. They are buying the house with the aid of an endowment mortgage from one of the well-known building societies. The mortgage deed is in the building society's standard printed form and incorporates the usual comprehensive general conditions found in a building society mortgage.

Your firm is on the society's panel of solicitors, and accordingly the society has instructed the firm to complete and perfect the mortgage. What steps will you take to achieve this in your dual role as solicitor for the buyer and solicitor for the mortgagee?

Commentary

This is a straightforward question provided you read it carefully and answer it methodically. You will notice that the mortgage is an endowment, so you will need to expand on the matters that are relevant to this type of mortgage. In particular, an assignment of a life policy to the building society is nearly always a requirement of the mortgagee.

You must also understand what is meant by 'perfect the mortgage'. Completing the mortgage is only part of the mortgagee's solicitor's job; the perfection of the security lies in the post-completion work, in particular the registration of it.

There is no magic in acting for a mortgagee as well as a buyer. After all, the interests of the mortgagee will nearly always coincide with those of the purchaser (although be aware that conflicts of interest can arise). The purchaser will want to buy and the mortgagee will want security upon a property which is free from unusual incumbrances and has a good and marketable title.

If you possess a sound knowledge of the conveyancing process and you adopt a systematic approach to your answer you are almost guaranteed to achieve high marks. Explain clearly, precisely and in chronological order each stage of the process, highlighting the areas of particular importance. Do not be afraid to spell out, for instance, that the buyers must execute the mortgage deed before the funds are released on completion!

Suggested Answer

The steps we would take to complete and perfect the mortgage on Coronation House can be summarised as follows:

1.   We would conduct all the usual pre-contract searches and enquiries for a property of this nature. For example, local search, index map search (if the title is unregistered) and standard enquiries of the seller's solicitors.

2. We would investigate title to the property in the normal way.

3. We would approve the draft contract and, provided we and our clients are satisfied on all points (including the terms and conditions of the mortgage offer), we would then exchange contracts.

4. Following exchange we would check the mortgage offer/instructions again, in particular the special conditions, and make sure there are no outstanding matters which need to be covered.

5. We would check the precise amount available from the mortgagee on completion. Will there be any retention in respect of works to the property? Will a mortgage guarantee indemnity premium be deducted from the gross advance?

6. By reference to our mortgage instructions, we would fill in the blanks in the mortgage deed and other security documentation in readiness for execution by our clients. For example, in the mortgage deed we would insert the property description (including any title number), names of borrowers and the initial rate of interest.

7. We would ask the clients to come into the office to sign the security documentation in the presence of a solicitor (many mortgagees insist on this in their standard instructions). All requisite documentation would have to be executed *before* completion.

8. Before obtaining the borrowers'/buyers' signatures to the mortgage deed we would explain to them its contents and effect. For example, it will probably contain covenants by the borrower to keep the property in good repair, not to sublet without the mortgagee's consent and not to carry out structural alterations. We would check for any interest penalty on early redemption and advise our clients accordingly (we should already have checked and advised on this when we received the mortgage offer before exchange!). Most importantly, the buyers must realise that their home is at risk if they default on the terms and conditions of the mortgage.

9. We would explain to the buyers the contents and effect of the Assignment of Life Policy Deed, which they will probably be required to execute because it is an endowment mortgage. They must appreciate that the effect of this is to transfer the benefit of the life policy to the building society,

so that in the event of their death, the policy proceeds are paid to the mortgagee to discharge the loan.

10. If not already done following exchange of contracts, the life policy should be brought into force (this is called 'putting on risk'). The age of the policyholder(s) is also normally proven to the life company by production of the policyholder's birth certificate (this is called 'admitting age').

11. We should have the original life policy in our possession on or before completion.

12. We would obtain the buyers' execution to all other necessary mortgage documents (e.g. bank mandate form, MIRAS forms etc.). Signatures should normally be witnessed by a solicitor. It is good practice to let the buyers have copies of the documents they have signed.

13. We would undertake all necessary pre-completion searches, including a bankruptcy search against the full names of the buyers/borrowers. The bankruptcy search is an essential requirement of all mortgagees.

14. Once we were satisfied on the title and the results of our searches, we would send our report on title and advance cheque request to the mortgagee in good time for the advance monies to reach our office by the day of completion. If the results of searches are still outstanding, our report would be qualified to say that the report is 'subject to satisfactory results of searches'.

15. The mortgage documents should not be dated until completion.

16. Following completion, we would perfect the mortgagee's security by attending to the crucial post-completion formalities. These would be: stamping the purchase deed, registering the dealing and mortgage at HM Land Registry, and sending the life company formal notice of assignment of the policy in favour of the mortgagee.

17. Upon completion of the registration at HM Land Registry, we would check the Charge Certificate to ensure that the entries are correct and then forward the Charge Certificate and other documents to the mortgagee for retention by it for the duration of the mortgage.

QUESTION 5

RICHARDS ABBEY AND PARTNERS, SOLICITORS
INTERNAL MEMORANDUM

To   The Trainee Solicitor

From   The Training Partner

Re our client Sanjay Miandad: proposed mortgage
We act for Sanjay Miandad of 24 Bromley Crescent, Drynoch, who intends to
lend £20,000 to his nephew, Javed Khan, to help him with his launderette
business, which is running into financial difficulties.

Javed Khan and his wife live in a leasehold flat in Drynoch which they bought
with the aid of a mortgage from the local building society. Mr Miandad has told
me that Mr Khan is happy to give our client a second charge on the flat to secure
the loan.

Mr Khan does not wish to incur the expense of instructing his own solicitor,
and in view of their close relationship he says he will gladly rely on our firm's
expertise in this area to prepare the necessary paperwork.

He wants us to draw up a mortgage this afternoon, collect it on his way home
from work and get his brother-in-law to sign it this evening before he flies to
Pakistan tomorrow.

What matters should we consider before advising our client to proceed with
these arrangements, if at all?

Commentary

These facts are typical of the kind of thing you will come across in practice.
The client has already reached agreement and decided in his own mind what
he wants from you. However, do not be brow-beaten by the client into doing
what he wants without considering carefully all the facts!

There are several areas of concern here, not least how you are going to react to
the time-pressure of the client's request for a document to be drafted
immediately. Never sacrifice carefully thought out advice in the interests of
speed and expediency. The client is not a trained lawyer and is unlikely to have

considered the full implications of his proposed course of action. That, after all, is your job, and you have a professional duty to ensure that vital issues are not overlooked.

Note the words in the question, 'if at all'. This should alert you to the possibility that the client may be best advised not to proceed in the first place.

You should recognise that a professional conduct issue has reared its head in the guise of r. 6 of the Solicitors' Practice Rules 1990 – acting for two parties in the same conveyancing transaction. Remember that conduct is a pervasive topic on the Legal Practice Course and is always likely to crop up in the context of a conveyancing problem. Rule 6 is an obvious area and you should be looking out for it, even in a situation like this which is not a buyer/seller-type problem.

Always have regard to whether the subject property is freehold or leasehold. If it is the latter – as in this case – there is likely to be a good reason for it, and you should be addressing your mind to possible leasehold issues which may be relevant. Here, it is the question of whether the landlord's consent may be required to the proposed charge by the tenant.

Lastly, a reminder that your answer should be given in the form of a concise memo in response to the partner's memo. Do not be tempted into writing an essay which will lose you marks for style.

Suggested Answer

RICHARDS ABBEY AND PARTNERS, SOLICITORS

INTERNAL MEMORANDUM

To   The Training Partner

From   The Trainee Solicitor

Re our client Sanjay Miandad

I refer to your memo regarding the above. I recommend that the following points should be considered before the client can be advised to proceed.

(a)   Mr Khan must be advised to seek independent legal advice before signing the mortgage. Rule 6 of the Solicitors' Practice Rules 1990 prohibits a solicitor from acting for both lender and borrower in a private mortgage at arm's length. Although it could be argued that this transaction falls within one of the exceptions to the rule (parties are blood related), the exceptions apply only if there is no conflict of interest. On the facts of this case I take the view that a conflict would arise if the mortgagor were seen to be relying on our advice and expertise.

(b)   As this is a proposed second charge we should inspect the first charge to establish whether the consent of the first mortgagee is required to the creation of the second charge.

(c)   If consent is required this should be obtained in writing before completion of the loan. The first mortgagee may require Mr Miandad to enter into a separate deed of postponement.

(d)   Importantly, the first mortgagee should also be asked to confirm the current amount outstanding so it can be checked whether there is sufficient equity in the property to cover the proposed advance.

(e)   The property is leasehold. The lease should be inspected to see if landlord's consent is required to charge the property. If so, consent must be obtained before completion otherwise the charge will not bind the landlord. Following completion it may be necessary to give notice of the charge to the landlord, and this should also be checked in the lease.

(f)   We should investigate title and conduct searches and enquiries in the same way as if our client were buying the property. Before we can advise our client to proceed we must be satisfied that the title is good and marketable and free from any unusual incumbrances.

(g)   We must obtain clear results to pre-completion searches, including a bankruptcy search against the full name of Mr Khan.

(h)   I note that Mr Khan lives in the flat with his wife. We must establish if she is a joint owner, in which case she will also have to join in the mortgage as joint mortgagor.

(i)   Even if Mr Khan is the sole legal owner, Mrs Khan may have an equitable interest in the property and will have statutory rights of occupation under the Matrimonial Homes Act 1983. She must give her written consent to the proposed charge and agree to postpone all rights behind our client's charge. Reasonable steps must be taken to ensure that she understands the nature of the transaction and the postponement of her rights (if any). To this end, I recommend we insist that she receives separate independent advice. This should be sufficient to counter any assertion by her at a later date that her husband exerted duress or undue influence on her (see *Barclays Bank plc* v *O'Brien* [1994] 1 AC 180).

(j) Does Mr Khan own the launderette premises? If so, have the parties considered the alternative possibility of Mr Miandad taking security on these premises? This avenue should be explored as it may prove less complicated.

(k) Given the important issues which need to be addressed, we cannot sensibly comply with our client's instructions to draft the mortgage immediately. If Mr Miandad is coming into the office this afternoon I will be happy to see him and explain the position.

Trainee Solicitor: time engaged 35 minutes.

8 Pre-completion Procedures and Completion

INTRODUCTION

This is a fascinating area of conveyancing that can be both practical and also involve the theoretical application of case law. You will have to be fully conversant with all aspects of pre-completion searches as this is one topic that comes up in exams time and time again. The reasons for this are really quite obvious; pre-completion searches are a critical part of conveyancing that can be fraught with all sorts of pitfalls for the unwary practitioner. In the first place there is the obvious but well repeated point that with two land law systems, registered and unregistered, there will always be confusion for the ill-prepared about which searches to make. Secondly, there is also the potential for confusion arising from the dual role of acting for the buyer and the lender at the same time. Thirdly, there is the variety of different but relevant searches that can confuse. The moral is, know your searches and you should do well.

Although conveyancing is about land law and its application, it is also about money and the transfer of valuable assets, both small and large. This is nowhere more clearly demonstrated than at completion. It is at this point in the proceedings that large sums of money will change hands. It is for this reason that questions in this area will require you to demonstrate an ability to handle elementary mathematics. Some examination authorities will specifically authorise you to take a calculator into the examination room. Always do so if permitted as it will be the case that most, if not all, of us will find them faster at computing the figures required. Be prepared to work out Value Added Tax, as of course this is payable not just on legal fees but also on estate agents' charges. Indeed, it is also important that you are aware of the prevailing rate for stamp duty, currently at 1% on all purchases over £60,000. (There will also be stamp duty on rents on the grant of a lease, but as this can be quite complicated it is unlikely that you will be required to calculate such an amount in an exam. However, you should be aware of the principles involved.)

Another area of potential confusion arises from the promulgation of the Law Society's National Conveyancing Protocol and the fact that some transactions will proceed within it and some will not. Those that do, will, in the absence of agreement to the contrary, complete in accordance with the Law Society's Code for Completion. Those that do not will only complete within the terms of the Code if the parties' solicitors specifically agree to adopt the Code. What this means for you is that you will be required to know the difference between the two systems as far as completion is concerned. You will also need to identify the weaknesses of both and how these can be addressed. You will need to know your case law.

You will have realised by now that every area of conveyancing can be separately identified but will usually be examined in the context of allied topics. A clear example in this area is set out in the first question, where you will need to consider from whom you have received instructions as well as the effect of a change of parties. Similarly, matters of professional conduct will surface, especially in the context of completion and the requirements of the Law Society's Code. Accordingly, throughout this whole area you should be continually aware of matters of professional conduct and whether or not they should be mentioned in your answer. Conflicts of interest will always need to be mentioned, and particularly in relation to possible completion arrangements.

QUESTION 1

Your clients, Mr and Mrs Clement Fazackerley, are purchasing from a Mr Leslie Markus his house, being 1 The Main Street, Lutterworth, for £75,000. They are buying with the aid of a mortgage of £50,000 from the Barchester Building Society for whom you are also acting. The title number is HD 362638. Contracts were exchanged two weeks ago and completion is due in two weeks' time.

Please list the pre-completion searches you would arrange and explain your reasons for doing so. What would change if your client was purchasing an unregistered property, and why? Would your answer be different if the seller were a limited company?

Commentary

This is a question that will appear in examination papers with monotonous regularity. If there is one area of paramount importance within pre-completion procedures then this must be it. Searches at this stage of a conveyance are of critical significance, and will therefore be central to the examination of your knowledge of the conveyancing process. As is always the case with examination questions, information is contained within it for a reason. For example, here you have been told that you also act for the Building Society. This should immediately sound alarm bells in your head that your set of double instructions will mean additional information required in your answer. Similarly, the reference in the latter part of the question to changes consequent upon the property being unregistered will require you to highlight the alternate searches required for unregistered land. The question also talks about 'searches you would arrange'. This is because you should also arrange to have the property to be purchased inspected before completion by the client. You should always refer to a pre-completion property inspection as a search in an answer of this kind. (Remember the effects of *Williams & Glyn's Bank Ltd* v *Boland* [1981] AC 487.) Lastly, you will also need to show the requirement for an extra search should the seller be a limited company.

Suggested Answer

The searches required in the several situations are as follows:

(a) Registered land –

    (i) Land Registry search;

    (ii) bankruptcy search against the buyers;

(iii)   inspection of the property.

(b)   Unregistered land –

(i)   land charges search;

(ii)   bankruptcy search against the buyers;

(iii)   inspection of the property.

(c)   Limited company seller, as above and also a search in the Companies Register.

(a)   Registered land. The buyers are purchasing a registered property, and as a consequence the first pre-completion search that should be carried out is an official search of the register at the Land Registry. Buyers should only accept as proof of title office copy entries, as searches cannot be made against mere photocopies. Since the introduction of new regulations (the Land Registration (Official Searches) Rules 1993) searches can only be made against office copy entries that are less than 12 months old. Accordingly, the buyers will want to check that there are no additional entries on the register that have not been seen and made since the date of the issue of the office copies. As it would appear that the clients are buying all of the seller's title the search is carried out on form 94A and the search will be from the 'search from' date of the office copy entries. The search will reveal whether or not there are any adverse entries made since that date, and the buyers are given a priority period of 30 working days. This priority period gives the buyers a time during which their registration of ownership at the Land Registry can take place without regard to any other application, adverse or otherwise, made during that period.

Apart from the buyers' instructions, there are also instructions from the mortgagees, and a bankruptcy search against the buyers must be made on behalf of the Building Society. The search is carried out at the Land Charges Registry on form K16. The purpose is, of course, to check that the buyers are not undischarged bankrupts. Any adverse entry disclosed could very well mean that the mortgage offer is withdrawn, and as a consequence any such entry has to be reported to the lender.

Lastly, the subject property should be inspected prior to completion. The reason for this is primarily to check on exactly who is in occupation. The existence of a third party occupant might amount to an overriding interest to which the purchase would be subject. (As was the case in *Williams & Glyn's Bank Ltd* v *Boland* [1981] AC 487.)

(b)   Unregistered land. If the property were unregistered then two of the three searches mentioned above would still apply and for the same reasons. Accordingly, the bankruptcy search would be carried out and the pre-completion inspection would still be necessary. However, if the land is unregistered an official search of the register at the Land Registry would be wholly inappropriate and should be replaced by a land charges search in the registers maintained by the central Land Charges Department in Plymouth. Section 198 of the Law of Property Act 1925 provides that registration is deemed to be actual notice of any registrable matter whether or not a search is carried out. It is therefore imperative to effect such a search against all estate owners on land charge form K15. A period of years is required on the search request for each estate owner, but if in doubt the period can be expressed to be from 1925 to the year the search is being made. Adverse entries will be disclosed on the search result, including a puisne mortgage (class C(i)), an estate contract such as an option to purchase (class C(iv)), or a restrictive covenant affecting the property (class D(ii)). Registrations under the Matrimonial Homes Act 1983 (class F) will also be disclosed. A buyer will have priority from the date of the search result to the intent that no registration made after the search result will be binding on the buyer if completion takes place within 15 working days of the date of the search result.

(c)   Limited company seller. If the seller were a limited company then there will be an alteration to the list of searches required and the additional search will apply to both registered and unregistered land. Where the seller is a company, a search of the Companies Register at Companies House should be carried out. This can be done either in person or through search agents. In the case of registered land, a companies search will be necessary because a buyer will wish to be sure that the company still subsists and has not been struck off the register, perhaps for failing to file returns. Of course, if the company is subject to winding-up proceedings these would also be shown by this search and would be information that a buyer would need to be aware of in the context of the imminence of completion. In the case of registered land there is no need to carry out a company search to check on financial charges made by the company as they will bind a purchaser only if they are registered at the Land Registry.

In the case of unregistered land, the company search is very important. The search will reveal floating charges, specific charges created before 1 January 1970, and the commencement of winding-up proceedings. All three items are of material importance to a buyer and would be clearly adverse. No purchaser should proceed until the seller has in the appropriate way shown how and when the adverse entry would be dealt with. Bearing in mind that any disposition by a company subject to winding-up proceedings is void (s. 127 of the Insolvency Act 1986), it will be appreciated just how important a company search can be. Lastly, it should be noted that there is no priority period of protection available for a company search. It should therefore be made just before completion.

QUESTION 2

Your clients, Mr and Mrs Gerry Desmond, are buying a house and paddock at 1 Alma Terrace, Hassocks, with the aid of a mortgage from the Kenlingsea Building Society for whom you also act. The house is registered with title absolute, while the paddock is unregistered. The unregistered title is simple, being just a conveyance made 16 years ago between the original sellers, Alan Estates Plc, and the present seller, Wayne Kingston Limited. This serves as the root of title and there are no other deeds involved in the abstract of title.

You have just been passed the file by your supervising partner who has pointed out that contracts were exchanged two months ago on 1 June and completion is due in two days' time, on 3 August next. The contract provides for vacant possession on completion. She has also said that everything has been done in readiness for exchange, but would you please check the papers, and in particular the searches. She adds that the person who had the conduct of this matter has now left the firm. All requisitions have been raised and answered, the purchase deed settled, and the firm is in funds in readiness for completion.

You have looked at the file and have noted that there is a clear land charges search result against Wayne Kingston for the proper 16-year period, and this search was issued by the Land Charges Department on 1 July. There is also a clear 94A search disclosing no adverse entries, that was issued by the Land Registry on 8 June. Please advise your supervising partner of the position on the file as far as pre-completion searches are concerned.

Commentary

This question is of course about searches again, but this time you are required to evaluate whether or not the position as shown in the question is acceptable. Clearly the position cannot be right, otherwise there would be little or no point to the question! So your job is to highlight just what is wrong with the file. Frankly, in the light of the several difficulties contained within the paperwork, it is not surprising that the person who previously had the conduct of the file has now left the firm!

You should expect just this kind of question in a conveyancing exam, and indeed you may to encounter similar problems in practice. Consequently, this style of question is one which you should anticipate, particularly where searches and time limits are concerned. Indeed, time limits can amount to a practitioner's nightmare, and for this reason alone an examiner will return to the topic time and time again. As to the format of the answer, you can either write an essay or you can prepare a memorandum of advice for your supervising partner. However, in either case it is best practice to show at the start of the answer the faults that you have identified so that the examiner's attention is seized from the very outset. After that you can go on to show why there are these faults and what should be done to remedy them.

Lastly, please be aware that the answer requires you to consider errors and omissions. As ever, with almost any examination question in the law you will need to highlight what has been left out as much as correct what has been stated.

Suggested Answer

RICHARDS ABBEY AND PARTNERS, SOLICITORS

INTERNAL MEMORANDUM

To: The Supervising Partner

From: The Trainee Solicitor

Re 1 Alma Terrace, Hassocks
I refer to the file that you passed to me concerning this proposed purchase by Mr and Mrs Desmond and set out below my report on the file as far as searches are concerned. To begin with, I can confirm that I have identified the following areas of difficulty that I will explain subsequently:

(a)   The land charges search is unreliable for two reasons.

(b)   The Land Registry search is unreliable.

(c)   There is no company search.

(d)   There is no bankruptcy search.

(e)   And there does not seem to have been any pre-completion inspection of the property.

(a)   The land charges search. This must be resubmitted to the Land Charges Department as the existing search is invalid. First, the search was made against the wrong name. The seller is Wayne Kingston Limited, while the search has been made against Wayne Kingston. For the search to be valid the full and proper name of the estate owner must be quoted. (See *Oak Co-Operative Building Society* v *Blackburn* [1968] Ch 730.) Secondly, the search is now out of date. An official land charges search provides a priority period of protection for a buyer such that no registration made at the Registry after the date of the search result will be binding on the buyer if the completion of the relevant transaction takes place within 15 working days of the result. On the facts contained within the file the search result is out of date and cannot be relied upon.

(b)   The Land Registry search. This must be resubmitted to the Land Registry as the existing search is out of date. An official search provides a priority period of protection for a buyer such that no application made at the Land Registry after the date of the search result will be binding on the buyer provided the buyer lodges his application for registration at the Land Registry within the priority period of 30 working days from the date of the result. From the facts within the file this cannot be done and the existing search cannot be relied upon.

(c)   Company search. A search of the file has failed to show a company search. The seller is Wayne Kingston Limited, a limited company. This seller is selling both registered and unregistered land, and in both cases a company search at Companies House is vital. In both cases a search will reveal if there are subsisting winding-up proceedings, or if the company has been struck off, say, for failing to file returns. In the case of the unregistered land the search will show many critical matters, including floating charges registered only at Companies House and pre-1970 specific charges. I therefore recommend an immediate company search; shall I instruct our search agents to proceed?

(d)   Bankruptcy search. We are acting for the Building Society as well as the buyers. We have an obligation to them to check on the status of the proposed borrowers. To do this a land charge K16 bankruptcy search at the Land Charges Department is required. It will reveal whether there are pending bankruptcy actions, or whether either client is an undischarged bankrupt. An inspection of the file has failed to show this vital search and one should be made immediately. If we did not carry out this search we would be in breach of our duty of care to the proposed lender. They require to know, before completion of the loan, that the proposed borrowers are persons to whom they may lend. Clearly any involvement in bankruptcy proceedings would need to be reported to the Building Society.

(e) Pre-completion inspection. There is no note on the file to show that anyone has carried out an inspection of the property. Similarly, I cannot see any letter to the clients suggesting that they themselves carry out such an inspection. This is an oversight and I would recommend that either I or the clients go and inspect the property now. I make this suggestion as I see that the contract provides for vacant possession on completion. It will be necessary to check the subject property to ensure that vacant possession will indeed be available and that there are no undisclosed third party occupants. If there are, their occupation may amount to an overriding interest. For this reason alone it is vital to inspect, and at the same time other checks can be made, such as for the continued existence of chattels to be left at the property at completion. Clearly if there is anything amiss then it would need to be resolved by the seller before completion. (Please see *Williams & Glyn's Bank* v *Boland* [1980] 2 All ER 408, which highlights the possible dangers of third party occupants.)

In all the circumstances I suggest that the position is retrievable by repeating the two out-of-date searches (the land charges search must be made against the correct name), by effecting a company search and a bankruptcy search, and by arranging an inspection of the property.

Trainee Solicitor: time engaged 35 minutes.

QUESTION 3

Your client is Daphne Scott, who is due to buy the freehold property being 21 Linden Lea, Liverpool, on the completion date being in five days' time. The purchase price is £89,000. Your client paid a deposit of £1,250 on exchange and a deposit of £250 was paid to the estate agents acting for the seller, Nigel Barton. You have mortgage instructions from the Cheshire Building Society, for a proposed loan of £52,750, from which you have noted the following:

(a) there is a repairs retention of £995;

(b) there is a indemnity policy premium charged of £575;

(c) there is a completion monies transfer fee charged of £23;

(d) and there is a Society minimum membership fee of £1.

Your principal has advised you that the firm's fees will be £295 exclusive and that the Land Registry fees are £180. You have checked the accounts ledger for the client in the accounts department and have noted the following debit entries in the office account:

1	local search fee	£75
2	coal search fee	£23.50
3	commons search	£10
4	land charges fee	£1
5	L.R. search fee	£5

Because completion is fast approaching, your principal has asked you to prepare a completion statement for the buyer immediately. You have also been asked to write a letter to Daphne Scott, enclosing the statement, to explain the contents and to explain how the shortfall is to be paid. Your principal will prepare the actual bill of costs. Please provide a draft of the statement and accompanying letter.

Commentary

It is now common practice in modern conveyancing exams to advise candidates to bring a calculator with them into the examination. This question shows why this is necessary! You can expect to find just such a question in your conveyancing examination, as examiners are keen to ensure that you understand the financial mechanisms involved. In the final analysis conveyancing is a practical subject, where legal theory is applied to commonplace situations. The most practical element of the whole process is completion, when the purchase price is paid and the deeds handed over. However, there are of course two sides to the transaction, and a buyer will be involved in financial matters just as much as the seller. It is for this reason that a completion statement will be required for the buyer and will have to be prepared by the buyer's lawyer.

This question looks quite straightforward. Indeed, in most respects that is true. However, as you will have come to expect, nothing in conveyancing is as simple as it seems. First, the legal fees are expressed to be exclusive. This should make you appreciate immediately that you must consider VAT. Secondly, the purchase price is £89,000, and this again should make you realise that not all the necessary facts and figures have been set out in the question. As the payment in question is the largest the buyer will have to make, it is important that it is not overlooked!

Lastly, as to the style of the answer, all you need to do is provide a short introduction and then set out the draft completion statement followed by the draft letter. An essay would be quite inappropriate.

Suggested Answer

There is set out below drafts of the completion statement and accompanying letter for Daphne Scott. Two points were not mentioned and which have been incorporated in the drafts, namely VAT on the legal costs and stamp duty of 1% of the purchase price.

(a)   Draft completion statement.

DRAFT COMPLETION STATEMENT

21 Linden Lea, Liverpool
Barton to Scott

Purchase price		£89,000.00
DEDUCT deposits paid		
On exchange	£1,250.00	
To Agents	£250.00	
	£1,500.00	£1,500.00
		£87,500.00
DEDUCT net mortgage		
Gross advance	£52,750.00	
less retention	£995.00	
less indemnity fee	£575.00	
less transfer fee	£23.00	
less membership fee	£1.00	
NET advance	£51,156.00	£51,156.00
		£36,344.00
ADD stamp duty at 1%		£890.00
		£37,234.00

ADD costs and other payments

	£295.00	
VAT thereon @ 17.5%	£51.63	
Local search fee	£75.00	
Coal search fee	£23.50	
Commons search fee	£10.00	
Land Charges fee	£1.00	
Land Registry fee	£180.00	
Land Registry search fee	£5.00	
	£641.13	£641.13
REQUIRED from you to complete		£37,875.13

(b)   Draft Letter to the client.

RICHARDS ABBEY AND PARTNERS, SOLICITORS

4 Red Lion Square London WC1

Partners

M. B. Richards
R.M. Abbey

Dear Ms Scott,

Re 21 Linden Lea, Liverpool

I refer to your purchase of the above property and now write to let you have details of the amount required by this firm to enable us to complete the transaction on your behalf. As you will recall completion is due in five days' time.

Please find enclosed a completion statement giving details of the amounts involved. The statement shows the purchase price, from which you will see the two deposit payments have been deducted, as well as the net amount available from the Building Society. To explain the deductions from the advance you should first refer to your mortgage offer. However, to clarify, all these deductions have been made by the Society in accordance with that offer. The net advance is the amount that we will receive from the Society. The repairs retention is, I think, quite clear, and once you have completed the works and the Society have approved them they will release these monies. The indemnity premium has been explained in the offer, but if you require further information please let me know. The transfer fee is a bank charge made and deducted by the Society for the transfer of the net advance to our account.

I have shown stamp duty as a separate item as this will be your biggest payment. This is a simple tax at 1% of the full purchase price, and I will have to pay this to the Inland Revenue within 30 days of completion to avoid a penalty fee being levied for late payment.

As to this firm's costs, please find enclosed a note of our charges [NB to be drafted by principal] which I trust meet with your approval and accord with the original estimate given to you at the start of the transaction. For the sake of clarity I have set out on the completion statement the legal fees and the VAT on them together with all other payments that lawyers call disbursements. In the main these are search fees to be paid on your behalf along with fees to the Land Registry for the registration of your ownership of the property. If any items are still unclear please do not hesitate to contact me and I will provide further detailed clarification.

In the end the amount required from you to enable us to complete is £37,875.13. Solicitors are required by the Law Society to be in possession of cleared funds to enable them to pay out monies from those funds. In effect this means that all cheques received must be fully cleared before payment is made. If you pay these monies by cheque then I will have to specially clear that cheque in view of the short period of time before completion. This will incur an additional disbursement, being a Bank special clearance fee. However, I can only accept such a cheque within the next two days otherwise there will not be enough time to clear the cheque. Accordingly, I would appreciate it if you could please let me have a payment of the sum concerned by a Banker's Draft which is tantamount to cash and does not need clearance. You can obtain this from your own bankers. However, as the draft is in effect cash please deliver it by hand.

If there are any points you are not clear on please let me know and I will do my best to assist, but in the meantime I await a banker's draft for the sum mentioned above to enable me to proceed.

Yours sincerely.

QUESTION 4

You act for Robert Morrison who has contracted to sell his freehold shop and upper part, being 88 Victoria Road, Newcastle, with vacant possession for

£119,950 to Alison Tasker. The property is registered. Completion is due in four days' time. Your supervisor is just about to go on holiday and has asked you to help with the transaction. You have to prepare a completion statement for the buyer's solicitors and a completion statement for the client.

You have looked at the file and have noted the following details:

(a) The selling agents hold a deposit of £495.

(b) A deposit was paid to the firm on exchange of £11,500.

(c) There is a first mortgage with Lloyds Bank where the redemption figure is £62,356.55.

(d) There is a second mortgage with ABC Loans plc where the redemption figure is £19,955.32.

(e) The estate agent's fees are £4,228.24 inclusive.

(f) Office copy entries of title cost £10.

(g) Our legal fees were originally quoted at £575 exclusive.

(h) The contract provides for the sale of chattels at a price of £775.

Please draft the statements required together with a letter to the client explaining the contents of his completion statement. Your supervisor will prepare the fee account which you may therefore ignore.

Commentary

This is another example of a conveyancing question that requires a calculator, but this time from the seller's perspective. If you are confident about your knowledge of the conveyancing process and also your mathematical ability then this is the question for you. Frankly, the question is perfectly straightforward and high marks can be obtained if you carefully structure the two statements. There is no mention of any allied purchase for your client, and as this would seem to be a business rather than a domestic conveyance you could ask the client if the net proceeds of the sale are to be issued direct to the client, or whether they can be placed on deposit.

Suggested Answer

There is set out below drafts of the completion statements and accompanying letter for Robert Morrison. It is assumed that a bill of costs will be prepared in addition to the documents set out below.

(a)   Completion statement for the buyer's solicitors

COMPLETION STATEMENT

88 Victoria Road, Newcastle
Morrison to Tasker

Purchase price		£119,950.00
DEDUCT deposits paid		
On exchange	£11,500.00	
To agents	£495.00	
	£11,995.00	£11,995.00
		£107,955.00
ADD amount payable for chattels		£775.00
TOTAL payable on completion		£108,730.00

(b)   Completion statement for the client seller

COMPLETION STATEMENT

88 Victoria Road, Newcastle
Morrison to Tasker

Sale price		£119,950.00
ADD amount payable for chattels		£775.00
		£120,725.00
DEDUCT mortgage redemption monies		
Lloyds Bank	£62,356.55	
ABC Loans plc	£19,955.32	
	£82,311.87	£82,311.87
		£38,413.13
DEDUCT estate agent's charges (incl. VAT)		£4,228.24
		£34,184.89

DEDUCT Land Registry office copies fee		£10.00
		£34,174.89
DEDUCT Legal fees		
Agreed costs	£575.00	
ADD VAT (17.5%)	£100.63	
	£675.63	£675.63
BALANCE DUE TO YOU, see letter attached,		£33,499.26

   (c)   Draft letter to the seller

RICHARDS ABBEY AND PARTNERS, SOLICITORS

4 Red Lion Square London WC1

Partners

M. B. Richards
R.M. Abbey

Dear Mr Morrison,

88 Victoria Road, Newcastle

I refer to your sale of the above property where completion is due in four days' time, and now write to provide you with financial details. Please find enclosed a completion statement giving details of all monies received, paid out and to be paid out. You will see that the sale price of the chattels has been added to the sale price of the property as of course both amounts will be paid on completion. The first deductions after that are the repayments of the two mortgages to the bank and to the loan company respectively. These have been calculated by the lenders and checked by us and include all interest payable up to and including the date of sale.

The estate agent's charges will be paid by us, in accordance with your letter of instructions received last week confirming that we should pay these. I can confirm that their account will be paid on the basis of their fees at 3% of the sale price with value added tax thereon. I will seek a receipted invoice from the agents and send it to you when I receive it as I imagine that you will require this for your accountants for tax purposes. The only other deductions are the Land Registry office copies fee and the costs of this firm. The Land Registry office copies fee is the amount they levy for official copies of your deeds that we are required to send to the buyers to prove your title to this property. As to our costs, these were originally quoted to you at the level of £575, being the amount you subsequently agreed, and they remain at this agreed level. As you will appreciate, these fees attract VAT at 17.5% amounting to £100.63. If you have any queries on this or any other points arising from the details supplied, please do not hesitate to contact me and I will do all that I can to clarify matters.

In the end I have shown the net proceeds of sale due to you on completion. I can either send this amount to you immediately on completion, or I can if you wish place the monies on deposit until you have made a further decision as to the ultimate destination for the monies. If you require the monies to be sent to you I can do this by cheque or by bank transfer. The latter is quicker but I would have to deduct the bank charges of about £23 for sending the money in this way. If I am to send the money by transfer I will require your full bank details. I await your instructions.

Yours sincerely,

Trainee Solicitor.

QUESTION 5

Please answer the following:

(a) You are effecting a personal completion of an unregistered sale of part of a freehold where you act for the seller who will be retaining the remainder of the land. There is a new house on the land being sold. The seller does have a mortgage but the sale price is not sufficient to discharge it. The bank has issued a release of the mortgage over the part being sold. There are no estate agents. The buyer's solicitors are just across the road and are therefore happy to complete in this way. Please list the documents you will hand over and also list anything you will receive. Are there any other steps or actions you will take at completion?

(b) Please state briefly the main provisions of the Law Society's Code for Completion.

(c) You are hoping to complete a purchase for a client by post where the Law Society's Code for Completion is not being adopted. This is because you have the seller's solicitor's undertaking to pay off the seller's mortgage.

Relying upon that solicitor's undertaking, you have sent off the completion monies. Is that undertaking sufficient?

Commentary

At last, a question for the supporter of the examination essay! It is in three parts and there are no indications of the individual marks for each. You are therefore entitled to assume that the marks will be allocated equally. This being the case, you should allocate your time in the same way. (By the same token, if marks are shown relate them to the time allocated for the question and apportion the minutes according to the marks available.) Of course there is no precondition that you stick rigidly to an essay format, as lists of relevant points in your reply are a boon to the marker. They immediately demonstrate the extent of your knowledge, and it is to be hoped that the enhanced speed with which the marking process can proceed will militate in your favour.

The global topic of completion has been dealt with in the question in three distinct ways. First, you have to consider a non-protocol, personal completion, the old style personal way of completing. This is followed by an examination of the Protocol procedure, and in particular the Code for Completion; this is the modern approach. Lastly, (c) is a question that should ring alarm bells in that it bears comparison to the Hong Kong Privy Council case that in part brought about the Law Society's completion code. In effect, you will score highly if you can identify the relevance and significance of the case examined in the following answer. You will have come across the case if you have actually read the Code for Completion as it is specifically referred to in note 4 to the Code.

Suggested Answer

(a)   I have instructions on an unregistered sale of part of a freehold property and I will be completing the transaction personally. In readiness for completion I have prepared a list of documents to be handed over, together with a list of items to be received. The documents to be handed over are:

(i)   The transfer deed duly executed by the seller. This may be in the form of a r. 72 transfer as the property is subject to compulsory first registration.

(ii)   There is a mortgage on the property and the mortgagees have issued a deed of release for the land being sold, and this release will be handed over.

(iii)   The house being new there will be NHBC Buildmark scheme documentation to be handed over.

(iv)   The property being newly erected there will be available on completion the original planning consent and building regulations approval to be handed to the buyer's solicitor.

(v)   There being no agents the keys to the new house should be available to be handed over.

The essential item to be received is a banker's draft representing the balance of the purchase price. A cheque cannot be accepted and the draft should be drawn on one of the main clearing banks.

As to other steps to be taken because the sale is of part, the following matters should be considered:

(i)   The seller will retain the deeds and consequently the abstract or epitome of title must be examined and marked up at completion. The original deeds must therefore be made available.

(ii)   A memorandum of the sale should be endorsed on the last conveyance of the whole (i.e., the conveyance to our client). (Please see s. 200 of the Law of Property Act 1925.)

(iii)   A copy of the transfer of part by r. 72 should be made up at completion and kept with the deeds. In this way there can be no doubt in the future for the seller as to the contents of the deed and the terms therein.

(b)   The Law Society's Code for Completion ('the Code') must be adopted by both sides in Protocol cases unless otherwise agreed. The main provisions are:

(i)   The crucial element of the Code is that the buyer's solicitor appoints the seller's solicitor as his or her unpaid agent for completion.

(ii)   The buyer's solicitor must provide full instructions for the 'agent' relating to the buyer's requirements. These instructions should clearly set out for the seller's solicitor what the buyer's solicitor requires him or her to do and what is to be sent on after completion has been effected.

(iii)   The seller's solicitor must confirm instructions from the seller to receive the sale monies and that he or she has been appointed the authorised agent of any mortgagee authorising the receipt of monies required to redeem the mortgage.

(iv)   The buyer's solicitor will send the completion monies by bank telegraphic transfer (a CHAPS payment) and on receipt the completion takes place. Until completion has taken place the seller's solicitor will hold the purchase monies to the order of the buyer's solicitor. At the point of completion the deeds and documents are held by the seller's solicitor as agent for the buyer's solicitor.

(v)   That day (i.e. the day of completion), the deeds and documents must be sent to the buyer's solicitor, and once posted properly they are at the buyer's risk.

(vi)   It should be noted that adopting the Code involves the giving of professional undertakings that will be enforced through the Law Society.

(vii)   The Code can only be used if there is no obvious conflict of interest. If such exists the appointment of an 'agent' would be inappropriate.

(viii)   Lastly, it should be noted that nothing in the Code shall override any rights and obligations of either the seller or the buyer under the terms of the sale contract or otherwise.

(c)   The circumstances that form the basis for this question are similar to those in the case of *Edward Wong Finance Co. Ltd* v *Johnson, Stokes and Masters* [1984] AC 1296. In that case it was held on comparable facts that the undertaking mentioned in the question was not sufficient.

In the above case, completion took place on the basis that the buyer's solicitors paid the completion monies relying on an undertaking given by the seller's solicitors to the effect that they would pay off the seller's mortgage. Unfortunately the seller's solicitors then absconded with the monies without, of course, paying anything to the mortgagee! The Court held that the loss had to be borne by the buyer's solicitors because the Court said they had failed to take all necessary and appropriate steps to protect their client's interests. In effect the Court said the solicitors were negligent because they did not seek confirmation that the seller's solicitors had the authority of the mortgagee to accept the monies. Notwithstanding that this is a case from Hong Kong, it will clearly apply in similar circumstances in England and Wales.

The only really safe arrangement is for the buyer's solicitors to obtain in writing an authority from the seller's mortgagee allowing the buyer's solicitors to pay the redemption monies to the seller's solicitor. If completion was in person two drafts could be handed over; one for the mortgagee and the balance to the seller's solicitors. This is of course a somewhat impractical suggestion, but if the buyers have cause for concern this is the only really safe approach. It is interesting to note that the Code does not include this requirement; and if this is necessary then, where the Code prevails, the alteration to the Code must be agreed by the parties, failing which the Code cannot apply. Accordingly it could be said that the code does not really address the problems in the *Wong* case, in that the buyers may still need the confirmation from the seller's mortgagee that the seller's solicitor is authorised to receive their redemption monies. Ultimately it is clear that the undertaking given is plainly insufficient as far as the buyers and their solicitors are concerned.

QUESTION 6

You have been consulted by Jeffrey Spearman about the family farm at School View, Diss. The farm has been in the Spearman family for generations and the freeholder was Jeffrey's father, Wilfred Spearman. Wilfred, with the intention of keeping the farm in the family and in consideration of one pound, granted to Jeffrey an option to purchase the land at the fixed price of £30,000. Neither Jeffrey nor his solicitors registered the option at the Land Charges Registry. Jeffrey is a tenant in occupation of the land.

Father and son subsequently had a blazing row about the management of the farm and Wilfred sought to get out of the option. He discovered that it was not registered, so he immediately conveyed the farm to his wife Edith for £500, even though the farm was actually worth £60,000! Jeffrey then attempted to exercise his option. He has told you that the farm is now worth over £100,000, and as such the option that his mother and father both knew about from the time it was granted is potentially of great value.

Jeffrey requires some advice. He has pointed out that the two matters that really bother him are, first, that £500 is simply not the true value and, secondly, that his parents have not acted fairly. What can he do?

Commentary

This is another example of a question where an essay-type answer will be acceptable. It is also an illustration of the type of question where a display of academic knowledge will be necessary rather than just your knowledge of the practical processes of conveyancing. This question straddles land law and the conveyancing requirements of the land charges provisions that relate to unregistered land. You will soon appreciate that the question is located in this chapter because of the need to make a land charges search to check on the registration of the option. You may also recognise certain features in the question that resemble the facts of a particularly important case from the 1980s that was concerned with the provisions of s. 13(2) of the Land Charges Act 1925, or what is now s. 4(6) of the Land Charges Act 1972. It is common practice for examiners to replicate the facts of an important case so that you can demonstrate your knowledge and your ability to examine and expound judicial reasoning. If you are acquainted with the facts of this case – and you should be – then you should not have difficulty in completing your answer.

Suggested Answer

Jeffrey Spearman wants to enforce an option against his parents to enable him to purchase the farm of which he is the tenant. He wishes to do so because if he can succeed with the option he will be able to buy a farm worth over £100,000 for just £30,000. The question is, can he force the exercise of the option by commencing proceedings against both parents? He will also want to know the effect of the non-registration of the option in the first place, as well as what would have shown up on a search at the Land Charges Registry, if anything. He will be concerned with the effect of that search result. He is also troubled about the payment made by his mother, which he considers so small as to be unreal, and that his parents have not acted in good faith towards him. All these matters will now be considered.

The facts within this problem bear a close similarity to the facts of the case of *Midland Bank Trust Co. Ltd* v *Green* [1981] AC 513 (on appeal from [1980] Ch 590). That case, and these facts, concerned the effect of non-registration of matters that should be registered as a land charge at the Land Charges Registry, and in particular an option to purchase. The Land Charges Act 1925 – and subsequently the 1972 Act – provided that registration constitutes actual notice of the matter so registered. In the *Midland* case, and on the facts of the question, registration will therefore constitute actual notice of the option. Accordingly, the effect of non-registration of an option is that it is void against a purchaser of a legal estate in the land for money or money's worth (s. 4(6) of the Land Charges Act 1972). In essence, therefore, this means that the statute clearly declares that if there is no protective entry (a C(iv) entry), then should the land concerned be sold for value the buyer will take free of the matter that should have been protected by the registration. However, in this case the seller and the buyer both actually knew of the existence of the option, and it could be argued that this awareness might amount to good notice of its existence. It seems that this is not the true position in law, however, and the *Midland* case sets the precedent that a buyer's actual knowledge of an unregistered but registrable interest is not good notice and is in fact immaterial and irrelevant. The law can therefore be simply stated: if there is registration there is protection; if there is no such registration there is no protection.

How did the father know that there was no registration? Of course he would have effected a search in the land charges register against himself to see if the option he granted to his son was protected by a C(iv) entry. The search result would have come back without any such entry on it, and in those circumstances and in the light of the decision of the House of Lords mentioned above Mrs Spearman could repeat the search, obtain the same result and buy the farm free of the option. There was no protective registration, and consequently Mrs Spearman could complete free of the option. To do this all she had to do was to issue a K15 land charge search request, receive back a clear result and then complete within the priority period of the search. The effect of such a search result is that it is conclusive in favour of the buyer and it confers priority on the buyer. The effect of this priority is that if completion takes place within 15 working days of the certificate the buyer has priority over any entry made after the certificate date and completion, and takes the property free of such entry. In these circumstances, if the son had made an application to register the option after the priority date on the mother's search she would take the property free of the option provided she completed the purchase within the priority period.

Jeffrey Spearman has also expressed concern about the amount paid by his mother to his father, which he considers to be unacceptably low. Therefore the question that must be asked is, was there a purchase 'for money or money's worth', as required by the Land Charges Acts? We know that at the time of the conveyance to the mother for £500 the farm was actually worth £60,000 and is now worth £100,000. If there was no such purchase then Mrs Spearman cannot take the farm free of the option. It is therefore interesting to note that in the *Midland* case, Lord Denning MR, in the Court of Appeal, found for the son because his view was that there was no purchase for money or money's worth as required by statute. It was his view that the statute required 'a fair and reasonable value in money or money's worth: not an undervalue'. He and the Court of Appeal were plainly of the view that the payment of just £500 was so small as to amount to an undervalue. There was therefore a subsequent appeal to the House of Lords. There the concept of a 'fair and reasonable' payment was rejected with a reversal and a finding in favour of the mother and father. Lord Wilberforce stated that all a purchaser need do was to pay 'valuable consideration' and that this included a nominal consideration. This being the case the payment of £500 was clearly valuable consideration and was thus sufficient for the land charges statutes, even though it was nominal in size. Accordingly, in view of the decision in the House of Lords on very similar facts, it is clear that Jeffrey Spearman can do nothing about the nominal consideration.

The son also expressed concern about the manner in which his parents had behaved towards him and felt that they had not acted in good faith. He is suggesting that a purchaser, to claim the benefit of the statutory protection, must act in good faith and that his mother had not acted in good faith as the conveyance to her was a deliberate attempt to defeat the son's option. Accordingly, can the equitable requirement be applied to the land charges legislation? Again in the *Midland* case, in the Court of Appeal, Lord Denning MR found for the son. He and the Court held the view that the mother had not purchased in good faith. He put forward the assertion that 'fraud unravels everything'. In effect he was saying that the conveyance was nothing more than a fraud on the son, and that as a consequence equity must step in to protect the son. Unfortunately this view was not replicated in the House of Lords. On appeal the House of Lords again reversed the lower court's decision by finding for the mother and father. Lord Wilberforce took the view that there was no requirement of good faith in what is now s. 4(6) of the Land Charges Act 1972. It was his opinion that 'it is not fraud to take advantage of legal rights the existence of which may be taken to be known to both parties'. (*Re Monolithic Building Co.* [1915] 1 Ch 643.) In his judgment he said that the mother 'would merely be taking advantage of a situation which the law has provided and the addition of a profit motive could not create an absence of good faith'. Accordingly, in the light of the decision in the House of Lords on very similar facts, it is plain that the son Jeffrey can do nothing about the apparent lack of good faith on the part of both of his parents.

Is there any other avenue of redress open to Jeffrey Spearman? In fact there is one obvious line to adopt, and that is for him to sue his solicitors for negligence. On the assumption he used solicitors in connection with the option then they were clearly negligent in failing to register the option and he should succeed in an action against them. (Indeed, in the case of *Midland Bank Trust Co. Ltd* v *Hett Stubbs and Kemp (a firm)* [1979] Ch 384, the solicitors were held to be liable in negligence.) This could go some way to compensate the son for his loss elsewhere.

9 Post-completion Procedures: Delays and Remedies

INTRODUCTION

Just when the practitioner thinks a sigh of relief is in order now that completion has taken place, it is suddenly realised that there is still more to do! Just because completion has successfully passed by does not mean that you can down tools and turn to something else. Stamping, registration and allied topics beckon.

This chapter deals with two areas that provide some of the more direct forms of question that you might encounter in a conveyancing examination. You will be concerned with time limits, with 'what if' scenarios, and with the mechanics of stamping and registration. In particular, delays and remedies are a fertile source for questions.

Apart from a knowledge of the work that is directly within the conveyancing process and which deals with the closing steps, you will also need a basic knowledge of the law of damages. You will need this in relation to breaches of the terms of conveyancing contracts. There will inevitably be questions centred around a 'what if' scenario arising from one party to the agreement failing to honour its contractual obligations. In these circumstances you will need to show your knowledge and understanding of what claims can arise, and what damages and other remedies can be attainable.

This is an area where lists come into play, for example lists of actions to be taken, documents to be supplied and payments to be made. As a result, do not be surprised if your answer must be written as a list. Indeed, for many practitioners lists are the way they make sure that they have done all that they need to do on any particular file. Checklists can assist even the most assiduous of conveyancers and should not be looked down upon. If a checklist saves you from acting negligently then it will have done its job – and probably saved yours.

In practice it is usually the buyer who fails to complete. In any event, if the completion date has passed by and a party to the contract (incorporating the Standard Conditions) has failed to complete, Standard Condition 6.8 will come into consideration. So far as completion is concerned, you are well advised to be fully aware of the terms of Standard Condition 6. You should be able to commit to memory the basic terms required in a notice to complete, and you should be able to confirm when it can be served and how long the period of notice will run and from when the period is to start. As to compensation, Standard Condition 7.3 is also of consequence.

As to case law, this is one particular area in the conveyancing process where you may be required to demonstrate a knowledge of various recent decisions. However, statute remains pre-eminent throughout, as is really the position for conveyancing generally. In the final analysis you will score high marks if you can show a strong grip of the practical procedures involved in this end of the conveyancing process.

QUESTION 1

RICHARDS ABBEY AND PARTNERS, SOLICITORS

INTERNAL MEMORANDUM

To   The Trainee Solicitor

From   The Training Partner

URGENT
Re our client Stewart Cunningham; sale of 6 Devon Rise, Newport and purchase of 10 Royce Avenue, Newport
We have a problem here which I would like you to look at urgently. Stewart Cunningham has exchanged contracts for the sale and purchase of the above properties and completion on both is set for next Friday. The contracts include the Standard Conditions of Sale (second edition). The client rang me this morning in a bit of a state to say that Mr Jenkins of 10 Royce Avenue was tragically killed last night in a terrible boating accident on Lake Windermere. The client went on to say that the deceased's wife understandably wants to call the whole deal off. Stewart Cunningham has said he will help in any way he can, but he's obviously worried about his own position, given that his buyers are expecting to move in on Friday, and there is a long chain above them. Stewart Cunningham is coming in this afternoon. Please consider the advice we should give him and prepare for the meeting later today.

Commentary

This is the classic kind of question you should always anticipate in this area, namely what can be done if a party to the transaction drops dead before completion? In effect you have to be sure whether the benefit or burden of the contract passes to the deceased's personal representatives, or whether it dies with the deceased. The question is a favourite with examiners because it is an easy and relevant 'what if' problem that can be set in conveyancing exams.

In this question the problem has been put forward in the form of an urgent office memorandum from the Training Partner to you, the Trainee Solicitor. This being the case you should construct your reply as an urgent memorandum in reply just in case the partner wants to see your notes before the meeting with the client. Please note that, as ever, one important bit of information has been left out of the question which means that your answer must provide alternate advice.

Suggested Answer

RICHARDS ABBEY AND PARTNERS, SOLICITORS

INTERNAL MEMORANDUM

To   The Training Partner

From   The Trainee Solicitor

URGENT

Re our client Stewart Cunningham; sale of 6 Devon Rise, Newport and purchase of 10 Royce Avenue, Newport

I refer to your urgent memorandum received this morning and set out below my notes that you may find of assistance for the meeting later today with our client. The principle in all cases of this nature is that the death of a party to the contract after exchange and before completion does not invalidate the contract. The benefit or burden of that agreement passes to the deceased's personal representatives who are then bound to complete according to the terms of the contract. The position is different if the deceased was a joint owner and I refer to this in the following notes:

(a)   Is the deceased's wife a co-owner? If the answer is no (that is to say the deceased was the sole owner), then the position in law will be as follows:

(i)   The contract for the sale of 10 Royce Avenue Newport is not discharged by the death of the seller. The personal representatives of the seller are bound to complete on Friday, otherwise there will be a breach of contract. They step into the shoes of the deceased seller and must perform all the obligations of the agreement entered into by the deceased.

(ii)   In order to complete the title, the personal representatives will need to obtain a grant of representation. Although they can apply for an expedited grant it is still unlikely to be issued by Friday, the date for completion. (It should be noted that normally the Probate Registry will not issue a grant of probate within seven days of the date of death, or 14 days in the case of an administration. Exceptions can be made in emergencies with the leave of two Registrars, and it is understood that these present circumstances would normally be accepted as an emergency.) If there is a will the executor's authority arises on death as it is derived from the will. If there is no will the administrator's authority will arise only from the grant. However, in either case a buyer will still require a certified copy of the grant without which his ownership will not be registrable.

(iii)   Delay therefore seems inevitable unless all parties in the chain can agree to postpone the contractual completion date for all the transactions in the chain.

(iv)   Although the deceased's wife has asked Stewart Cunningham to call off his purchase, we cannot advise him to do so, unless he is willing and able to move into temporary accommodation. The reason for this is of course that he is bound to complete his own sale of 6 Devon Rise and give vacant possession on Friday, failing which he will be in breach of his sale contract.

(v)   Stewart Cunningham could try to contact all the sellers and buyers in the chain of transactions to see if they are willing to call off their transactions, but frankly I am of the view that this an impractical suggestion.

(vi)   The personal representatives will be advised by their own solicitors to complete as soon as possible, to try to mitigate any liability for the deceased's estate. Delay will result in a claim by Stewart Cunningham for interest under Standard Condition 7.3, or damages. His claim will include any compensation he has had to pay to his purchaser. This could be avoided by the personal representatives allowing Stewart Cunningham into possession of 10 Royce Avenue before completion of his purchase, thus enabling him to complete his sale on time. The rights of Stewart Cunningham and the personal representatives will then be governed by Standard Condition 5.2, where the buyer will occupy the property as a licensee and not a tenant. The detailed terms of the occupancy are set out in Condition 5.2.2 (a–h).

(vii)   If the widow has a related purchase due to be completed on the same day she will be in breach twice over if she fails to complete on Friday. If our client is forced to complete his sale and cannot complete on the purchase any loss he suffers can be claimed against the personal representatives, including the cost of temporary accommodation for our client.

(viii)   If necessary we should consider the possibility of applying for an order for specific performance against the personal representatives if they insist they will not complete in any event. Furthermore, it is unlikely that time was of the essence in the purchase contract but you can serve a notice to complete to make it so. Under Standard Condition 6.8 the notice will cause time to be of the essence and the notice can be served upon the personal representatives or, if none, on the Treasury Solicitor on behalf of the President of the Family Division. (Until a grant of letters of administration is issued the property vests in the President of the Family Division.) Of course this tactic is only of help if our client wishes to bring the contract to an end, because without a grant the personal representatives cannot complete. It will serve to reinforce the buyer's concern by putting further pressure, in terms of time, on the other side in the hope that this will urge them on to obtain the grant of representation and complete.

(b)   If the wife *is* a co-owner:

(i)   Is she a joint tenant or a tenant in common? If a joint tenant, she can convey as beneficial owner, acquiring her late husband's equitable interest by survivorship. To complete the title all she has to do is produce and hand over a certified copy death certificate at completion. Of course the transfer will need to be redrawn. Just to make sure that there is no question of any severance of the joint tenancy, another check of the office copies and the final Land Registry search is recommended.

(ii)   If the title is unregistered you will again need to consider whether the joint tenancy has been severed. In view of the provisions of the Law of Property (Joint Tenants) Act 1964, you can assume that there has been no severance if the widow sells as beneficial owner or the conveyance says she is solely and beneficially entitled. Further, there should of course be no memorandum of severance endorsed on the conveyance to Mr and Mrs Jenkins (see s. 1(1)(a) of the Law of Property (Joint Tenants) Act 1964).

(iii)   As a final check a land charges search should be repeated against the deceased and the wife to make sure that there are no bankruptcy matters registered, as bankruptcy will sever the joint tenancy.

(iv)   If the deceased was a tenant in common with the wife, another trustee must be appointed to enable her properly to convey the property and thereby overreach the beneficial interests under her late husband's estate. The purchase deed will have to be amended to reflect any changes, but it is to be hoped that delay in completion will be avoided.

Lastly, in view of the circumstances and the possibility of delay, you should consider registering the contract either as a C(iv) land charge if the title is unregistered, or as a caution if the title is registered.

Trainee Solicitor: time engaged 50 minutes.

QUESTION 2

RICHARDS ABBEY AND PARTNERS, SOLICITORS

INTERNAL MEMORANDUM

To   The Trainee Solicitor

From   The Training Partner

<u>Re our client the Malhamshire Building Society and their sale of 46 Long Churn
Crescent, Settle</u>
We act for the above local building society who are selling as mortgagee in
possession. Contracts were exchanged a month ago and completion was due
yesterday. As you will know, the society are important clients of ours and we
must do our utmost to protect their interests at all times. Unfortunately,
notwithstanding that the contractual date for completion was yesterday, the
buyer has failed to complete. I rang the other side's solicitors who told me they
were not in funds and were having difficulty getting instructions from their
client purchaser who seems to have suddenly become somewhat elusive. The
sale price for this freehold cottage is £57,000. We have a stakeholder deposit
of £5,500 in our client deposit account and the contract incorporates the
Standard Conditions of Sale, second edition.

Roberta Salter, the Malhamshire's local manager, has been on the telephone to
me this morning saying she has another buyer interested who can proceed to
exchange immediately, albeit at a lower price of £56,000. She believes that the
offer is genuine and that the buyer could indeed exchange very swiftly. What
are our options for advice for the clients in the light of these circumstances?
Can I please hear from you today in view of the buyer's default.

Commentary

This is another question that you could almost predict will appear in a
conveyancing examination when there is to be a question about one party to the
contract failing to complete and what the other party can do about it. Failure to
complete is a fairly common occurrence in practice, and so examiners will want
to be sure that you know how to deal with these circumstances. You will need to
know the relevant conditions in the second edition of the Standard Conditions and
you should be able to draft a simple notice to complete if that is what the question
requires. This should not present you with a difficulty as the operative words in
such a notice simply repeat the appropriate part of Standard Condition 6.8.

This is also an area where case law will come into consideration, particularly concerning the question of damages. You will need to know the basic law about the measure of damages for breach of contract so far as it relates to contracts for the sale and purchase of land. You may also need to demonstrate when and if a party to the contract is entitled to seek an order for specific performance. Lastly, you should by now appreciate that if the question is set in the form of an office memorandum your reply should be couched in the same terms.

Suggested Answer

RICHARDS ABBEY AND PARTNERS, SOLICITORS

INTERNAL MEMORANDUM

To   The Training Partner

From   The Trainee Solicitor

Re our client the Malhamshire Building Society and their sale of 46 Long Churn Crescent, Settle

I refer to your memorandum received earlier today and now write to respond as follows. However, to assist I can confirm that, should your time be limited, the essence of my advice is contained in the final point numbered 9.

1.   The purchaser is in breach of contract because he has not completed on the contractual completion date. It should be noted that late completion is a breach on the part of the defaulting party that will enable the injured party to claim damages for any loss suffered as a consequence of that delay. (See *Raineri* v *Miles; Wijeski (Third Party)* [1981] AC 1050.)

2.   However, you have not said whether or not time is of the essence of the contract, but I will assume that time is not of the essence so the client has no grounds for treating it as discharged by breach. In effect when time is not of the essence the agreement on its own does not entitle the injured party to terminate the agreement.

3.   To remedy this problem, we can make time of the essence by serving a notice to complete upon the purchaser's solicitors. (I can confirm that Standard Condition 1.3.2 states that giving a notice or delivering a document to a party's solicitor has the same effect as giving or delivering it to that party.)

4.   May I please refer you to Standard Condition 6.8. If we are 'ready able and willing to complete' we can serve notice to complete, making it a term of the contract that completion must take place within 10 working days of the giving of the notice, excluding the day of service. A party is 'ready able and willing' if that party could be but for the default of the other party (Standard Condition 6.8.2). As the amount to be paid on completion would enable the property to be transferred freed of all mortgages it is clear that the seller must be deemed to be 'ready able and willing to complete'. Standard Condition 6.8.4 (b) provides that on receipt of a notice to complete if the buyer paid a deposit of less than 10%, the buyer is forthwith to pay a further deposit equal to the balance of that 10%. I have noted from your memorandum that the buyer was £200 short of a 10% deposit, and in theory we can demand of the other side the additional deposit. Of course if they have no funds this demand may be somewhat worthless. The amount will still form part of our claim for damages.

5.   If the purchaser does not comply with the notice – that is to say by completing within the time limits prescribed by the completion notice – our clients can then treat the contract as discharged. If this happens then the building society can forfeit the buyer's deposit. Thereafter they can also seek to sell to the other interested party. Such sale must of course proceed on the basis that the price and other terms still acquit our clients of their obligations on a sale as a mortgagee. (Please see *Cuckmere Brick Co. Ltd* v *Mutual Finance Ltd* [1971] Ch 949, where it was held that a mortgagee must obtain the proper or 'market' value of the premises. However, in *Palk* v *Mortgage Services Funding plc* [1993] 2 WLR 415, CA, it was held that the mortgagee cannot delay the sale to the detriment of the mortgagor.)

6.   I have noted that the sale price in the present contract is £1,000 more than that offered by the new buyers. It may help you to know that any loss incurred on the resale can be recovered as damages under *Hadley* v *Baxendale* principles, that is to say loss arising naturally from the breach (*Hadley* v *Baxendale* (1854) 9 Exch 341). However, any claim must be reduced by the amount of the forfeited deposit. See also Standard Condition 7.5.2. Having said that, the effect of s. 49(2) of the Law of Property Act 1925 should be noted. This provision allows the court a wide discretion to order repayment of the deposit, and it will do so dependent upon various factors like the conduct of the parties, the size of the deposit or the significance of other matters in question.

7.   Actual financial loss can also be claimed provided that the loss was as a result of the breach. Under this heading our client could claim our costs incurred in the abortive transaction up to the time of sale.

8. The client also has the option of seeking a decree of specific performance from the court against the defaulting purchaser. However, this is an equitable remedy that will come into play only if damages prove to be insufficient compensation for the breach. Accordingly this remedy would normally be used only as a last resort, say, where the seller has no reasonable prospect of selling the property in the foreseeable future. It should be noted that as this is an equitable remedy the other maxims apply. This being so, a decision to go for specific performance should be made reasonably promptly otherwise 'delay will defeat equity'. Bearing in mind that there is already another interested party, the option of specific performance would not seem appropriate. Indeed, it is the clients' duty to mitigate their loss by trying to re-sell without any delay. This being the case the Society are probably under an obligation to accept such an offer, bearing in mind it is very close to the original sale price. (You should bear in mind that if the client is not seen to be attempting to mitigate the loss the award for damages could be reduced for failure to mitigate.)

9. In conclusion, my recommendation is for the immediate service of a notice to complete upon the buyer's solicitors pursuant to Standard Condition 6.8, bearing in mind the buyer has become somewhat elusive. If the purchaser still fails to complete, we should rescind the contract, forfeit the deposit, proceed with the sale to the other purchaser and seek additional compensation, if appropriate. If I can assist you further please let me know.

Trainee Solicitor: time engaged 45 minutes.

QUESTION 3

(a) The sale of the freehold at 'Deepdale', 27 Langcliffe Drive, Skipton for £55,000 has today been completed by a transfer. The purchaser has simultaneously mortgaged the property to secure a loan of £35,000. How will the deed of transfer and mortgage be stamped? How will you deal with the PD form?

(5 Marks)

(b) Your client, Fred Davis, has today completed his purchase of two adjoining sites from the same seller, James Brown. There is one sale contract describing the two pieces of land together and providing for a sale price of £80,000. Fred intends to develop both sites immediately. Two transfers were prepared so as to show one at £50,000 and the other at £30,000. What is the stamp duty liability, if any, for your client bearing in mind the figure of £60,000 in the usual certificate of value?

(5 Marks)

(c)   You have just been instructed by Margaret Smith, who has passed you the deeds of her home at 69 Widecombe Way, Hove. When she bought, she did her own conveyancing and paid £70,000. She has given you all the deeds, saying it was an unregistered title but there should be no problem because she only completed the purchase this year; in fact four months ago. You have checked and the title is in order up to the conveyance to the client which has not been stamped. She now wants to sell quickly as she has a very keen buyer at £80,000. She wants to move abroad with all expedition, and this is the reason for the proposed quick sale. Please advise her.   (10 Marks)

Commentary

Practitioners, as well as being lawyers, must also be unpaid tax collectors! In fact the involvement of stamp duty in many transactions is the reason why this kind of question may well appear. Indeed, it could be said that stamp duty occurs in all transactions, even if it is just a question of certifying that there is no stamp duty payable. The importance of this question is that if you know the area of the law concerned you can earn high marks without having to spread the knowledge in your answer too widely. In this case the number of marks, out of 20, are shown in the body of the question. Accordingly, apportion your time in the same proportions so that the section that earns the most marks enjoys the main thrust of your time and effort.

Apart from indicating in your answer the need for stamping and registration, it is important also to highlight what the position is if a client fails to stamp or register a purchase deed. You will see that this is certainly needed in (c) if high marks are to be obtained. Always consider the ramifications of oversights, as the examiner will want you to show an understanding of all facets of the scenario set out in the question.

This question also contains another example of a problem requiring you to comment on what has not been highlighted, as well as the obvious matters for you to consider in your answer. The question seems to be about stamp duty alone but there is more to the third section, as will be shown from the answer set out below. You will need to address more than just the tax angle to score well.

Lastly, this is an example of a question that can be answered in the form of an essay. Clearly, you will need to construct your answer in three parts, thereby addressing the individual units in the body of the question. You will also need to advance evidence to back up your assertions, particularly when dealing with information that has not necessarily been mentioned or referred to in the question. Please see the paragraph above!

Suggested Answer

(a) The transfer, being a transfer on sale of a fee simple, must bear the 'produced' stamp (known also as the 'particulars delivered' or 'PD' stamp) required by s. 28 of the Finance Act 1931 as amended. Generally, a transfer is subject to *ad valorem* stamp duty at the rate of £1 for every £100 of the consideration, that is to say at 1%. Where, however, the consideration is £60,000 or less and the transfer bears the appropriate certificate of value, no duty is payable. It should also be noted that conveyances or transfers for sums exceeding £60,000 bear stamp duty upon the whole consideration, not just upon the excess above £60,000. Stamp duty on mortgages was abolished by s. 64 of the Finance Act 1971, so mortgages post-1971 do not need to be stamped. Accordingly, in this example there will be no stamp duty on the mortgage deed, and with a certificate of value incorporated into the transfer no stamp duty on the transfer. Because there is no stamp duty, the PD form can be sent with the Land Registry application for the registration of the transfer of the property. In cases of this nature the Land Registry will deal with the particulars delivered form and PD stamp along with the registration itself.

(b) It is true to say that the figure in the stamp duty certificate is at present £60,000. However, that does not mean that if you apportion a purchase price between properties, so as to allocate an amount to each property of less than £60,000 that there will not be stamp duty payable. If you refer to the certificate of value you will see that it states: 'It is hereby certified that the transaction hereby effected <u>does not form part of a larger transaction</u> or series of transactions in respect of which the amount or value or aggregate amount or value of the consideration exceeds £60,000.' As will be seen from the underlining, the certificate refers specifically to part of a larger transaction, and as such the certificate could not be used for the transfers. Each transfer would need to be stamped at 1% of the stated consideration to be considered to be valid deeds. It would not help to make each property the subject of a separate contract between the parties as this would be considered to be a series of transactions that would again be caught by the wording in the certificate of value. Again, each transfer would need to be stamped at 1%.

(c) Margaret Smith has two major difficulties facing her that will inhibit her wish to sell the property quickly and move abroad. First, the conveyance has not been stamped and, secondly, the title has not been sent to the Land Registry for first registration. Until both the processes have been completed she will be unable to prove title, and consequently will not be able to sell.

Dealing first with the unstamped deed, Margaret completed recently at a price on the purchase of £70,000. Stamp duty should have been paid within 30 days of the date of the deed in the sum of £700. Until the duty is properly paid, s. 14(4) of the Stamp Act 1891 provides that the deed cannot be produced in court as evidence, and as a result the deed cannot be relied upon to prove title. She is plainly over the time limit for stamping purposes and, as such, until the deed is stamped the title will be unacceptable to a buyer. Late stamping is possible but the Revenue will raise a penalty fee for late payment. The Land Registry will not accept for registration an unstamped deed. She needs to submit the conveyance immediately to the Revenue with a payment of £700, and ask for an indication of the penalty fee so that it can be paid promptly. It is also assumed that the deed does not have the PD stamp on it and, as such, along with ad valorem stamping, the PD process must also be completed.

Turning now to the question of registration, the property is in Hove and is thus in an area of compulsory registration, as all of England is compulsorily registrable. We have checked the title and it is in order, and we must therefore assume that there are no other dispositions prior to the conveyance to the client that might have induced registration. This conveyance will certainly induce first registration being a transfer for value of the freehold estate. Obviously the conveyance will need to be fully stamped and the PD stamp must also be made. Thereafter the title documents will have to be sent to the Land Registry with the necessary registration fee. If an application for first registration is not made within two months of the date of the deed, in theory the buyer loses his or her right to that legal estate. However, a late application can be made, and if it is accepted by the Land Registry, as mostly they are, then the applicant will eventually receive a Land Certificate confirming her ownership of the legal estate. Again it is clear from the facts that the client is out of time for the submission of the registration application and as such has no title to sell. (Please see s. 123(1) of the Land Registration Act 1925, which makes the conveyance void in relation to the legal estate until such time as registration is made.) In this case our client wants to sell quickly and move abroad. It should therefore be noted that it is possible to ask the Land Registry to expedite the registration application. An expedition fee will be payable for this facility. Accordingly, once the conveyance has been stamped the registration application should be made, and a letter explaining the reasons for the late application should be sent with the other deeds and documents. A request for expedition should be made and the expedition fee paid. Once the application has been successfully concluded title can be proved and the sale can proceed, and the client can then move abroad.

QUESTION 4

Re sale of 4 Common Way Redditch and purchase of 8 Middle Way Redditch

Your clients are Mr Mohammed Rashid and Ms Janet West. They are selling the freehold at 4 Common Way for £65,000. It is registered under title number TL 132435. There are two mortgages on this property, the first being an endowment mortgage with the Malhamshire Building Society and the second with Branklays Bank. The redemption amounts are £30,045.60 and £16,255.98 respectively. They are contemporaneously buying the leasehold property at 8 Middle Way for £75,000 with the aid of a repayment mortgage of £50,000 from the Malhamshire. Estate agents Browning and Associates are acting on both transactions. 8 Middle Way is also registered, under title number TL 615243. Your clients are buying and selling as tenants in common. Completion has now taken place in both the sale and the purchase.

Please list the steps you will take following completion in respect of both transactions. Within what period should the registration application be made? Please draft a letter to the clients reporting completion and advising them of the steps you will be taking to finalise matters. Please also advise them as to the way they will be holding the property.

Commentary

This is a straightforward question that simply requires you to show that you know what steps are taken in both a sale and a purchase once completion has taken place. It is often mistakenly thought that once completion has been effected there is nothing more to be done. Clearly you need to show to the examiner that you appreciate that there are several critical steps to be taken to protect your clients' interests on a sale as well as a purchase. You will be aware of the more obvious and pressing needs, such as stamping and registration, but you will also need to show you are aware of other important points like re-assignment of life policies previously part of an endowment mortgage. Indeed, you will also need to show that you are aware that ultimately a practitioner is there to make money in the form of costs, and that it is after completion that these monies can be yours. It is of course a cardinal sin not to remember this element of the process!

Remember the question asks for lists, and that is exactly what the examiner will want to see as your answer. This being the case, do not write an essay but actually provide two separate lists as requested setting out all the steps concerned. The question contains no tricks, no missing elements and no ambiguities. All you need to do, therefore, is marshal your information and make sure you include all the detail required and you will score high marks. In effect the question requires you to demonstrate your ability to apply your knowledge in an orderly and efficient manner, something you will need to show just as well in practice.

Lastly, remember that there are two additional points at the end of the question that should not be overlooked. First, you need to consider what the examiner wants you to highlight about the fact that the clients are tenants in common and, secondly, you must indicate when the registration application must be made.

Suggested Answer

Re sale of 4 Common Way Redditch and purchase of 8 Middle Way Redditch

A. Specimen steps to be taken following completion

1. Telephone the clients to report the successful completion of both transactions. Advise that you will be writing to confirm.

2. 4 Common Way Redditch
   (i) Write to the first mortgagee, the Malhamshire Building Society enclosing a cheque for redemption monies, £30,045.60, Form 53 (the Land Registry discharge of mortgage form) for sealing, together with the life policy mortgage or assignment for release and re-assignment. Usually the first mortgagee will have allowed for redemption to be by cheque, but there will be exceptions where the redemption monies should then be sent by bank telegraphic transfer.
   (ii) Telegraphically transfer to Branklays Bank the redemption monies required to redeem their loan in the sum of £16,255.98.

(iii)   Write to Branklays Bank confirming the above method of payment and the sum sent, and enclose Form 53 for their second charge for execution and return. Ask for their written confirmation that your undertaking to the Bank is now fully discharged.

(iv)   Pay the estate agent's commission account if instructed to do so by client. (Browning and Associates of Redditch.)

(v)   Transfer payment of your professional costs from client to office account.

(vi)   Write to the local water authority and council tax office advising them of the sale and purchase details, stating that no apportionment of water rates and council tax was made, and requesting any refund due or apportioned demand to be sent to the clients at their new address.

(vii)   Give notice of re-assignment of the life policy to the life company at their head office. Send the original policy to the clients for safe-keeping, with all assignments and re-assignments and receipted notices concerning the same. (The life office will require all these documents should a claim arise under the terms of the policy.)

3.   8 Middle Way Redditch

(i)   Report the completion of new mortgage to the mortgagee, the Malhamshire Building Society, using their standard report form if supplied with mortgage instructions.

(ii)   Within 30 days of the day of completion arrange for the PD stamp to be made on the purchase deed and then stamp the purchase deed with £750 being 1% of the purchase price (£75,000).

(iii)   Within the priority period (30 working days) disclosed on your Land Registry search (94A), apply to the Land Registry on Form A4 for registration of the clients as proprietors of this title. If there was a mortgage on the seller's title, there is no need to wait for the discharge of the seller's mortgage (Form 53) to be received from the seller's solicitors. This can follow later if the priority period is about to expire. If completion is delayed a second search can be made to obtain a further priority period.

(iv)   If not already done, draft and obtain clients' execution of a trust deed recording their beneficial interests in the property in view of their ownership as tenants in common.

(v)   If required by the terms of the lease, give notice of assignment and charge to the Lessor's solicitors and pay any registration fee prescribed by the lease.

(vi)   Transfer your costs from client to office account.

B.   Draft letter to clients on completion

RICHARDS ABBEY AND PARTNERS, SOLICITORS

4 Red Lion Square London WC1

Partners
M. B. Richards
R. M. Abbey

Mr M. Rashid and Ms J. West
8 Middle Way
Redditch
Malhamshire

Dear Mr Rashid and Ms West,

Re your sale of 4 Common Way and purchase of 8 Middle Way Redditch

I refer to my telephone conversation with you today and I am pleased formally to confirm completion today of your sale and purchase of the above properties. I trust that the move went smoothly, but of course if there are any points outstanding that I can assist with please do not hesitate to contact me.

First, concerning your sale, I have paid off both your mortgages on completion and the amounts so paid were as previously indicated by me in correspondence. In accordance with your written instructions, I have paid the commission account of your estate agents, Browning and Associates of Redditch. I have written to the local water authority and district council advising them of the sale and purchase and requesting a refund of water rates and council tax, or apportioned demands to be sent to you at your new address. I will arrange for your life policy to be re-assigned and will give notice of re-assignment to the life company. I enclose the original policy for safe-keeping. When the completed re-assignment and receipted notice are to hand I will send these on to you. Please keep all these deeds and documents and the policy itself in a safe place as they will all be required should a claim on the policy arise.

Turning to your purchase, the transfer deed is being stamped with the requisite amount of stamp duty and thereafter the deeds will be sent to the Land Registry for the registration of your ownership along with your new mortgage. I shall attend to the registration procedure. The application for registration of title at the Land Registry should take about one or two months. When it is completed I shall send you a copy of the title showing you both as registered owners. I shall then forward the deeds to your Building Society for retention for the duration of the loan.

Lastly, I would remind you of my previous advice that you both need to consider the preparation of a formal document that will clearly record the basis of your joint ownership of the property. You will both also need to consider making wills as in your particular circumstances there is no automatic transfer of a deceased's share in the house to the survivor. This would have to be covered by mutual wills. May I suggest that you consider this and contact me to arrange an appointment to discuss the documents further?

I should like once again to take this opportunity of thanking you for your instructions and to wish you all the very best in your new home.

Yours sincerely,

Trainee Solicitor.

10 Leaseholds

INTRODUCTION

Leases are a popular area for questions in conveyancing examination papers, if only because they are in themselves complex and difficult documents. Indeed, the law relating to leaseholds is fraught with difficulties and there are always potential, substantial pitfalls for conveyancing practitioners. In fact the subject itself is so large that it could, and does, command a book on its own. It is this aspect that gives you your first problem – just what is likely to appear?

The first question below demonstrates that, like many subjects in conveyancing, you cannot expect this topic to be neatly compartmentalised. Each area touches and concerns another, and you should expect questions to cross over various areas. However, Question 2 demonstrates that you will come up against some questions concerning leases that are particular and will require specialist knowledge, such as the likely contents of a residential lease. It also shows that a question can contain several aspects and that you will be required to demonstrate a good working knowledge in each disparate area.

The third question highlights the need for you to be thoroughly familiar with the likely provisions in a residential lease, by actually asking you to list the major provisions expected in such a deed. This is the type of question that could almost be predicted as being attractive to examiners because it will test your knowledge of the core areas, relating to residential leases. The final question shows that you cannot always expect general questions on leases, as this particular one pinpoints two discrete areas of leasehold conveyancing. What it also does is to show that when you are asked to give advice you must do so and actually come out with a positive recommendation, particularly when this is in your client's best interests. The answer also demonstrates a continuing theme in conveyancing, i.e. the considerable importance and effect of statute.

It will soon become clear to you that to achieve high marks in this area you will need to be thoroughly conversant with the contents of residential leases, both for a house and for a flat in a block. You will also need to be aware of how statutes affect leasehold conveyancing, and in particular you should review the effects of the Leasehold Reform Act 1967, Part I of the Landlord and Tenant Act 1987 and the Leasehold Reform, Housing and Urban Development Act 1993. An understanding of the Landlord and Tenant Act 1985 is also recommended.

Lastly, while you should be familiar with the major contents of a lease you will need particular knowledge of a few tenants' covenants. These will include repairing covenants, covenants concerning alienation, user and alterations and additions. You will benefit from acquiring this detailed knowledge because it repeatedly forms the basis for many of the questions encountered in this area.

One final word of warning. Because the area is so detailed you will again need to exercise some discipline when answering broad-based questions. You will be tempted to throw as much information as you can remember at the examiner. However, this can be counter-productive as it will lead to an unstructured, waffling answer. Instead you should adopt a plan for your answer to the question and stick to that plan when writing.

QUESTION 1

RICHARDS ABBEY AND PARTNERS, SOLICITORS

INTERNAL MEMORANDUM

To   The Trainee Solicitor

From   The Senior Partner

Re our client The Megalopolis Bank Plc

The Bank have offered financial assistance in the form of a proposed advance by way of a first mortgage of £75,000 to Mr and Mrs Chatterway in their proposed purchase of the leasehold dwellinghouse, number 102 Seaview Road, Whitegates, for the residue of a term of 99 years from 1 January 1944 at a yearly rent of £25. The purchase price is £100,000 for this four-bedroomed house in one of the more select areas of Whitegates.

The Bank have instructed us to look after their interests in taking a first charge over the property. Mr and Mrs Chatterway are separately represented by Over Eager AND Co. You will be aware that the Bank will require a report on title with particular reference to the lease. The bank manager has seen a copy of the purchase contract and is a little worried because it refers to the lease being registered with good leasehold title. He thinks that there might be a problem because the Chatterways came to the Bank for the loan after exchange of contracts and it could be that they have had problems raising a loan. We therefore need to exercise some discretion in this case. However, completion is next week, so we shall need to work quickly on the preparation and submission of the report on title.

Please list and explain the documents we shall need to inspect before we are able to give a satisfactory report on title to the Bank. In particular, please let me have your thoughts about the nature of a good leasehold title and the term of the lease.

Commentary

This is an interesting question in that while it is about a lease, it is from the perspective of a lender proposing to make a loan secured on the leasehold title. You will need to consider what constitutes an acceptable title for a mortgagee and what does not. In these circumstances, where a lease is involved, you will need to show why a particular leasehold may not be acceptable. Accordingly, there are two elements to this question: first, whether or not the title offered as a security is acceptable and, secondly, what you as a solicitor for the lender will need to see to enable you to check and report on the title for the bank. The particular point that will need detailed consideration is of course the question of a good leasehold title. You will only be able to score high marks if you can demonstrate a clear appreciation of the nature of such a title and its limitations. Now that all of England and Wales is subject to compulsory first registration this kind of question is going to be more popular with examiners particularly as the question of good leasehold titles remains an area of current concern.

Please note that the question asks you to list the documents required. Accordingly, you should make sure that in your answer you do exactly that – list the documents. Of course each part of the list will include your reasons for the inclusion of that particular document.

Suggested Answer

RICHARDS ABBEY AND PARTNERS, SOLICITORS

INTERNAL MEMORANDUM

To   The Senior Partner

From   The Trainee Solicitor

Re our client Megalopolis Bank Plc: 102 Seaview Road, Whitegates
With reference to your recent memo concerning the above property, I set out below a list of the documents we will require together with my comments on the good leasehold title and other pertinent factors that will be of concern to the client.

Dealing first with the good leasehold title, as you will know this title is issued by the Land Registry when the superior or freehold title has not been deduced. Because the freehold has not been deduced it cannot be produced to the Registry, who therefore issue a good leasehold title instead of an absolute title. In these circumstances we shall need to inspect office copies of the leasehold title to confirm that the title is in fact only good leasehold. Assuming this to be the case, then there is no guarantee that the lease has been validly granted; and also, if the freehold title contains a defect, the fact that the lease has been registered with a good leasehold title does not release the leasehold from any knock-on effect of the freehold title defect. (See s. 10 of the Land Registration Act 1925.) This could mean that the landlord might not have the right to grant the lease in the first place; but as the title was not deduced no one has checked on this threatening possibility. It is therefore clear that we cannot report to the clients that the leasehold title is good and marketable without also having investigated the freehold title.

Accordingly, we shall need to inspect the following documents:

(a) Office copies of leasehold title including filed plan. This of course constitutes the registered element of the title to the lease.

(b) On the assumption that the freehold title is unregistered, evidence of such freehold title from a point at least 15 years ago and down to the date the lease was granted will be required. This is necessary to get around the problems with the good leasehold title.

(c) Land charges search or Land Registry search in respect of the freehold title, depending on whether the freehold is unregistered or registered. We will need to check whether any adverse entries existed at the time of the grant of the lease.

(d) Contract. This is required to confirm the terms of the transaction and also to see if the contract allows the buyer to investigate the superior title. It probably does not, whereupon the buyer is likely to be in difficulties in satisfying our requirement on behalf of the Bank.

(e) Copy of lease. This will need to be seen to make sure that none of the tenant's covenants is particularly onerous or unusual, and in particular that there is not a prohibition in the lease against creating mortgages or assigning the lease. It would also be prudent to check on whether the lease requires the lessor's consent to the creation of a legal charge over the leasehold title.

(f) Replies to requisitions on title. These should be seen to check on the questions raised by the buyer to avoid duplication by us in our own requisitions of the buyer's solicitors. It is also appropriate to check that the necessary arrangements have been proposed for the redemption of all existing mortgages to ensure that there will be no obstacles to our client Bank's mortgage being a first charge.

(g) Result of Land Registry search of leasehold title. To check on any adverse entries and to ensure that if there are any, they are dealt with to our entire satisfaction on or before completion.

(h) Replies to pre-contract enquiries of the seller's solicitors. To check on the answers to see if any matters have been disclosed that could be disadvantageous to our clients or their proposed mortgage.

(i) Local search. To check on any adverse entries or replies made by the local authority.

(j) Other searches. We should consider whether other searches are required, such as a coal mining or commons registration search. This will depend on the location of the property and I can give further assistance once the copy title details are to hand.

It should be mentioned that s. 77 of the Land Registration Act 1925 as amended by the Land Registration Act 1986, allows for the conversion of a good leasehold title to an absolute title if the Registrar is satisfied as to the freehold title and indeed any intermediate title. In effect this necessitates the production to the Registry of the superior title or titles and the Registry's acceptance. This will require the Registrar to be satisfied that the original lessor had the power to grant the lease in the first place and that if there any incumbrances that affect the lease they are disclosed.

One further item should be mentioned to the Bank, and that concerns the residue of the term granted by the lease. I believe we should highlight the fact that this lease was granted in 1944 and that as a consequence there are fewer than 49 years left to run. I am aware that some lenders are reluctant to lend on a lease with fewer than 50 years to go, bearing in mind that a lease is in effect a 'wasting asset' in that as each year passes the term is correspondingly shorter and of less value. However, I have also noted that the property in question is described as a leasehold dwellinghouse, and it may well be that the owner of the property could qualify as a tenant capable of enfranchising, of demanding the freehold, pursuant to the provisions of the Leasehold Reform Act 1967. If the freehold can be acquired in this manner then of course it could remove both difficulties, namely the problem with the good leasehold title and the difficulty over the residue of the term of the lease.

Trainee Solicitor: time engaged 40 minutes.

QUESTION 2

Your client, Dorothy Anderton, inherited two adjoining semi-detached homes and moved into the one on the right looking at the properties from the road.

Both are freehold. The other house was originally tenanted by an elderly single woman who has recently died, so that this property is now vacant. Dorothy has decided she wants to sell the vacant property. However, she wishes to continue to exert a measure of control over the next-door property even after it has been sold. Her motivation is to ensure that the adjacent property does not adversely affect the value of her own. In particular, she has written a letter to you asking you how this can be achieved for the following:

(a)   that the house will remain a residential property;

(b)   that it will always be well maintained;

(c)   that it will not be altered or extended without her prior approval; and

(d)   all fences between the two houses will be maintained by the next-door owner.

You consider and suggest to Ms Anderton that the best way of achieving these objectives is by a new long lease. Please list with explanations the main provisions you would incorporate in such a lease. Is there any complication that you need to refer to the client concerning your suggestion?

Commentary

If any question on leases might be predicted, this must be it. This is a decidedly broad question, but particular in its requirement for you to demonstrate a good working knowledge of what should be in a lease. However, the lease contents must be in accordance with the client's requirements. Accordingly, what is required is a list of the main provisions with a specific analysis of the four particular items set out in the body of the question. Of course the difficulty in answering a question of this nature is selecting what should go in and what you can safely leave out. Many residential leases of this kind can stretch to over 50 pages and may contain more than 60 covenants for the tenant to perform. It is therefore not difficult to see why you must discipline yourself by adhering to what are the main lease provisions, with specific reference to the four items in the question.

In the light of the demands of this type of question, you should keep a careful eye on the clock to make sure that you do not exceed the time allotted to the writing of this answer. The best way of doing this is to plan your answer carefully before starting and then make sure you stick to the plan, even if, with the pressure of time, you end up with numbered points at the conclusion of your answer rather than full paragraphs. At least this way you will be able to show to the examiner the extent of your knowledge and still be able to devote enough time to your other answers. As to format, you could answer the question by way of an essay, or you could adopt a letter form in reply to the letter mentioned as written by the client. Lastly, you must consider what the examiner might want to see in your answer as a complication, and here you will need to show an understanding of the effect of the Leasehold Reform Act 1967.

Suggested Answer

The following are the main provisions that I consider should be in the lease of Ms Anderton's adjacent property:

(a)(i)   After setting out the parties to the deed, the lease must commence with a clear and precise description of the property, together with a plan if necessary. The main reason for this is to ensure certainty as to the extent of the property comprised in the lease.

(ii)   This should be followed by a statement of the rights accruing to the property, along with the rights to which it is subject. This again is to ensure certainty, particularly as to rights of access or parking etc.

(iii)   There should be a clear statement as to the term of the lease and the annual rent to be paid, and whether or not the rent is fixed or subject to upward only increases. All leases should contain such critical components.

(iv)   After these provisions there should then be listed the tenant's covenants, including a covenant to pay the rent. One particularly important provision is a covenant restricting the tenant's use of the property. This is of special concern for Ms Anderton and can be addressed by a covenant by the tenant restricting his or her use of the property to residential use only for the occupation of the family of the tenant solely. The covenant can be absolute or qualified by reference to the lessor's consent, and if it is so qualified it is not implied that consent may not be unreasonably withheld (c.f. the position regarding a qualified prohibition against alterations; see **(c)** below). However, for the sake of certainty the advice to Ms Anderson should be to insert in the lease an absolute covenant by the tenant not to use the property other than as a private dwellinghouse for the occupation of the tenant and the tenant's family.

(**b**)(i) Ms Anderton requires the house to be well maintained, and to accomplish this she can insert in the lease a covenant on the part of the tenant to put and keep the premises in good and substantial repair and condition. This places an extremely heavy burden upon the tenant, such that the tenant will have to put the property in good repair even if it was not in such good repair at the start of the lease. The clause could be further amplified to extend the tenant's liability to replace worn and damaged parts of the property, including brick, stonework, roofing materials and ironwork.

(ii) To further ensure proper maintenance the lease should also contain two further clauses: one requiring the tenant to redecorate the interior at least every five years; and the other requiring the tenant to redecorate the exterior every three years. These clauses would operate on a rolling cyclical basis, thus ensuring continued maintenance throughout the lease term.

(**c**) Ms Anderton requires the tenant to seek her permission for any proposed alterations or additions. This can again be ensured by a tenant's covenant not to alter or add to the property without the prior written permission of the lessor. The covenant is qualified, and as such statute implies that consent cannot be unreasonably withheld in the case of improvements (s. 19(2) of the Landlord and Tenant Act 1927). It is suggested that to avoid any difficulty in this respect the covenant be made absolute. The reason for this kind of covenant is to stop unwelcome, unsightly or unbalanced alterations that could affect the lessor's next-door property.

(**d**) To ensure that the boundary fences are maintained there should be inserted in the lease a covenant on the part of the tenant not to allow the boundary fences to fall into disrepair but to maintain all of them, whichever they are, in good and weatherproof condition. This will put an obligation on the tenant to repair all the fences in accordance with the client's requirements.

The lease should also require the tenant to insure the property to the full reinstatement value and to use all insurance monies received in reinstating the property. This is to ensure that the property is repaired after being damaged by any insurable risk.

The lease should also contain a forfeiture clause, to the intent that should the tenant be in breach of any covenant the lessor can forfeit the lease. This is of course the reason for making all the restrictive covenants, in that the forfeiture clause enables the lessor to exert a sanction against the tenant of the ultimate loss of the residue of the lease term.

So far as any covenants by the lessor are concerned, there need only be one, being the covenant by the lessor allowing the tenant quiet enjoyment of the premises. This is best made an express covenant as the lessor may want to limit the possible effects of an implied covenant at common law.

Lastly, there should be a covenant by the tenant to repair as a party structure equally with the adjoining owner (i.e., our client) any walls, foundations, roofs or roof timbers used in common with that adjoining owner. This must be included as the properties are semi-detached.

Furthermore, if the premium for the lease is less than £60,000 there should be an Inland Revenue stamp duty certificate of value, without which the tenant would be obliged to pay stamp duty at 1%.

There is one complication that should be mentioned to the client, and that is the effect of the Leasehold Reform Act 1967. This statute applies to long leases such as this (s. 3 of the Leasehold Reform Act 1967 as amended) and where there is a low rent as there will be for this lease (s. 4). If the tenant occupies the property for at least three years then the tenant will be allowed to demand the freehold from Ms Anderton. On paying the open market value the tenant may enfranchise. If the lease is in its early stages the value will be low, and on acquisition the lessee can merge the lease into the freehold. The Act does set out what terms are to be in the freehold transfer. The statute contemplates the inclusion of such terms as are required to put the parties in the same position as they were under the lease.

QUESTION 3

You have been consulted by Standard Grand Estates Plc about their intended development in Brixton. They have purchased a mansion block of flats and intend to sell all 80 flats once they have been fully refurbished. They want to know from you how to deal with the question of subsequent repairs or redecoration required to the block. They wish to know this in the light of their clear requirement to be released completely from any such involvement. Their instructions are that once the leases have been granted, they simply want to collect the rents and do nothing else. They have asked you how this might be accomplished. In your advice please indicate the appropriate method of complying with their instructions and how it might work in practice.

The company have also indicated that once all the flats have been sold they may well want to sell their freehold reversion by auction. However, they believe there maybe a problem about this and have asked you for your advice. Please indicate what this problem might be and how it could affect your client.

Commentary

This is a two-part question that covers, first, how to deal with repairing obligations that avoid any liability on the lessor's part and, secondly, the effect of Part I of the Landlord and Tenant Act 1987. The answer required is in the form of an essay, but you are being asked for your advice. In these circumstances the structure of the essay must be clear and direct and must provide the advice required by your clients. This can be in an essay or in a letter of advice, but either way the advice must be directed to the particular areas concerned. If you know the law the second part of the question is simple – all you need to do to obtain high marks is to show how the statute will affect the proposed sale. The first part of the question is more demanding. You will need to be aware of at least two distinct ways in which the requirements of the client can be accommodated, and then you will need to recommend one against the other. Good advice examines the possibilities available to the client and then puts forward a choice for the client to consider. Because, in the main, law is a set of boundaries showing what people cannot do rather than what they can, lawyers can easily fall into the trap of simply being negative in their advice. A good lawyer will help the client by showing what the client can do as well as what the client cannot do.

Suggested Answer

The advice required by Standard Grand Estates Plc ('the company') is in two parts, the first concerning future maintenance of the block and the second relating to a statutory provision that could upset their auction plans, namely Part I of the Landlord and Tenant Act 1987.

Future maintenance arrangements

The company wish to grant 80 leases on the basis that they are not involved in the subsequent upkeep of the block. This is an area of real concern for the client because potential mortgagees will lend on the security of the leases only if they are satisfied with the repairing arrangements for all the block. They will take the view that the leases must contain terms that ensure that the block is well maintained so that the value of their security is upheld. The company have a choice – they can either go for the simple option and impose on all their lessees repairing covenants, or they can create the more complicated situation of a third party to all the leases, namely a management company assigned the responsibility of the repair and upkeep of the block. There is the alternative of the lessor providing these services, but this is of course exactly what the company wish to avoid. Each option will be considered in turn, with a recommendation for the company after that.

The simple option of the imposition of repairing covenants is the easiest to arrange but does have considerable practical disadvantages that may outweigh the attraction of simplicity. It is true to say that in a long lease the tenant is normally expected to be responsible under the lease covenants for the maintenance and upkeep of the demised premises. However, there are inherent problems with this arrangement in the case of flat leases in a block where there are many flats, such as in this mansion block in Brixton. It is not difficult to imagine the piecemeal or patchwork effect that might arise if the tenants were each individually responsible for repairs. Some leaseholders may well be diligent and comply in full with their obligations. However, undoubtedly there will be others who will not, and consequently the block will suffer from uneven care and attention. Indeed, when considering the main structure, unless there are very detailed and lengthy definitions within the leases it may not be clear just who will be expected to repair what. For example, should those flat owners on the top floor be the only ones responsible for repairing the roof? If so they are unlikely to sell, as of course most buyers would be very reluctant to proceed with a purchase that could involve such an onerous obligation. As can be seen, this patchwork approach is fraught with difficulty and has the major disadvantage for the client of making the flats harder to sell. This alone may be enough to persuade them to consider the other option, that of the management company.

The leases could be drafted so that there are three parties to the lease, being the lessor, the lessee, and a management company. The lessor would grant the leases to the lessees on the basis that in future the lessor simply collects the ground rent, while the management company is charged with the responsibility of the future repairs to the block. All tenants will be under an obligation to pay service charges either in advance or on demand. The best element is, however, that each individual lessee will have a say in how the maintenance company acts. This is because the leases will provide for each of them to be a member of the management company. This can be by individual shares, or by being simple members if the company is one limited by guarantee. (The latter is suggested as it does away with the necessity of share certificates, etc.) The lease will further say that no lease transfer registration can take place without there being a prior transfer of membership, such as a transfer of the management company share from the seller to the buyer. The attraction to the company of this arrangement is that it is preferred by mortgagees, and this will in turn lead to the flats being more readily saleable. Further, there will be an element of democratic control available to all tenants as far as repairs are concerned, and this in itself could be a strong selling point. Accordingly the best advice for the company must be for them to set up a management company to look after future repairs.

Auction plans and Part I of the Landlord and Tenant Act 1987

The company may wish to sell their freehold reversion at auction once all the leases are sold, and have enquired about whether this could be a problem. Unfortunately there could be a difficulty caused by the effects of the statute mentioned above ('the Act'). The Act gives tenants in a block such as this a right of pre-emption where the lessor intends to dispose of the freehold. The lessor must give notice of the proposed disposal to the tenants (s. 5 of the Act) and the notice will give them the right to buy the lessor's interest. At least 50% of the flats must be held by qualifying tenants (in effect long leaseholders) and the block must contain two or more flats. It is clear that both these pre-conditions apply in this case and the Act will therefore apply to any such sale by the company. An auction is clearly a disposal contemplated by the Act (see s. 4 of the Act) and the company will be obliged to offer the reversion to the tenants before the auction. If at least half of the qualifying tenants take up the offer the lessor will be obliged to sell on the same terms as those that gave rise to the notice. It is presumed that the price will therefore be not less than the auction reserve price.

The Act contains clear provisions should the lessor sell without serving the necessary notices. Section 11 provides for a notice to be served by the tenants on the buyer requiring information about the sale, and s. 12 then contains a provision to force the buyer to transfer the freehold to the tenants on the same terms as were made for the disposal to that buyer. However, any dispute about the terms, including the price, can be referred to and decided by a Tribunal. A further practical problem is that the time constraints contemplated by the Act are lengthy. For example, the period during which the tenants must respond to the notice is in effect two months with further time delays possible. Accordingly, the timing of the disposal may be greatly delayed by the effect of the Act.

Lastly, it should be noted that the Leasehold Reform Housing and Urban Development Act 1993 ('the LRHUDA') confers a right of collective enfranchisement upon certain tenants holding long leases in blocks of flats. Accordingly there is also the possibility that in time the LRHUDA could further complicate matters for Standard Grand Estates Plc.

QUESTION 4

Bianca Constantinou is the sole owner of a residential leasehold flat in a block of flats in Bradford. The lease is for 99 years from 25 December 1991 at an annual rent of £100. She works as a journalist and is away from home quite a bit working on assignments for her newspaper. She arrived back home yesterday to find to her astonishment that the landlord had entered her flat, changed the locks and stuck up a notice on the front door. This said that the lessor company had taken peaceable repossession of the flat as a consequence of a breach of a covenant in the lease by Ms Constantinou. It went on to say that consequently she no longer had a lease. She now wants to know what her position is as she has nowhere to live.

Commentary

This is a question that requires, in a good answer, precise knowledge of the law relating to the determination of a tenancy, and in particular the common forfeiture provisions in a lease. It is particularly interesting to note that the question is silent as to the actual nature of the alleged breach. This should immediately make you realise that there could be alternative answers required, and indeed this is the case. You will need to show that you understand the difference between breaches of covenants that relate to the non-payment of rent and those relating to other covenants not concerned with rental payments. You will also need to demonstrate in your answer that your information is up-to-date. The law has been substantially affected by several recent cases about just this kind of difficulty, and you will therefore need to refer to these in your answer. In particular you will need to know the facts of and decision in the House of Lords case of *Billson* v *Residential Apartments Ltd* [1992] 1 AC 494. This was a difficult case that caused considerable alarm in the profession until the decision in the House of Lords. It is therefore no surprise to see it appear as the source of an examination question. It is an important case concerning leases, and you should acquaint yourself with it as it will be a fertile area for future examination questions.

The question is short, and as such it is clear that you are expected to fill in the gaps in your essay-style answer. It is in effect almost an 'academic' style examination problem, but of course the decision does have profound consequences for all practitioners.

Suggested Answer

Ms Constantinou is the owner of a long leasehold estate of a residential flat where the lessor company has purported to take possession and has forfeited her lease as a result of an alleged breach of covenant. This situation raises several queries that will need to be considered in turn, to enable her position to be explained:

(a)   Does her lease contain a forfeiture clause?

(b)   Is there a breach of covenant?

(c)   If there is a breach, is it for non-payment of rent or for breach of some other covenant?

(d)   In both cases, can the lessor simply effect re-entry and take possession so as to forfeit the lease?

Each point will be discussed below. It should nevertheless be remembered that there is a discretion for the court to grant equitable relief against forfeiture. (See *Shiloh Spinners Ltd* v *Harding* [1973] AC 691.)

(a)   The lessor is seeking to forfeit the lease. However, it should be noted that the lessor's right to forfeit the lease must be expressly stated in the deed as it will not be implied by operation of law. In these circumstances if there is no forfeiture clause in the lease the lessor is not entitled to forfeiture and his actions will therefore be unlawful. If it is assumed that there is such a clause, we must go on to answer the subsequent queries set out above concerning the circumstances of this matter.

(b)   The facts as stated do not actually indicate the exact nature of the alleged breach. Ms Constantinou's solicitor must be satisfied as to the actual existence of a genuine breach of covenant. Action could be taken over a trivial breach but the courts do not look kindly upon landlords starting proceedings in these circumstances (see *Re Vanek and Bomza* (1977) 74 DLR 175). The practitioner must look at the lease covenants, ascertain the facts relied upon by the lessor that purport to be the alleged breach, and then judge whether there might indeed be such conduct on the part of the lessee so as to add up to a breach of covenant.

(c)   On the assumption that there is a breach, further enquiries need to be made to ascertain whether the breach results from non-payment of rent or is a breach of some other covenant in the lease. In either case, the lessor, in the light of a known breach, must either waive it or enforce the forfeiture by re-entering the demised premises. This enforcement is a legal interest (see s. 1(2)(e) of the Law of Property Act 1925). However, in this case it should be noted that the premises are residential, and by s. 2 of the Protection From Eviction Act 1977 it is unlawful to enforce a right of re-entry where such a lease is involved 'other than by proceedings in court'. Failure to observe this provision can incur a criminal liability under the Act. The re-entry could also be considered harassment of the tenant.

(d)   Where there is forfeiture for non-payment of rent, most modern leases by an express term preclude the necessity for any formal demand for the monies outstanding. However, the Court has for many years had the ability in equity to reinstate the lease provided the arrears and all costs are paid by the tenant. It is only in exceptional cases that the courts do not grant relief from forfeiture, provided of course the arrears and all resulting costs are paid.

Forfeiture for breach of non-rent covenants takes a different course, being governed by statute. Section 146 of the Law of Property Act 1925 requires the service of a statutory notice upon the tenant before re-entry can be enforced. Indeed, the tenant must be given time to comply with the notice, and a reasonable period can be considered to be three months; and only after that period has elapsed, if the tenant is still in breach, can the right of forfeiture be enforced. Of course the breach may not be capable of being remedied. Even then a section 146 notice must be served. Whether the breach can be remedied or not does not stop the possibility of the court granting the equitable relief against forfeiture under s. 146(2). Relief may be available by this section if the lessor is 'proceeding by action or otherwise' to enforce such a right of re-entry or forfeiture.

This area of law was considered in the House of Lords in the case of *Billson* v *Residential Apartments Ltd* [1992] 1 AC 494. In this case the question of the tenant being granted relief from forfeiture was considered when the lessor had forfeited the lease for a breach of covenant by peaceably re-entering the premises. In this case there was a forfeiture clause, there was a breach of the covenant not to make alterations without the lessor's prior consent, by the lessee of course carrying out unauthorised alterations, and there was subsequent forfeiture. The lessor did serve the required s. 146 notice, but two weeks later, with no remedial action having occurred, the lessor, at 6 a.m., peaceably re-entered the premises. Subsequently, and four hours later, persons authorised by the tenant broke back into the property to regain access for the tenant. The lessor immediately commenced proceedings claiming that the landlord was entitled to possession having taken peaceable possession and having therefore forfeited the tenant's lease. The lessor argued that because repossession had taken place, s. 146(2) could not apply and that matters were at an end. In the lower courts the decisions went against the tenant because the tenant had not applied to the court for relief prior to the lessor taking possession. The contention was that the landlord having taken possession, there was no pending action and as such s. 146(2) could not apply. In the House of Lords a contrary view was taken and expressed by Lord Templeman, who asserted that the phrase 'or otherwise' allowed the tenant to seek relief when the landlord had taken back possession. In effect the decision meant that relief would be available both in proceedings commenced by the lessor and if the lessor had taken possession, and that s. 146(2) applied to both situations.

In summary, then, relief from forfeiture will be available in all save the most exceptional circumstances. This being the case, and applying the *Billson* decision to the circumstances relating to Ms Constantinou, it would seem that there is a real possibility that the lessor has overstepped the mark but that in any event relief should be available. The nature of the breach should be ascertained, and following an inspection of the terms of the lease advice given on the forfeiture clause and the relevant covenant. Even if the breach is irremediable, relief may still be available, and certainly the court has the power to grant such relief (see *Scala House and District Property Co. Ltd v Forbes* [1974] QB 575). The tenant should commence an immediate action for relief against forfeiture along with an order allowing immediate repossession by Ms Constantinou. Ms Constantinou will also have to be aware that the court may grant relief only on condition that she pays the lessor's costs together with any compensation the court deems appropriate.

11 New Properties

INTRODUCTION

You will appreciate from your studies that the sale of a new property is a more complicated transaction than the sale of an existing one, and as a result it commends itself to the examiner! There are several reasons for the added complexity. First, a new property on an estate will comprise part of the developer's title to the whole estate, and a conveyancer must therefore have regard to 'sale of part' considerations such as the grant and reservation of new easements and the imposition of new covenants. There is a clear overlap here with the general topic of the draft contract, which we considered in Chapter 3, and Question 1 in this chapter provides a typical example of a question concerning a contract for the sale of a new property.

The National Protocol is not normally used by a developer's solicitor, but the spirit of it is usually invoked as the solicitor will invariably send out a comprehensive package of documents at the beginning of the transaction to assist the buyer's solicitor. As you will see from the suggested answer to Question 2, you will need to appreciate the items that are relevant, and why.

Where the property is in the course of construction there will also be a complication over the timing of completion, because the builder/developer will not know precisely the date when the building will be physically completed. Accordingly, the builder cannot agree a fixed completion date and this can have a knock-on effect where the buyer of the new property has a related sale. This is one of the points raised in Question 4.

There are obvious planning considerations where a property is newly constructed; and it must be remembered that as well as the dwelling itself, one must have regard to the estate roads, drains and sewers, and their future maintenance and adoption by the local authorities. In this respect, you will appreciate the overlap with the material you covered earlier in the course when you considered town and country planning, searches and enquiries. Remember that enquiries over and above the standard pre-contract enquiries will be appropriate where your client is buying a new property. This aspect is also dealt with as part of Question 4.

QUESTION 1

Explain what particular matters you would include in a contract for the sale of a residential freehold property in the course of construction on a new housing estate. You may assume that the estate is being developed by a well-known and reputable builder. You should confine your answer to matters relevant only to new properties and make reference to matters which both parties would wish to see dealt with in the contract.

Commentary

When you come across a question like this it is important not to panic and write everything you know about contracts for the sale of land. You will appreciate in reading this chapter that the question concerns new properties, but in the pressure cooker atmosphere of the exam room crucial matters can get overlooked. The question asks specifically for matters which are peculiar to the sale of a *new property in the course of construction* and you should concentrate your mind on this, not contractual matters of a more general nature. Notice also that the house has not yet been built, which is a crucial factor in the form the contract will take.

The question invites a wide discussion of the contract from both the seller's and buyer's perspective. Do not be afraid to put each side's case – you will be given credit for explaining why the seller wants something included but the buyer does not, or *vice versa*. You have not received a memorandum so your answer can be given in the form of an essay.

Suggested Answer

This transaction is a sale of part of the seller's title and so the usual sale of part considerations apply. The seller will want to negate any implied grant of easements in favour of the buyer under s. 62 of the Law of Property Act 1925 and the rule in *Wheeldon* v *Burrows* (1879) 12 Ch D 31. The contract should make appropriate provision for the grant and reservation of new easements and the imposition of new covenants. The easements will cover such matters as rights of way and the right to run services over the remainder of the estate, and the right to enter to inspect, maintain and repair accessways and services. The buyer must be satisfied that the new covenants do not unduly restrict the buyer's intended use and enjoyment of the property. Typical covenants include: restricting the use to residential only, not making any alterations without the seller's consent (the buyer should be advised to limit this in time to say, three years), and maintaining one or more fences around the plot. It should be noted that the easements and covenants will actually be created in the purchase deed, not the contract, but the contract will govern the contents of the purchase deed, so the contract will normally stipulate the exact wording of the easements and covenants.

Another important consideration on a sale of part is to ensure that the contract contains a full and accurate description of the property being sold. This should be done by reference to a scaled plan attached to the contract showing the individual plot edged red. The description will be short with the added words, 'more particularly described on the plan', thereby indicating that the plan is to prevail in the case of conflict or uncertainty (*Neilson* v *Poole* (1969) 20 P & CR 909).

The builder cannot be absolutely sure when the house will be physically completed and ready for the buyer to move in. A fixed completion date therefore cannot be agreed on exchange of contracts. The contract should provide instead for legal completion to take place within a certain period after the seller's solicitors have notified the buyer's solicitor that the property has been physically completed and is fit for occupation. The period in question must be sufficient to allow time for the buyer to carry out the pre-completion searches, to request the drawdown of any mortgage advance and for the buyer's (and probably mortgagee's) surveyor to carry out a final inspection of the property. Fourteen days should be sufficient and is normally acceptable to both builder and purchaser.

One point to note where the buyer is purchasing with the aid of a mortgage is that the mortgagee will not release the mortgage advance until the property has been completed to the satisfaction of the mortgagee's surveyor. The buyer's solicitor should therefore consider a provision in the contract whereby the buyer cannot be forced to complete until the mortgagee's surveyor is satisfied in this respect.

The buyer will also require a 'long stop date' for completion, being a date, say six or nine months hence, after which the buyer may withdraw from the contract. Without this provision, if the property was never physically completed or the seller's notice was not served, the contract would remain open indefinitely, a state of affairs which ultimately would be unsatisfactory for both parties.

The builder/seller will want to ensure that the buyer carries out the investigation of title before exchange and that no requisitions may be raised on the title after exchange. This will be covered by a Special Condition. The buyer should be happy with this provided he has enough time to carry out the title investigation.

Assuming that the property will not be finished by the time contracts are exchanged, the seller should be responsible for it between exchange and completion. However, Standard Condition 5.1 is not appropriate as the seller will not be transferring the property in the same physical state as it was at the date of the contract. This condition should therefore be excluded or amended, although the Special Condition doing so must make it clear that the risk remains with the seller until legal completion. Otherwise, the open contract position would apply and the buyer would assume the risk from exchange.

The builder is described in the question as 'well-known and reputable', so presumably the company is registered with the National House Building Council (NHBC). The new property will therefore have the benefit of the NHBC Buildmark scheme which provides a 10-year insurance for structural defects. The contract should specify that the builder will provide NHBC protection and that the NHBC documentation will be supplied to the buyer before completion.

The property is in the course of construction, and the buyer would prefer to see a contractual obligation on the builder/seller to build the property and the rest of the estate in a good and workmanlike manner in accordance with the planning permission and the agreed plans and specifications. The buyer would also want the right (together with the buyer's mortgagee) to inspect the property during its construction and again, finally, when it is finished. Associated with this will be a provision requiring the seller to rectify any minor defects (known as 'snagging items') either before legal completion, or within a specified time thereafter. A snagging list is normally prepared by the buyer's surveyor on final inspection. A prudent buyer would also insist on a clause in the contract whereby the seller agrees to remove all builder's rubbish before completion, to erect boundary fences, and to landscape the garden and adjoining areas. The builder may prefer to confirm these points in its solicitors' replies to pre-contract enquiries rather than amend its standard form of contract.

While it may be the intention of the builder to build the property in accordance with the agreed plans and specifications, the builder may wish to reserve a right to vary the method of construction or the materials used in the construction. The buyer will be reluctant to accept such a clause unless it is qualified to provide that such variation will not diminish the value of the property or the accommodation to be provided.

Like anyone in business, the builder will be keeping a watchful eye on cash-flow and will therefore normally expect to receive a full 10% deposit from the buyer on exchange of contracts. Normally, the builder will want the deposit to be held by its solicitor as agent for the seller rather than as stakeholder, so that the deposit can be released to the builder as soon as the contracts are exchanged. The seller's solicitor should therefore cover the point and amend the Standard Conditions by a Special Condition to this effect. Conversely, the buyer would prefer the deposit to be held by the seller's solicitor as stakeholder, so that it remains secure in the solicitor's client account until completion! The argument can be put forward on behalf of the buyer that it may be several months before the transaction is completed, and if the deposit is released to the seller and the seller later defaults (for example, because of insolvency), the buyer as unsecured creditor may never recover the deposit.

Lastly, if the buyer is paying an additional price for 'extras' (e.g. specially designed kitchen or bathroom fittings) then, having regard to s. 2 of the Law of Property (Miscellaneous Provisions) Act 1989, the contract should specifically deal with this by itemising the extras and clearly stating the additional sum.

QUESTION 2

RICHARDS ABBEY AND PARTNERS, SOLICITORS

INTERNAL MEMORANDUM

To   The Trainee Solicitor

From   The Conveyancing Partner

Re Newbuild Ltd

Several years ago we acted on the acquisition of a greenfield site by Newbuild Ltd, a major player in the UK building industry. The acquisition was financed by Acto Finance Ltd, who took a first fixed charge on the site together with a floating charge over the company's assets. Newbuild Ltd has recently begun developing the site and is in the course of constructing 30 freehold detached houses. It has instructed us to act on the sale of the individual plots.

Please prepare a memo listing and explaining the items we should send to each buyer's solicitors.

Commentary

This question is in the form of a memo and asks for a memo in reply, so do not write an essay on the subject! As you have to list *and explain* the items, it may be worth spending a few minutes first, jotting down on a piece of rough paper the items that you feel are relevant. That way you can calculate how long you will spend on each explanation. It would be frustrating to find near the end of the allotted time for this question that you have spent practically the whole time discussing at some length the contract and purchase deed, but left yourself no time to explain the other items. You may appreciate their significance, but unless you can actually put it down on paper, sadly you will fail the question, and this is something that regrettably happens all too often.

With the reference to fixed and floating charges, you may think that a comprehensive knowledge of secured lending is required in order to achieve high marks on this question. It is not – all you need do is stick to basic conveyancing principles. Every conveyancing student, whether specialising in commercial property or not, should appreciate the requirements for the release or discharge of a mortgage on completion of a sale of land.

Once again, ensure that your answer is germane to the question. You are told that the properties are freehold so you will get no marks for discussing leasehold issues; nor will you get any credit for writing about mutual rights of support (because the properties are detached!). Note also that the builder is a 'major player in the UK building industry', a clear pointer to registration with NHBC. Do not make the mistake, though, of saying that the NHBC documents will be included in the pre-contract package – these are not released to the buyer until after exchange.

Suggested Answer

RICHARDS ABBEY AND PARTNERS, SOLICITORS

INTERNAL MEMORANDUM

To   The Conveyancing Partner

From   The Trainee Solicitor

Re Newbuild Ltd
I refer to your memo and report that in my opinion the following items should be prepared by us (or obtained) and sent to each buyer's solicitors as and when sales are agreed subject to contract:

(a)   The draft contract with a copy for the buyer's solicitor's use. On the sale of a new property the form of purchase deed is usually stipulated in the contract, and this is permitted by s. 48 of the Law of Property Act 1925. To comply with s. 2 of the Law of Property (Miscellaneous Provisions) Act 1989, the contract must incorporate all the terms agreed by the parties.

(b)   The draft purchase deed will be prepared by us at the same time as the draft contract and annexed to it. The draft contract and purchase deed together will be sent in duplicate to each buyer's solicitors. We will inform the other side that no amendments of substance to the documentation will be accepted. This is prudent policy for a seller of multiple plots on a building estate, who will prefer to have uniformity and standardisation of its legal documentation. The purchase deed will set out expressly all necessary grants and reservations of easements together with the new covenants being created.

We are not told whether the land is registered or unregistered. If the land is registered a Land Registry transfer will be the appropriate purchase deed. We can ask the Land Registry for prior approval of the form of transfer. If the land is unregistered a draft conveyance will be appropriate (or if we prefer, a transfer under Land Registry r. 72 as the plots will be compulsorily registrable).

(c)   The buyers will require evidence of our client's title to the site so that the title can be investigated in the normal way. If the land is registered we will supply office copy entries of title and filed plan. The filed plan may be too large and unwieldy, in which case it will easier for us to send the Land Registry a plan showing the layout of the estate and ask them to issue a Form 102 for each plot shown on the plan. The Form 102 will certify that the property to which it relates is within our client's title. It will also indicate those entries on the filed plan that affect the plot in question. Form 102 will help the buyer's solicitors when they do their pre-completion Land Registry search, because they can simply quote the plot number on the Form 102 when the search application is made.

If the land is unregistered we should prepare an abstract of our client's title, or alternatively an epitome of title with copy documents attached. It may be worth considering applying for voluntary first registration of our client's title as deducing title to registered land is likely to be simpler. We should especially consider voluntary registration if the unregistered title is complex.

(d)   Replies to buyer's enquiries before contract. We should prepare our own, which we can gear specifically to the purchase of a new dwelling on a housing estate. In this event we shall be diverting from the standard forms under the National Protocol and so we must advise the buyers' solicitors that the Protocol is not being used. This can be done in our initial letter (see (h) below).

(e)   Replies to standard pre-completion enquiries and requisitions on title. As our client has mortgaged the site, each prospective buyer will require confirmation that on completion the mortgage will be discharged by Acto Finance over that plot. Each buyer will also require a letter of non-crystallisation from Acto Finance in respect of the floating charge. Other matters that can be dealt with in these replies are the arrangements for collection of keys on completion and the furnishing of our bank details for transmission of funds by the buyers' solicitors on completion.

(f)   Copies of the planning permissions for the development and any building regulation approvals (although the latter are unlikely to be available yet). The buyers will want to be satisfied that the local planning authority has authorised the construction of the estate and that the builder has complied or will comply with all conditions of the planning permissions. We could advise the buyers' solicitors of any reserved planning matters in our initial letter (see (h) below).

(g)   Copies of agreements and supporting bonds under the Highways Act 1980, s. 38, and the Water Industry Act 1991, s. 104.

The roads and street lighting on a new estate will become adopted by the local authority (and thus maintainable at the public expense) only after the estate has been physically completed. The local authority is empowered to make up the roads and charge the house buyers for the cost of doing so. The buyers will therefore require our client builder to enter into an agreement with the local authority under s. 38 of the Highways Act 1980, in which the builder agrees to make up the roads and street lighting to an adoptable standard and the authority agrees to adopt them subsequently. The buyers will be concerned that the builder may default in making up the roads (e.g. because of liquidation) resulting in the local authority making them up and charging the cost to the buyers. To protect against this, the s. 38 agreement is supported by a bond or guarantee from the builder's bank or insurers which provides for the buyers to be indemnified for any costs paid to the local authority should the builder default.

Our client should complete a similar agreement and supporting bond in respect of the making up and adoption of the drains and sewers on the estate. This agreement is made with the local water authority under s. 104 of the Water Industry Act 1991.

(h)   A standard letter for each buyer's solicitor enclosing the package of documents. The letter can confirm that we do not intend to use the Protocol. It can also provide useful general information about the new estate, covering such matters as the anticipated dates for physical completion of the houses and details of where plans and specifications can be inspected. A general information pack could also be provided. We can make it clear at this early stage that no material amendments to the draft documentation will be accepted.

As a large reputable building company, Newbuild Ltd will of course be registered with the National House Building Council (NHBC). Accordingly, our letter will confirm that our client is so registered and that we shall forward the appropriate NHBC documentation to the buyers' solicitors following exchange of contracts.

Trainee Solicitor: time engaged 45 minutes.

QUESTION 3

RICHARDS ABBEY AND PARTNERS, SOLICITORS

INTERNAL MEMORANDUM

To   The Trainee Solicitor

From   The Conveyancing Partner

Re Mr and Mrs C. Langley buying plot 71, The Saltings, Hythe
As you know, we are acting for Mr and Mrs Langley in their purchase of the above new freehold property from Constructalotta Ltd who are registered with NHBC. Ceridig Langley has just rung to say that he does not understand the defects insurance position on the property and would like a letter from us explaining the NHBC Buildmark scheme. Please would you write to Mr Langley today at 2 Bugs Bottom Cottages, Abby Road, Blakey, explaining to him how the Buildmark scheme works.

Commentary

This is a straightforward question requiring you to explain how the NHBC defects insurance scheme operates; but it is important to appreciate that your answer will take the form of a letter of advice to your clients, not an essay. As always, keep the letter clear and to the point. Remember that you are writing to a client not a lawyer, so avoid convoluted or highly technical language.

Suggested Answer

RICHARDS ABBEY AND PARTNERS, SOLICITORS

4 Red Lion Square London WC1

Partners
M.B.Richards
R.M.Abbey

C. Langley Esq.,
2 Bugs Bottom Cottages,
Abby Road,
Blakey

Our ref: MR/TS/PP

[Date]

Dear Mr Langley

Plot 71, The Saltings, Hythe
I refer to your recent telephone conversation with our Mr Richards in which you asked for some general guidance concerning the operation of the NHBC Buildmark scheme. I am pleased to advise you as follows.

The Buildmark scheme is used where a builder registered with the National House Building Council (NHBC) sells a newly constructed house or flat which the builder has built or converted. I confirm that the builder of your house, Constructalotta Homes Ltd, is registered with the NHBC and you will therefore receive the benefit of the scheme.

In essence, the Buildmark scheme will offer you protection in the form of an insurance policy against structural defects in the property which may arise during the first 10 years. The scheme is in two parts, comprising separate agreements in the form of warranties given by the builder and the NHBC respectively. I will advise you on each part of the scheme in turn.

First, the builder agrees that the new dwelling will be constructed in a good and workmanlike manner and in line with the requirements of the NHBC. The builder also agrees to put right any defects in the property, notified to the builder in writing, which occur during the first two years (known as the initial guarantee period) and which occur as a result of the builder's failure to comply with the NHBC requirements.

Secondly, the NHBC give separate warranties which will compensate you against any loss you may suffer as a result of: (a) the builder becoming insolvent before the dwelling is finished, (b) the builder failing to fulfil its own warranty to correct defects arising in the initial guarantee period, and (c) any defects or major structural damage to the property which occur during the eight years following the initial guarantee period. This eight-year period is known as the structural guarantee period.

In the contract for the sale of the new house we will ensure that there is an obligation on the part of Constructalotta Homes Ltd to provide you with full NHBC insurance cover without any extra cost to you or Mrs Langley. The builder will also agree to supply us with all the relevant NHBC documentation before completion.

The procedure is as follows. Once contracts are exchanged (which is when the terms of the contract become binding) the builder's solicitors will send us the following papers supplied by NHBC:

1. offer of cover form (BM1);

2. acceptance form (BM2); and

3. the Buildmark booklet (BM3) which sets out the terms of the scheme.

The acceptance form is signed by you (or by us on your behalf) and returned to NHBC. As soon as the NHBC receive the signed acceptance form, the cover will begin in respect of the builder's warranties and for any loss which is caused as a result of the builder becoming insolvent.

Once the NHBC have approved the completed dwelling on its final inspection, they will issue a notice of protection of cover for the full 10-year period (BM4). This is issued in duplicate. We place one copy with the deeds of the property (which will be held by your building society), and the other is given to you together with the offer of cover form and the Buildmark booklet.

If, unfortunately, you have to make a claim under the scheme, this will be dealt with by the NHBC regional office where a Freephone service is provided. If there are defects which are the responsibility of the builder, having arisen during the initial guarantee period, the regional office will normally arrange a conciliation meeting with the builder at the property. Where a claim is made during the structural guarantee period, the regional office will carry out an inspection to confirm the validity of the claim and the work to be carried out by the NHBC.

I trust this letter has helped to clarify how the NHBC Buildmark scheme works, but if you have any queries or wish to raise any further questions, please do not hesitate to contact me.

Yours sincerely.

QUESTION 4

RICHARDS ABBEY AND PARTNERS, SOLICITORS

INTERNAL MEMORANDUM

To   The Trainee Solicitor

From   The Training Partner

Re 36 Highfields, Barton St. Mary
The firm has been instructed by Mr and Mrs Lavery to act for them in their purchase of the above freehold dwellinghouse which is in the course of construction by the seller/builder, Buildwell Ltd.

(a)   The seller's solicitors are not using the National Protocol so please consider what relevant pre-contract enquiries we should raise of Buildwell Ltd's solicitors.   (10 Marks)

(b)   Mr and Mrs Lavery have a property to sell, the net proceeds of which they are utilising to help finance the purchase of 36 Highfields. Do you foresee any problem regarding synchronisation of completion of their sale and purchase and, if so, how can this be overcome?   (8 Marks)

Commentary

In part (a), you are told that the builder's solicitors are not using the National Protocol, and this is quite normal on the sale of a property on a new estate. As mentioned earlier, the builder's solicitors will often still adopt the spirit of the Protocol by supplying a package of documents including replies to standard enquiries. However, in this question you should start from the premise that no replies to enquiries have been given at all.

You will note the word 'relevant', and it is important to confine your enquiries (especially those of a general nature) to those that are pertinent to this type of property, i.e. one that is not built yet, otherwise you will risk wasting valuable time and marks. Two examples of general enquiries to avoid would be to ask the builder what fixtures and fittings are not included in the sale, and to ask for details of who is in occupation! You will see how the suggested answer deals first with the general enquiries and then the additional ones.

Note the slightly greater marks allocation for part (a) and structure your reply memo accordingly. Part (b) concerns the perennial problem of synchronisation where the client has a related sale, and should present no problems to those of you who have revised this topic well.

Suggested Answer

RICHARDS ABBEY AND PARTNERS, SOLICITORS

INTERNAL MEMORANDUM

To   The Training Partner

From   The Trainee Solicitor

Re 36 Highfields, Barton St. Mary
In response to your memo concerning the above, I will deal with each point in turn.

(a)   We must have regard to the fact that this a new property in the course of construction. Consequently, as well as raising some general pre-contract enquiries, we must also consider some additional enquiries which will be relevant on the purchase of a new property. I have given some thought to this and set out below my explanation of some general enquiries followed by some more specialised additional enquiries.

General enquiries
1.   We should ask the seller whether it is aware of any past or current disputes regarding the land or its use and, if so, to provide details.

2.   Is the seller aware of any rights or informal arrangements affecting the property, other than those disclosed in the draft contract? If so, we would require details and copies of any supporting documents.

3.   Following on from this, if the title is registered, we would want confirmation that the seller is not aware of any overriding interests as defined by the Land Registration Act 1925, s. 70(1).

4.   We would ask the seller to confirm that all restrictions affecting the property or its use have been observed and performed, for example, restrictive covenants apparent from the title. If any person's consent or approval has in the past been required, we would want to see written evidence of that consent.

5.   The seller must supply copies of all planning consents and building regulation approvals relating to the development. Linked to this, we would seek confirmation that the builder/seller has complied with (or will prior to completion comply with) all conditions attached to the planning consents and building regulation approval, and generally all the requirements of the local planning authority.

6.   We would ask for particulars of any other notices (that is, apart from planning) relating to the property, or its use or enjoyment, of which the seller is aware.

Additional enquiries
1.   Perhaps the first additional enquiry could be a simple request for confirmation of how many houses/units will be constructed on the estate, and how many of these have been sold to date.

2.   As this is a new development, it is unlikely that our clients' house will abut a public highway, but instead it will be served by a private, unmade road leading to a public road. Accordingly, we must be satisfied that the seller has entered into an agreement with the local authority under s. 38 of the Highways Act 1980 to make up the estate roads to an adoptable standard, and that a supporting bond is in place. We would ask the seller to supply copies of these documents.

3.   While mentioning the estate roads, we might care to raise the practical question of when the seller expects to lay the final wearing surface to the roads.

4. In conjunction with additional enquiry 2 above, the position regarding the estate drains and sewers must also be investigated. The property is unlikely to be drained directly into the mains yet, and if this is the case we would require copies of the seller's agreement with the local water authority under s. 104 of the Water Industry Act 1991 to make up the drains and sewers to an adoptable standard. We would also want to see a copy of the supporting bond.

5. We would ask the seller to confirm that it will pay for all charges for construction and connection of the drainage and sewage systems, and of all other services of which the property will have the benefit, e.g. electricity, gas, telephone. The developer may also be able to supply a plan showing the proposed route of all services to and from the property, and this could be requested.

6. We would seek confirmation that the property is to have the benefit of the NHBC 'Buildmark' scheme providing insurance protection against structural defects for up to 10 years, and that the seller will supply us with all the necessary documentation.

7. The draft contract will normally provide for legal completion to take place only after the new property has been physically completed. If the seller will not agree any material amendments to the draft contract, we should ask the seller to confirm that our client buyer will not be called upon to complete until not only the property but also all services are finished and reasonable access to the property has been provided.

8. If the contract permits the seller the right to vary the construction or dimensions of the property but, as above, the seller will not agree to qualify that right in the contract, we must seek to protect our client's position by raising an enquiry along the following lines: Does the seller have any plans to vary the construction or dimensions of the property and can the seller confirm that any such variation will not diminish the accommodation to be provided or the value of the property?

9. Lastly, to end on a practical note, the plot number of the property will invariably not be the same as the postal address. We could therefore ask the seller to supply the postal address of the property.

(b) As Mr and Mrs Lavery's purchase is dependent upon completion of their sale, we must ensure that each transaction is completed on the same day. In this way, the sale proceeds will be readily available to apply towards the purchase price of the clients' new property, and Mr and Mrs Lavery will be able to move out of one property and into the other on the day of completion.

As their new property is in the course of construction, the builder/seller will be unable to agree in the contract a fixed completion date. Instead, the contract will contain a provision whereby completion will take place a given number of days after the seller's solicitors have notified us that physical completion of the new property has taken place.

The property our clients are selling is not of course a new property but an existing one, and it would be customary in a contract of this nature to agree a fixed completion date. However, if that were to occur here, Mr and Mrs Lavery would have no guarantee that the completion dates on their sale and purchase would coincide.

I would therefore recommend that we do not agree a fixed completion date on the sale, but seek to agree a condition in the sale contract regarding completion similar to that in the purchase contract. That is to say, completion shall take place a specified number of days after we, as the seller's solicitors, notify the buyer's solicitors in writing that our clients are ready to complete. We would want to serve this notice once we receive the completion notice on our clients' purchase. In order to give ourselves some leeway, the notice period in the sale contract should be say, one day less than the notice period in the purchase contract. As an example: if the purchase contract specified 14 days' notice of completion then, upon receipt of the same, we would prepare the sale contract notice and the following day serve it on the buyer's solicitors notifying them that completion will take place in 13 days time, i.e. the same completion day as the purchase.

If our clients' buyer insists on a fixed completion date (for instance because there is a chain behind), we must advise Mr and Mrs Lavery that they will be unable to synchronise the two completions. If they still wanted to proceed, I would advise them that they have two options: (i) either to seek bridging finance to complete the purchase first, or (ii) more usually, to complete the sale first and move into temporary accommodation until completion of the new property. Whatever they decide, we must still in any event make sure that the *act of exchange of contracts* is synchronised, so as to prevent Mr and Mrs Lavery ending up with two properties or none at all.

Trainee Solicitor: time engaged 1 hour.

12 Putting it all Together: the Process as a Whole

INTRODUCTION

We hope by now, at the final stage of the book, that you will immediately appreciate the significance of this section of questions. Conveyancing is not just about the transfer of title; it is of course the process as a whole that enables that transfer to take place. We have in the preceding chapters considered each part of that process. We must now put all those parts together to see the whole picture. You should therefore understand the importance of the following questions, because the examiner will want to be sure that you have fully grasped the complete process rather than merely understood parts of it in the hope that you will thereby be able to answer discrete questions. It is undoubtedly the case that in conveyancing the examiner will want to be sure that you can complete the whole jigsaw. After all, this is what a practitioner must do; and it is for this reason, if for none other, that these questions will arise in your examination. To this end the examiner may set questions that either bring together several disparate elements or stretch across the whole subject. Either way, it will be your job to exhibit an understanding of the subject that will enable you to cope with both types of questions. To help you we will consider both types in this chapter.

Dealing first with the kind of question that brings together several distinct elements, the crucial piece of advice we can give you is *read the question carefully*. The point is that the question might start out to be the kind you want, but because there are several sections, that last section might just be on a topic that you were not expecting. There is always the temptation to see a friendly topic in the first paragraph of a question and to think that this is the one for you.

There is then nothing more destabilising than to launch into the answer and find two-thirds of the way in that you cannot actually give an answer to the final part. The moral is, do not let initial relief and over-confidence inhibit the necessity for you to read the whole of the question all the way through just to make absolutely sure that it really is one for you. Examiners know that these kinds of questions can be unpopular, but then they are not there to be popular; they are there to test your knowledge and how you apply it, and these questions do just that! In these circumstances you can almost expect to find one of them in most conveyancing examination papers. If you find yourself in the unenviable position of not being able to find a last question you know you can answer, *then* think about attempting a multi-section question where you believe you can properly answer at least 75% of the sections. It is normally poor examination technique to do this, but clearly when you have no choice there is little else you can do. Simply do your best in the sections that you can answer and make at least a structured attempt for the part that troubles you even if this means you will score perhaps only style marks. A few additional marks obtained in this way are better than leaving the section unanswered.

Questions that stretch over the whole subject are perhaps just as awkward to answer for a set of different (and sometimes similar) reasons. However, you must always expect at least one question of this type in almost every conveyancing exam. Indeed, where examination papers contain one compulsory question, it is a strong probability that if there is an element of compulsion it will apply to just such a comprehensive question. The reason for this is perfectly plain – these questions inevitably test your overall knowledge of conveyancing and how you can apply it generally. For this reason it is again of real importance that you always read the whole question very carefully, including any documents annexed to it. It is good practice while you are going through the body of the question and those documents simply to note down any immediate thoughts that might occur to you. For example, you may see that there is a time limit that has been exceeded, or that there is an inconsistency in the chronology of the question. Wherever you can, always make a note of such matters so that you do not later overlook what could turn out to be of material importance. Your task will end up being very much the same as you will find in the office should you decide to become a conveyancing practitioner. You will need to understand and analyse overlapping subjects in an exam in just the same way as you will in the office. The process is the same – you will need to identify the problem areas and address them with solutions of your own. These solutions will be your advice to the client, or in an examination situation your answer to the question. In providing your answer, our advice to you must be to avoid superficiality and try to structure your answer in such a way as to be seen to be incisive when giving an in-depth reply. The risk with questions of this type is that they can entice you into thinking that you should simply write down all you know about what you think might be the subject of the question. This is a recipe for disaster. You need to show an ability to be clear yet concise, structured, thorough and focused. Do not allow yourself to go on a ramble through your knowledge of conveyancing, however extensive that may be. The examiner will want to see your direct route to the correct answer.

Lastly, these questions have answers that are longer than many of the others in this book. This is deliberate, as in many examinations longer answers will be expected as more marks covering the assorted subjects are likely to be on offer for these questions.

QUESTION 1

You are instructed on behalf of Susan Yates in relation to her proposed purchase of a bungalow at 13 Cockfosters Way, Southgate in North London, presently owned by Bazlur Ahmed. The property is leasehold under a lease for 125 years from 25 December 1959 at an annual rent of a peppercorn, if demanded. The property is registered with an absolute title under title number NGL 362638. It has the benefit of a 10-year timber treatment guarantee from A1 Timbers (Acton) Limited. Ms Yates is purchasing the property for £95,000 and will be doing so with the aid of a mortgage for £45,000 from the Greenside Building Society, who will be instructing you along with Ms Yates. The seller's solicitors have sent you photocopies of their client's Land Certificate, from which you have seen that there is a first mortgage with a building society followed by a second mortgage with a bank. There is also a notice registered on the title under the provisions of the Matrimonial Homes Act 1983, as well as a covenant in the Charges Register not to use the property as a retail shop.

(a)   Please indicate with reasons the papers you will look for when title is deduced.

(b)   What will you do about the notice and the covenant? Please show the essence of your proposed advice to the client.

(c)   Please set down all the searches you will make before completion and say for whom they are being made and for how long they will remain in force.

(d)   Please set down the documents you require on completion.

Commentary

This is a typical example of the 'sweeping up' kind of question, where from one set of facts you must answer several different sections all on different points. You must start with what is required as evidence of title. You must then deal with a restrictive covenant, as well as a Matrimonial Homes Act 1983 notice. You are then required to jump to final searches, followed by completion! As you can see, in one question you are being asked, in effect, to jump from the beginning of a transaction when you will inspect the title right down to the end and the completion process. Moreover, in the operation you are also required to consider notices and covenants along the way together with searches. You will therefore appreciate that this is a classic example of the kind of question considered in the introduction to this chapter and it will pose all the problems highlighted by us. We therefore suggest you look again at that introduction to appreciate further what can be done in the circumstances of such a broadly based examination question. In particular, this is a clear example of where you must read the question carefully and where you should carefully note down, as you are reading, all the salient facts. Then pause and think (P.A.T.), and sketch out your answers to each section so that you can feel sure that you will be able to complete all parts of the question. Only after you have gone through this important process should you actually embark upon your written answer.

On a matter of style, the answers required are as mixed as the topics in the question. The first section is in effect looking for a list with reasons. The second section should be answered on the basis of advice to the client, either as a file memorandum or as a letter. The third section requires a list with further information; while the last section is really just a list of deeds and documents. Your answer should reflect these differences and should not be in the form of a unified essay.

Suggested Answer

(a)   Please find listed below, with reasons, the deeds, documents and other papers I would require as evidence of the seller's title:

(i)   First and foremost, I will require a full set of office copy entries that have been properly issued by the Land Registry. The seller has at present submitted mere photocopies, and these are no longer acceptable. The reason for this is that the search must show a 'search from date' and that date must be a date from office copies that are less than 12 months old calculated from the date of the search request. Because section 113 of the Land Registration Act 1925 confirms that office copies are guaranteed as to their accuracy by the State, mere photocopies are not acceptable notwithstanding the provisions of s. 110 of the same statute.

(ii)   I will also require an office copy of the filed plan to ensure that the extent of the property is shown correctly and in full.

(iii)   I will also need to see and check any documents referred to on the registers of title number NGL 362638. I need to do this as these documents could contain onerous or unusual covenants, or conditions that might adversely affect this property.

(iv) I will also require any subsequent deeds that have affected the original lease such as deeds of variation or supplemental deeds that may have in any way affected or altered the original terms and covenants.

(v) I will require a full and complete copy of the lease showing all Inland Revenue stampings and the execution of it by the original lessor. I need to check all the contents of the lease, and in particular the lessee's covenants, so that I can give Ms Yates full details. It should be remembered that the lease could contain a covenant requiring the lessor's licence to assign which would have to be obtained before completion could take place.

(b) RICHARDS ABBEY AND PARTNERS, SOLICITORS

File note:

Re Ms S. Yates and her purchase of 13 Cockfosters Way, Southgate
I set out below as a file record the essence of my proposed advice for the client in connection with two matters of concern affecting her proposed purchase, being a restrictive covenant and a Matrimonial Homes Act 1983 notice.

(i) The Restrictive Covenant.
Ms Yates will need to be advised of the existence of this covenant and the fact that it will be binding on her, to the effect that she will not be able to use the property as a retail shop. If she has that intention in mind she should be advised to withdraw from the transaction and seek another property elsewhere. It may be of use to explain that to try to have the covenant removed could prove to be a costly, lengthy and ultimately fruitless task.

(ii) The Matrimonial Homes Act 1983 notice ('the notice').
It is assumed that the notice has been registered by the seller's spouse, Mrs Ahmed, under the terms of the Matrimonial Homes Act 1983 ('the MHA'), which protects the spouse's rights of occupation in the property even though she is not shown as a registered proprietor. Because the notice has been registered our client is deemed to have good notice of the spouse's rights and cannot buy free of her minor interest. However, s. 4 of the MHA implies in circumstances such as prevail in this case that the seller will before completion discharge the notice. To do this the seller must complete Form 202 and must support the application with sufficient evidence that the registration should be cancelled. Typically this will be a signed form of release by the spouse, a decree absolute or a court order for the release.

It is assumed that contracts have not yet been exchanged. In these circumstances the contract should be altered to require the seller to provide on completion:

(1)   form 202 duly completed; and

(2)   sufficient evidence for cancellation.

There should be an additional condition in the contract requiring the spouse to release her interest in the bungalow obtained as a result of the provisions of the MHA, to consent to the sale and to release any equitable interest she may have. If the spouse will not sign the contract incorporating such a release then our client must be advised not to proceed as it would be unsafe to do so.

(c)   I set out below the searches required, and for whom they are obtained and for how long they last:

(i)   Property inspection. The bungalow must be physically inspected just before completion to ensure that there are no undisclosed third party occupants. This will be for both the buyer and the mortgagee. This search is effected just before completion as of course it is not a time constrained search.

(ii)   Land Registry search. A search must be made at the Land Registry on Form 94A for both the buyer and the mortgagee. We are acting for both these parties and the search should accordingly be in the name of the mortgagee. In this way the buyer will have the protection of the search result as well, and consequently two Form 94A searches will not be necessary. The priority period for this search is 30 working days from the date of the search certificate.

(iii)   Bankruptcy search. Because we act for the mortgagee, a bankruptcy search is required for the lender against the buyer. This is made on Form K16 and the result speaks from the date of the issue of the search.

(d)   Please find set out below the documents required on completion:

(i)   The first Charge Certificate.

(ii)   Form 53 for the first mortgage or undertaking from the seller's solicitors in the Law Society form of wording.

(iii)   The second Charge Certificate.

(iv)   Form 53 for the second mortgage or undertaking from the seller's solicitors in the Law Society form of wording.

(v)   Transfer duly executed.

(vi)   Form 202 duly completed.

(vii)   Form of evidence supporting release of MHA Notice.

(viii) Original lease.

(ix)   Any other deeds and documents relating to the lease, such as licences, variations etc.

(x)   The original timber guarantee, and if possible the original report and estimate.

(xi)   Pre-registration deeds, if any.

(xii)   The keys, if available, i.e. not with the estate agents.

QUESTION 2

You have received instructions from Patricia O'Hanley in connection with her proposed purchase. She has told you that she will be buying a brand new house presently being built by Random Site Developers (Keele) Plc in Stoke on Trent. She believes that the present description is Plot 27, The Hawthorns Estate, Horwood, and that the property is freehold.

You have had a preliminary letter from the developer's solicitors confirming that they will not be using the National Protocol and telling you that the property is registered and that the documentation will follow shortly. Please list, with reasons, what documents you expect to receive from the seller's solicitors and when, throughout the whole conveyancing process.

Commentary

This is a splendid question for highlighting how an examiner can, in two short paragraphs, require you to show not only the main steps in a standard conveyance but also how the steps will vary when there is a sale by a developer of a new property. As you will see from the following answer, the suggested approach that will earn high marks is once again to set out the answer in list form with explanations contained in the list. Do not misread the question by thinking that the Protocol applies! In many cases in practice developers do not use the Protocol as this could put them to extra expense. However, it is also the case that they do supply a copious package of documents at the outset. This does not mean that you should overlook the fact that there will be other documents available throughout the course of the transaction, and also of course at completion. Remember the question does refer to 'the whole conveyancing process' and you should therefore list all the documents you think are relevant from start to finish. Because of the number of documents involved do not be overzealous in your explanations – you only have a given amount of time to answer the question.

Suggested Answer

Please find set out below, with reasons for their inclusion, the documents to be received on behalf of Ms O'Hanley and when:

(a)   At the very outset of the transaction the developer will send the following items in an opening package:

(i)   The draft contract in duplicate which is of course fundamental to the whole transaction. This will usually be in a standard form common to all the plots in the development. In view of s. 2 of the Law of Property (Miscellaneous Provisions) Act 1989, the agreement must be in writing signed by all the parties and contain all the terms agreed. This being the case, a developer will insist upon a contract so that all the terms can appear within it to ensure the complete validity of the transaction.

(ii)   Details of the developer's title. The developer's solicitors have confirmed that the title is registered, and as a consequence the evidence of the developer's title will comprise office copy entries and an office copy filed plan. It is imperative that office copies are supplied that are less than 12 months old as without them the buyers will not be able to submit a search request to the Land Registry. It is possible that if the estate is large the Land Registry will issue, and the developer will therefore supply in lieu of the filed plan, Form 102. This will be the confirmation from the Registry that the plot is within the seller's registered title and it will also say which (if any) of the entries on the title affect this particular plot.

(iii)   Copy planning consents. This being a new property, it is vital that a buyer's solicitor makes sure that the new house is being erected lawfully, that is to say with the consent of the local planning authority. Furthermore, the planning consents may include conditions affecting the property, and the buyer's solicitor will want to check these to make sure that they are being fully complied with, and to seek the seller's written confirmation that this is indeed the case.

(iv)   Copy building regulations approval. The same is true for these approvals and the situation is much the same as for (iii) above. In some cases these documents may be issued by other approved authorities rather than the local authority. An example of an alternative authority able to be involved in this way is the National House Building Council (NHBC).

(v)   Form of draft transfer of part. Because this sale is one of many on the estate the seller will want to impose upon all the buyers similar covenants and conditions, and this is a compelling reason for requiring the transfer to be in the seller's format. It will be the case that if such a transfer is required it will have to be incorporated in the contract as a document annexed thereto, in view of s. 2 of the Law of Property (Miscellaneous Provisions) Act 1989. For this reason the draft transfer will be issued at this early stage along with the draft contract.

(vi)   Replies to enquiries before contract. Most developers will, to save time, have standard answers ready to a standard set of preliminary enquiries. Indeed, once these have been issued many will try to avoid answering any specific enquiries! Many of the answers will of course be apparent from the documents supplied in this package.

(vii)   Replies to requisitions on title. If it saves time to reply to standard enquiries it must be true of replies to standard requisitions on title. As the title is registered it should be possible to issue replies at this stage that are really perfectly straightforward. The requisitions should be fairly simple bearing in mind the need to issue reasonably up-to-date office copies for the purposes of the buyer's Land Registry search.

(viii) Copy road-making agreement and bond. Where there is to be a new road on the estate the developer will enter into an agreement with the local authority whereby the developer will make up the road and the authority will adopt it thereafter as a public highway (s. 38 of the Highways Act 1980). The bond is a guarantee that there will be sufficient funds to complete the road. Without this arrangement the road will continue to be a private roadway with all the attendant problems about rights of way. There could also be a potential road-making financial liability for frontagers should the road be adopted by the authority some time in the future.

(ix)   Copy drainage agreement. Following the terms of s. 104 of the Water Industry Act 1991, the developer will have entered into an agreement with the local water authority whereby the developer will build the new drainage system and the authority will adopt that system thereafter. Again, it is important to the buyer to ensure that there will not be an extensive private drainage system serving the property that could incur large maintenance bills for the owner in the future.

(b)   On exchange of contracts the seller's solicitor will issue the seller's signed contract. This is of course the documentary evidence of the binding agreement between the parties and the terms thereof. By the same token the seller will hold the buyer's signed part of the agreement.

On exchange the seller's solicitors will also supply the NHBC documentation. Almost all builders will be in the NHBC buildmark scheme that provides insurance protection against structural defects affecting the property during the first 10 years of its life. Without this most mortgagees will not normally lend on a new property. Because this is the case, it vital for all solicitors acting for a buyer to ensure that this documentation will be forthcoming, and a condition in the contract to that effect is appropriate. The seller will provide an offer form, an acceptance form and a buildmark scheme booklet. The buyer must complete and send the acceptance form to the NHBC for the insurance cover to be ready on or after completion.

(c)   On completion the following will be required:

(i)   The transfer of part, duly sealed by the seller company. This is of course the crucial document to the whole process, without which the seller cannot be registered at the Land Registry as the registered proprietor of this particular freehold plot. The transfer will in most cases include a plan showing the extent of the property being transferred, and this should also be sealed by the seller.

(ii)   Consent of the seller's mortgagee. The office copies of the seller's title will show if there is a registered mortgage. If there is then Form 53 (the release form relevant to registered land) as to the part being sold will be required so as to release the plot from the effect of the seller's mortgage. A plan will be attached to Form 53 showing the full area of the plot to be sold. An undertaking to supply Form 53 and the plan is acceptable from a solicitor for the developer in the Law Society form of wording.

(iii) Deposit number. This being a sale of part of the seller's land, the Land or Charge Certificate must be put on deposit at the Land Registry to meet this sale of part. This will enable a new title to be issued to the buyer out of the seller's title. This may be shown on the replies to requisitions on title, but if not, it must be supplied on completion otherwise the buyer's registration application cannot proceed. An undertaking to lodge the certificate and to supply the deposit number within a specified period, say 14 days, may be acceptable.

(iv) If a precautionary company search has been made, and if it disclosed a floating charge that was not disclosed on the Land Registry search, then the seller's solicitors must hand over a certificate of non-crystallisation to confirm that the charge has not become fixed. (This search will also show if there are problems about impending insolvency, and if this is the case then the seller must resolve this difficulty before completion.)

QUESTION 3

Outline the main stages in a residential registered conveyancing transaction highlighting the differences between National Protocol and non-National Protocol cases. You may assume that the third edition of the Protocol applies and that the title to the property being transferred is freehold.

Commentary

This is probably the shortest question you have encountered in the book, but does that mean the answer will be the easiest? Well, as you will now appreciate, nothing in conveyancing should be taken just at face value! The question is short and appears simple, but it poses two major problems for you. First, you have to work out the structure of your answer and, secondly, you have to work out how you can integrate and highlight the Protocol changes. As to the structure, the real problem is deciding just what needs to be in the answer and what you can safely leave out. If you know your material well the danger is you could develop an unrestrained and unstructured answer that will not earn good marks. What you need is a well-ordered tersely written guide to this kind of conveyancing, with clearly marked references to the Protocol along the way. This is how you can address the second problem – that of integrating the Protocol into your answer. The simplest and most efficient approach is for you to answer the question by following a traditional style transaction with diversions into the Protocol when there are obvious differences between the two.

So, to earn high marks in an answer of this kind you must make sure you adopt a concise structure and that you stick to it from start to finish. However, before you write the answer you must decide what will be in your answer and what you can safely leave out. In the end it is a matter of prioritising your information as succinctly as possible given the limited amount of exam time you will have for each question.

Suggested Answer

Any conveyance can be broken down into the following main sections:

  (a)   Before contract negotiations.

  (b)   Exchange of contracts.

  (c)   Post-contract proceedings.

  (d)   Completion.

  (e)   Post completion arrangements.

These will be examined in turn for a traditional style of conveyancing transaction, but highlighting differences with the Law Society's National Conveyancing Protocol (the Protocol).

  (a)   Before contract negotiations. In this section the main stages for a seller will be:

  (i)   taking instructions;

  (ii)   obtaining the title deeds;

  (iii)   drafting the contract and sending it to the buyers with a copy for their use. In the old style of conveyancing only incumbrances on the title were disclosed at this stage, although it is now common practice to issue full title details with the draft contract as is the case with the National Protocol;

  (iv)   replying to pre-contract enquiries;

  (v)   receiving back the draft contract approved, or agreeing terms as amended by the buyer;

(vi)   engrossing the contract and having it signed by the seller;

In this section the main stages for the buyer will be:

(i)   taking instructions;

(ii)   issuing all necessary pre-contract searches;

(iii)   issuing pre-contract enquiries;

(iv)   approving replies to enquiries and approving or amending the contract and returning it to the seller's solicitors;

(v)   if the client has a mortgage, ensuring an offer of mortgage has been issued and that all conditions therein can be fulfilled;

(vi)   obtaining the deposit and signed contract from the buyer.

The main differences in this section that will arise should the Protocol be adopted do so because the scheme contemplates a package of documents and papers being issued by the seller at the earliest stage possible. It should be remembered that the Protocol was conceived to try and reduce delays in the conveyancing system. To streamline the process it requires the seller's solicitor to issue as much as possible at the earliest stage. This being the case in Protocol matters, it is possible for the seller to issue along with the draft contract full details of the title, replies to enquiries in a form called the Property Information Form, and the Fixtures, Fittings and Contents Form. In these circumstances all the buyer has to do is carry out appropriate searches, approve the contract and complete the mortgage negotiations.

(b) Exchange of contracts. Contracts will be physically exchanged to create a binding agreement. This can be done in person, by post (or document exchange) or on the telephone between solicitors provided the Law Society's Code for Exchange is adopted following agreed formulae depending on the particular circumstances. Immediately following exchange the seller will hold the buyer's contract and *vice versa* and the seller will hold or use the deposit paid by the buyer in accordance with the terms of the contract concerning the same. There are no real differences in this section between the traditional system and the Protocol, although traditionally exchange was by post rather than over the telephone.

If the contract provides for the risk in the property to pass to the buyer on exchange, then the buyer's solicitor will have to ensure that the property is insured immediately following exchange.

(c)   Post-contract proceedings. In this section the main stages for the seller will be:

(i)   issuing details of the title, if the old style traditional method has been adopted (which is very rare);

(ii)   replying to requisitions on title;

(iii) approving the draft transfer and, if unaltered, using the top copy as the engrossment;

(iv)   obtaining the seller's execution on the engrossment in readiness for completion;

(v)   if the seller has a mortgage, obtaining a redemption figure;

(vi)   preparing a completion statement and sending it to the buyers.

In this section the main stages for the buyer will be:

(i)   if not done before exchange, checking the title and raising requisitions;

(ii)   drafting the transfer and sending it to the seller's solicitors with a copy for their use;

(iii) if the transfer has been amended, approving the amendments, engrossing the transfer and sending the engrossment to the seller's solicitors;

(iv)   engrossing the mortgage, getting the buyer to execute it and sending a report on title to the lender to seek the mortgage advance;

(v)   obtaining the balance of the purchase monies from the client;

(vi)   sending out all searches and approving the results, and arranging for the property to be inspected.

If the Protocol has been adopted then there will be no necessity for the title to be checked at this stage, as of course this will have been done before exchange. Strictly speaking, requisitions are therefore not necessary, although there is a new Protocol form of requisitions that asks about completion arrangements. This form is actually called the completion information and requisitions on title form.

(d)   Completion. At the completion stage the deeds are passed over to the buyer's solicitor in exchange for the balance of the purchase price. This is usually completed by post. The buyer sends the monies by a CHAPS payment, a computerised inter-bank cash transfer, and the seller sends the deeds by mail. The main difference between a Protocol and a non-Protocol case is that in all Protocol cases the Law Society's Code for Completion will apply unless otherwise agreed between the parties. In non-Protocol cases the parties must elect to adopt the Code.

(e)   Post-completion arrangements. In this section the main stages for the seller will be:

(i)   if there is a mortgage to redeem, sending the redemption monies and form 53 for sealing to the lender;

(ii)   on receipt of the sealed Form 53, sending it out to the buyer's solicitors;

(iii)   paying any estate agents if instructed so to do by the seller;

(iv)   accounting to the client and transfering costs.

In this section the main stages for the buyer will be:

(i)   reporting completion to the client and the lender, if any, and account to the client;

(ii)   checking that the property is fully insured;

(iii)   if required, stamping the transfer ad valorem and the PD stamp;

(iv)   sending the deeds to the Land Registry within the search priority period for registration;

(v)   following registration sending the deeds to the client or, if there is a mortgage, to the lender;

(vi)   transfering costs.

At this stage there is really no difference between Protocol and non-Protocol cases. This is really to be expected, bearing in mind that the purpose of the scheme is to speed up the conveyancing process. So, once completion has taken place there is really nothing more to streamline and matters can therefore take their normal course.

QUESTION 4

You have been instructed by the High Windmill Equitable Building Society in connection with a proposed loan to Winston Asika that is to be secured on Mr Asika's proposed purchase at 32 Serial Link, Selby, Yorkshire. The property is a pretty cottage located at the edge of town. Mr Asika recently applied for a mortgage on the property, having started negotiations himself and having conducted his own conveyancing. You are not instructed by him and are simply looking after the interests of your building society client.

Completion is due in exactly one month's time. You wrote to the buyer confirming instructions with a request that he tell you if he is still doing his own conveyancing. He has now replied saying that he is, and he has sent to you the documents he believes you require. They are:

(a)   the contract showing the title is an unregistered freehold free from incumbrances;

(b)   the root of title, being a conveyance between Jane Smith (1) and Paul Jones (2) dated 5 May 16 years ago;

(c)   the only other deed in the title being a conveyance on sale dated six months ago between Paul Jones (1) and the seller (2);

(d)   A clear local authority search result disclosing nothing of an onerous or unusual nature;

(e)   standard pre-printed pre-contract enquiries with acceptable answers;

(f)   a copy of the standard requisitions on title that he has sent to the seller's solicitors, along with a form of draft conveyance that closely follows the format of the most recent deed to the seller.

Please comment on the sufficiency of the documents supplied and list with reasons any other documents you will request. Please also list the subsequent steps you will take to perfect your client's security.

Commentary

This is a complex question that covers many different aspects of conveyancing and from a different angle, namely that of a mortgagee. But do not be deceived into thinking that is all that this question is about! The facts in the question contain several hidden problems, as well as pieces of information that are there but do not need further consideration. For example, you do not need to comment further on the contents of the local search in view of the statement in the question that there are no adverse entries in it. However, how old is it? If it is more than two months old it will not be acceptable by the time completion takes place. Similarly, there are acceptable replies to standard enquiries before contract, but are there further specific enquiries that need to be asked?

Beyond these two examples there are further topics that a good answer will have to address. As you will have seen before, in more demanding questions, the crucial elements are those that are not stated in the body of the question rather than those that are. This question is certainly demanding and is no exception. Remember there are three parts to your answer: (1) your comments on the documents listed; (2) a list with reasons of any further documents required; and (3) a list of subsequent steps to be taken to perfect your client's security.

Suggested Answer

At the outset it is appropriate to say that at the moment the papers supplied are insufficient and that there are substantial problems with the paperwork and the title such that at this time a clear report to the lender would not be possible. I set out below the reasons for this detrimental overview. Accordingly, I will start with my view of the documents supplied, this will be followed by further documents required, and I will finish with a list of steps to be taken to perfect the security.

(1)   The documents supplied

Regrettably the documents supplied are not as straightforward as might have been hoped and my comments on their sufficiency are as follows:

(a)   The contract. This would seem to be acceptable except that there are severe problems with the title, and as such the contract may not be acceptable in its present form. Please see my comments further on in relation to the conveyance to the seller.

(b)   The root of title. This would seem sufficient, although it is not clear if the conveyance is for value which would be preferable to a voluntary conveyance. It is at least 15 years old and is therefore potentially a good root. (See s. 44(1) of the Law of Property Act 1925 as amended by the Law of Property Act 1969.)

(c)   The major problem with the title stems from the conveyance to the seller that was completed six months ago. The deed itself may well be properly constructed, but the problem is that it was a conveyance on sale, for valuable consideration, and as such should have induced first registration of this title. Since 1 December 1990, the whole of England and Wales is an area for compulsory first registration. (Please see the Registration of Title Order 1989, SI 1989/1347.) In these circumstances, where there is a conveyance on sale since that date, the legal estate comprised in that conveyance must be submitted to the Land Registry for first registration within two months of the date of the deed. (See s. 123 of the Land Registration Act 1925.) Section 123 goes on to say that the deed will be void as regards the conveyance of the legal estate if the two-month time limit is not adhered to. Accordingly, the seller at this time has no legal estate to sell and the buyer will have no legal estate to mortgage in favour of the Society! (See *Pinekerry* v *Needs* (1992) 64 P & CR 245.)

(d)   The contents of the local authority search result appear to be satisfactory, but how old is the search? If it is more than seven or eight weeks old it will be out of date by the time completion is due. At completion it will be about three months old and really should not be relied upon when that old.

(e)   The replies to enquiries seem acceptable, but have all necessary enquiries been made? It would seem that there are special and specific enquiries that could be made pertinent to this particular property and transaction. For example, is the seller aware of mining operations within the locality of the property?

(f) Standard requisitions are acceptable, but there must now be additional requisitions that will relate to the title and the fact that the seller has no title to sell and must immediately apply for late first registration. The draft conveyance could be sufficient, but in the circumstances it would probably be better to adopt the form of transfer stated in r. 72 of the Land Registration Rules 1925 that could be used in first registration cases.

(2) Further documents required

(a) Public index map search. The property is not registered, but should have been when the seller bought the property. It is therefore necessary to submit a late first registration application; but before this goes off, an index map search should be sent to the Land Registry. This search is vital because it will reveal if some or all of the property is already registered or is subject to a pending application for registration. The search result will also show if there is a caution against first registration. A clear result will be required by any prudent mortgagee.

(b) The property is in Selby in Yorkshire. This is an area that to common knowledge is one affected by coal mining. (Even if it were in another area of Yorkshire, a coal mining search could still be required and the Law Society's booklet of coal mining areas should always be consulted for counties like Yorkshire.) In these circumstances a coal mining search result is absolutely vital to the lender, and indeed to the buyer. The search result will show if the property is in an area of active coal mining, proposed coal mining or past coal mining. It will also disclose underground workings that could give rise to subsidence and whether or not there has been compensation paid in respect of past subsidence damage. A clear result will be required by a prudent mortgagee.

(c) A commons registration search will be required as the property seems to be on the edge of town. The search result will reveal if the property is affected by any registrations under the Commons Registration Act 1965, including common land rights and other adverse matters. A clear result will be required by a prudent mortgagee.

(d) Purchase deed. A redraft of this would be sensible given the problems with the title, and it should follow the requirements of r.72 of the Land Registration Rules 1925.

(e) Local search. If necessary another local search result will be required to ensure that there is a result less than three months old at the time of completion.

(f) Enquiries and requisitions. Additional enquiries and requisitions should be raised that are specific to the property and the title, and particularly to the buyer's requirement of the seller to apply for an expedited late first registration application.

(g) There seems to be no final search in the Land Charges Registry. In view of the fact that the property remains unregistered it is vital to carry out such a search as this will certainly be required by the Land Registry on the application for first registration.

(3) Steps to be taken to perfect the security
The following steps will be required to ensure that the Society has a valid and enforceable first charge against this freehold property:

(a) First and foremost, the seller must be required to make title by submitting an expedited late first registration application. Once this has been completed, proper title must be deduced by way of office copy entries and an office copy of the filed plan.

(b) The local search must be renewed and the result approved.

(c) A coal mining as well as a commons registration search must be obtained and the results approved.

(d) A bankruptcy searc ı must be made against the borrower Winston Asika and the result must be clear. The Society cannot lend to an undischarged bankrupt and would not want to lend to someone involved in pending insolvency proceedings.

(e) A Land Registry search must be made in the name of the Society in connection with their proposed loan and the result must not disclose any adverse entries. A search in the name of the buyer would not confer any priority on the Society and it is for this reason that the search must be in the name of the Society.

(f) A mortgage form must be sent to Mr Asika for him to sign, along with a strong recommendation that he take legal advice on the terms and effect of the mortgage. The mortgage will be in the Society's standard form, and as such no amendments by the borrower to the contents of the mortgage will be permitted. His signature should be witnessed by a solicitor or licensed conveyancer.

(g)   A report on title should then be submitted to the Society confirming that the property will now be an acceptable security for their loan, and the advance monies should be requested.

(h)   On receipt of the mortgage advance Mr Asika should be requested to attend at our offices to complete. In exchange for the deeds the advance monies can be passed to him. Completion must take place within the priority period of the Land Registry search.

(i)   Completion should be reported to the Society.

(j)   After completion and still within the search priority period, the registration application should be submitted to the Land Registry for the registration of the first mortgage in favour of the High Windmill Equitable Building Society.

(k)   Once the registration application has been completed the Charge Certificate should be checked for errors made by the Land Registry; and if it is all correct the Charge Certificate and other deeds and documents should be sent to the Society for it to retain until the loan has been repaid.

QUESTION 5

(a)   Arthur Black wants to buy Pussy Cottage, Skelmersdale, from Richard Diver at a price of £45,000. The parties have negotiated the terms of the transaction without using agents. Arthur does not need a mortgage and can proceed quickly because Richard needs to move out expeditiously. To cement the deal, Arthur paid Richard a deposit of £450 in cash and they shook hands and agreed to complete in exactly three weeks' time. A receipt was issued signed by Mr Diver recording the parties, the property and the price. Two days later Arthur called around again to find Richard already packing, and so he paid him another £4,050 to make up the full 10%. Two days later Arthur got a note from Richard to say he had another higher offer and was not going to sell to him. Arthur believes he has a legal contract and wants to enforce the agreement. Can he?

(5 Marks)

(b)   Diana Spense has agreed to buy the freehold house at 11 Hiphigh View, Stiltown in Wiltshire from Charles Quince at a proposed price of £100,000. The property was part let with there being an elderly tenant living in the top floor under a shorthold tenancy agreement, but the rest of the house on the other three floors is empty. Ms Spense has had a survey which confirmed that the property was in good order, and as she is a cash buyer contracts have been exchanged with completion being two months hence. The contract states that the property is sold subject to and with the benefit of the tenancy of the top floor. Since exchange the tenant has left and Charles Quince wants to re-let to ensure his rental income continues. Can he?   (5 Marks)

(c)   Tim Harris has exchanged contracts on his purchase of 33 Monument View, Madeley Heath, Lincolnshire, and is due to complete next week. The contract incorporates the Standard Conditions of Sale (second edition). At the weekend there was a cold snap and a pipe froze in the house. When the thaw set in on Monday, a pipe burst causing damage to the property that will cost a minimum of £6,500 to put right. Tim wants to know if he is liable to pay for the repairs required as a result of the frost damage. Is he?   (10 Marks)

Commentary

This three-part question is contained within this chapter as it is a good example of how an examiner will sometimes mix several different topics into a one multi-part question. In this case you have subjects based on topics from areas both before as well as after exchange of contracts. The intention of the examiner is of course to test the breadth of your knowledge. In this particular example you must also be able to exhibit an ability to demonstrate your knowledge of case law and to apply that knowledge to the scenarios within the question.

The first part of the question goes to the heart of any conveyance, namely the existence or otherwise of a contract. You will be required to show your knowledge of the recent statutory changes in this area. The second part deals with changes to the property or the occupants after exchange and before completion. There is much case law on this, and you will need to be able to refer to cases and substantiate your assertions. The last part touches upon the thorny problem of insurance and who does what when the property is affected by an insurable risk. In this part a good knowledge of the Standard Conditions will be required.

You will therefore appreciate that this kind of question is perhaps more academic than some others you will have encountered. Furthermore, it is the kind that can be answered in an essay format. It is also the case that a good answer will require an overall knowledge of the whole process of conveyancing. Lastly, you should note the apportionment of the available marks and adjust your time and answer accordingly to ensure that your effort in the third section is greater than in the first two. After all, half of the available marks can be obtained in this part alone.

Suggested Answer

(a)   Arthur Black ('the buyer') wants to try to force Richard Diver ('the seller') to sell to him Pussy Cottage for £45,000. He believes that there is an agreement between them and wants to enforce it. In essence, therefore, what is needed is to establish whether or not there is a binding agreement between the buyer and the seller that can be enforced, if necessary, in the courts.

Whether or not the buyer will be able to enforce the agreement depends on whether s. 2 of the Law of Property (Miscellaneous Provisions) Act 1989 has been complied with. This requires that a contract for the sale and purchase of an estate in land must be in writing, must contain all the terms expressly agreed and be signed by all the parties. In this case there may have been a document purporting to be a deposit receipt that could be construed as a contract. However, if it was a contract, and while it was in writing, it may not have contained all the express terms, and it was certainly not signed by all the parties. If the facts of the purported contract are examined it will be seen that all the terms were not recorded in the receipt as it did not mention the size of the deposit to be paid or the date for completion. Of greater consequence is the fact that the buyer did not sign the document. Without all the signatures on the receipt there is no possibility of it being construed as a contract. Accordingly in these circumstances it is clear that there can be no enforceable and binding contract between the buyer and the seller as a result of the operation of statute.

Lastly, it is of interest to note that had this set of facts occurred before the above Act became effective (27 September 1989), then these circumstances could well have given rise to an enforceable agreement. This would have arisen from the effects of the now repealed s. 40 of the Law of Property Act 1925 and the outmoded doctrine of part performance. However, on the present facts and current law no contract can exist between Arthur Black and Richard Diver.

(b)   Ms Spense has contracted to buy a part possession property from Mr Quince and completion is due shortly. The tenant mentioned in the contract has vacated and Mr Quince wishes to replace the departed tenant with a fresh tenant. Whether or not he can do this depends upon his duty to take reasonable care of the property now that contracts have been exchanged.

Once contracts have been exchanged the seller is required to take reasonable care of the property. While the seller remains the legal owner, the buyer has an equitable interest as a result of the contract. The case of *Clarke* v *Ramuz* [1891] 2 QB 456 established that there is a duty on the seller to maintain the property in the condition it was in at the date of the contract. Does this therefore mean that the logical extension of this duty is to maintain the occupancy of a tenant, albeit a new one? In fact the case of *Abdulla* v *Shah* [1959] AC 124 made it clear that it is a breach of the seller's duty to take care if the seller lets the property and thereby creates a protected tenancy. Indeed, if the contract between the parties incorporates the Standard Conditions then condition 3 applies. Condition 3.2.2(b) requires the seller to inform the buyer without delay if the lease ends, and the definition of 'lease' includes a tenancy. The seller is then to act as the buyer reasonably directs although the buyer is to indemnify the seller against all consequent loss and expense.

Accordingly, if the Standard Conditions apply the seller cannot re-let without the buyer approving; and even if they do not apply the seller could be in breach of the duty to take reasonable care.

(c)   Tim Harris is the contractual purchaser of 33 Monument View, where completion is due next week. Due to a cold snap the property has been damaged by a burst pipe and the cost of repair could exceed £6,500. Not unnaturally, the buyer wants to know if he is liable in view of the expense involved. In the absence of any conditions in the contract the insurance risk passes to a buyer on exchange of contracts. This is because the insurable risk runs with the buyer's equitable interest, being the beneficial owner behind the trust of the legal estate. (See *Lysaght* v *Edwards* [1876] 2 Ch D 499.) However, in relation to the purchase by Mr Harris, the buyer's liability will be controlled by the effect of the Standard Conditions.

Standard Condition 5 provides that pending completion the responsibility for the property rests with the seller. Condition 5.1.1 says that the seller will transfer the property in the same physical state as it was at the date of the contract (except for fair wear and tear), which means that the seller retains the risk until completion. Condition 5.1.2 enables the buyer to rescind the contract if the property, at any time before completion, has been damaged so badly that it has become unusable for its purpose. It is not clear from the facts above if this is so, but judging from the amount concerned, £6,500, it is unlikely that the property has become completely unusable. In these circumstances it may well be that the remedy of rescission will not be available to Mr Harris.

Accordingly, it is clear that the Standard Conditions under which Mr Harris contracted to buy the property ensured that the seller retained the risk until completion unless the Special Conditions amended Standard Condition 5.1. The facts set out above are silent as to whether or not there are any Special Conditions. In the absence of Special Conditions the Standard Conditions apply and the risk remains with the seller. This being so it should also be noted that Standard Condition 5.1.3 states that the seller is under no obligation to the buyer to insure the property! This is really a very unsatisfactory state of affairs in that the Standard Conditions on the one hand require the risk to remain with the seller and yet on the other hand do not require the seller to insure! This undesirable circumstance might have been altered by a Special Condition requiring the seller to insure, but again, from the facts it is not clear if there was such a Special Condition.

To sum up, the contract would appear to make the seller responsible for the insurance risk for this property, and as such Mr Harris must hope that the seller is insured. (In passing it should be noted that a prudent solicitor acting for a buyer under a Standard Condition contract should always ask if the seller has the property insured, and should also change the contract to make sure the seller's insurance continues right up to completion.) As the risk is with the seller and damage has occurred, the seller should deal with the repairs; but if the property is unusable the buyer may have a right to rescind. Lastly, to complicate matters further there is the difficulty that even if the seller is insured the insurance company could repudiate the claim. Many policies provide that if the property has been empty for more than 30 days the cover they offer will not extend to damage occasioned from certain risks, including water damage!

Appendix 1: Chapter 3, Question 1

Draft contract for sale of 19 Minster Yard, Blakey

AGREEMENT

(Incorporating the Standard Conditions of Sale (second edition))

Agreement date   :
                                               come House

Seller   : Reverend Giggs of 19 Minster Lane
                                               Blakey Cornshire

Buyer   : Martin Dobson and Sandra Ince of 24
                                               Lady Jane Court Blakey Cornshire

Property (freehold/leasehold)   : All that land and building erected
                                               thereon known as 19 Minster Yard
                                               Blakey Cornshire which is more par-
                                               ticularly delineated on the plan an-
                                               nexed hereto and thereon edged red

Root of title/Title Number   : Conveyance on sale

Incumbrances on the Property   :

Seller sells as   : Legal owner

Completion date	: 4 weeks from the date hereof
Contract rate	: 4% above the Law Society interest rate for the time being in force
Purchase price	: £190,500
Deposit	: £19,050
Amount payable for chattels	: Nil
Balance	: £171,550

The Seller will sell and the Buyer will buy the Property for the Purchase price.

SPECIAL CONDITIONS

1. (a) This Agreement incorporates the Standard Conditions of Sale (Second Edition). Where there is a conflict between those Conditions and this Agreement, this Agreement prevails.

    (b) Terms used or defined in this Agreement have the same meaning when used in the Conditions.

2. The Property is sold subject to the Incumbrances on the Property and the Buyer will raise no requisitions on them.

3. The chattels on the Property and set out on any attached list are included in the sale.

4. The Property is sold with vacant possession on completion.

(or)

4. The Property is sold subject to the following leases or tenancies:

5. The latest time for completion shall be 12 noon.

6. The deposit shall be held by the Seller's solicitors as agent for the Seller.

7. The Buyer having previously inspected the Property admits entering into this Agreement in reliance upon the knowledge gained from such inspection and not from any statement or representation made by the Seller or any person on behalf of the Seller before the date hereof.

Seller's Solicitors   :

Buyer's Solicitors   :

Appendix 2: Chapter 3, Question 2

Copy title entries of 13 Augustine Way, Kerwick
Specimen Register

HM Land Registry

TITLE NUMBER: CS72510

Edition date: 31 August 1990

Entry No.	A. PROPERTY REGISTER containing the description of the registered land and the estate comprised in the Title
	COUNTY DISTRICT CORNSHIRE MARADON
1.	(19 December 1989) The Freehold land shown edged with red on the plan of the above Title filed at the Registry and being 13 Augustine Way, Kerwick.
2.	(19 December 1989) The land has the benefit of a right of way on foot only over the passageway at the rear leading into Monks Mead.

Entry No.	B. PROPRIETORSHIP REGISTER stating nature of the Title, name, address and description of the proprietor of the land and any entries affecting the right of disposing thereof TITLE ABSOLUTE
1.	(31 August 1990) Proprietor(s): PAUL JOHN DAWKINS and ANGELA MARY DAWKINS both of 13 Augustine Way, Kerwick, Maradon, Cornshire.
2.	(31 August 1990) RESTRICTION: Except under an order of the registrar no disposition by the proprietor(s) of the land is to be registered without the consent of the proprietor(s) of the Charge dated 29 July 1990 in favour of Weyford Building Society referred to in the Charges Register.

Entry No.	C. CHARGES REGISTER containing charges, incumbrances etc. adversely affecting the land and registered dealings therewith
1.	(19 December 1989) A Conveyance of the land in this title and other land dated 19 May 1924 made between (1) Allen Ansell (Vendor) and (2) Frances Amelia Moss (Purchaser) contains the following covenants:- "And the purchaser for herself her heirs executors administrators and assigns hereby covenants with the Vendor his heirs and assigns that she will perform and observe the stipulations set out in the First Schedule hereto so far as they relate to the hereditaments hereby assured THE FIRST SCHEDULE above referred to (a) No caravan shall be allowed upon the premises and the Vendor or owner or owners of adjoining premises may remove and dispose of any such caravan and for that purpose may forcibly enter upon

Continued on the next page

Specimen Register

HM Land Registry

TITLE NUMBER: CS725

Entry No.	C. CHARGES REGISTER (continued)
	any land upon which a breach of this stipulation shall occur and shall not be responsible for the safe keeping of any such caravan or for the loss thereof or any damage thereto or to any fence or wall
	(b) No earth gravel or sand shall at any time be excavated or dug out of the land except for the purpose of excavations in connection with the buildings erected on the land and no bricks or tiles shall at any time be burnt or made nor any clay or lime be burnt on the land."
2.	(19 December 1989) The passageway at the side included in the title is subject to rights of way on foot only.
3.	(31 August 1990) A Transfer of the land in this title dated 29 July 1990 made between (1) JOHN EDWARD CHARLES BROWN and (2) PAUL JOHN DAWKINS and ANGELA MARY DAWKINS contains restrictive covenants. NOTE:- Copy in Certificate
4.	(31 August 1990) REGISTERED CHARGE dated 29 July 1990 to secure the moneys including the further advances therein mentioned.
5.	(31 August 1990) Proprietor(s): WEYFORD BUILDING SOCIETY of Society House, The Avenue, Weymouth, Cornshire.

* * * * * END OF REGISTER * * * * *

NOTE A: A date at the beginning of an entry is the date on which the entry was made in the Register.

NOTE B: This certificate was officially examined with the register on **31 August 1990.**
          This date should be stated on any application for an official search based on this certificate.

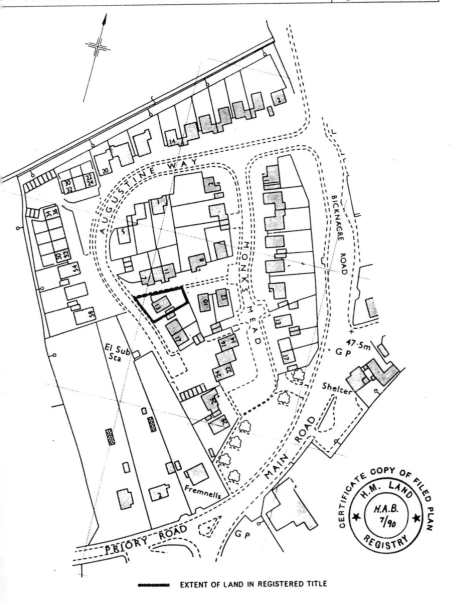

	TITLE NUMBER
H.M. LAND REGISTRY	**CS72510**

ONANCE SURVEY\nN REFERENCE	TL 7802	SECTION U	Scale\n1/1250 Enlarged from 1/2500
NTY CORNSHIRE	DISTRICT MARADON		© Crown copyright 1977

AUGUSTINE WAY

BICKNACRE ROAD

MONKS MEAD

El Sub
Sta

47·5m
G P

Shelter

MAIN ROAD

Fremnells

PRIORY ROAD

G P

CERTIFICATE COPY OF FILED
H.M. LAND
H.A.B.
7/90
REGISTRY
PLAN

EXTENT OF LAND IN REGISTERED TITLE

Appendix 3: Chapter 3, Question 2

Suggested draft contract for sale of 13 Augustine Way, Kerwick

AGREEMENT

(Incorporating the Standard Conditions of Sale (Second Edition)

Agreement date	:	
Seller	:	ANGELA MARY DAWKINS of 13 Augustine Way Kerwick Maradon Cornshire
Buyer	:	ANDREW PEACH of 25 Woodlands Road Kerwick Maradon Cornshire
Property (freehold/~~leasehold~~)	:	13 Augustine Way Kerwick Maradon Cornshire registered at HM Land Registry with Title Absolute
~~Root of title~~/Title Number	:	CS 72510
Incumbrances on the Property	:	Entries 1, 2 and 3 in the Charges Register of the Title
Seller sells as	:	Beneficial owner
Completion date	:	
Contract rate	:	The Law Society's interest rate from time to time in force
Purchase price	:	£70,000
Deposit	:	£7,000
Amount payable for chattels	:	£500
Balance	:	£63,500

The Seller will sell and the Buyer will buy the Property for the Purchase price.

The Agreement continues on the back page.

WARNING
This is a formal document, designed to create legal rights and legal obligations. Take advice before using it.

Signed

Seller/Buyer

STANDARD CONDITIONS OF SALE (SECOND EDITION)

(NATIONAL CONDITIONS OF SALE 22nd EDITION, LAW SOCIETY'S CONDITIONS OF SALE 1992)

GENERAL

Definitions

1 In these conditions:

(a) "accrued interest" means:

(i) if money has been placed on deposit or in a building society share account, the interest actually earned

(ii) otherwise, the interest which might reasonably have been earned by depositing the money at interest on seven days' notice of withdrawal with a clearing bank

less, in either case, any proper charges for handling the money

(b) "agreement" means the contractual document which incorporates these conditions, with or without amendment

(c) "banker's draft" means a draft drawn by and on a clearing bank

(d) "clearing bank" means a bank which is a member of CHAPS and Town Clearing Company Limited

(e) "completion date", unless defined in the agreement, has the meaning given in condition 6.1.1

(f) "contract" means the bargain between the seller and the buyer of which these conditions, with or without amendment, form part

(g) "contract rate", unless defined in the agreement, is the Law Society's interest rate from time to time in force

(h) "lease" includes sub-lease, tenancy and agreement for a lease or sub-lease

(i) "notice to complete" means a notice requiring completion of the contract in accordance with condition 6

(j) "public requirement" means any notice, order or proposal given or made (whether before or after the date of the contract) by a body acting on statutory authority

(k) "requisition" includes objection

(l) "solicitor" includes barrister, duly certificated notary public, recognised licensed conveyancer and recognised body under sections 9 or 32 of the Administration of Justice Act 1985

(m) "transfer" includes conveyance and assignment

(n) "working day" means any day from Monday to Friday (inclusive) which is not Christmas Day, Good Friday or a statutory Bank Holiday.

2 When used in these conditions the terms "absolute title" and "office copies" have the special meanings given to them by the Land Registration Act 1925.

Joint parties

If there is more than one seller or more than one buyer, the obligations which they undertake can be enforced against them all jointly or against each individually.

Notices and documents

1 A notice required or authorised by the contract must be in writing.

2 Giving a notice or delivering a document to a party's solicitor has the same effect as giving or delivering it to that party.

3 Transmission by fax is a valid means of giving a notice or delivering a document where delivery of the original document is not essential.

4 Subject to conditions 1.3.5 to 1.3.7, a notice is given and a document delivered when it is received.

5 If a notice or document is received after 4.00pm on a working day, or on a day which is not a working day, it is to be treated as having been received on the next working day.

6 Unless the actual time of receipt is proved, a notice or document sent by the following means is to be treated as having been received before 4.00pm on the day shown below:

(a) by first-class post:	two working days after posting
(b) by second-class post:	three working days after posting
(c) through a document exchange:	on the first working day after the day on which it would normally be available for collection by the addressee.

7 Where a notice or document is sent through a document exchange, then for the purposes of condition 1.3.6 the actual time of receipt is:

(a) the time when the addressee collects it from the document exchange or, if earlier

(b) 8.00am on the first working day on which it is available for collection at that time.

VAT

1 An obligation to pay money includes an obligation to pay any value added tax chargeable in respect of that payment.

2 All sums made payable by the contract are exclusive of value added tax.

FORMATION

Date

1 If the parties intend to make a contract by exchanging duplicate copies by post or through a document exchange, the contract is made when the last copy is posted or deposited at the document exchange.

2 If the parties' solicitors agree to treat exchange as taking place before duplicate copies are actually exchanged, the contract is made as so agreed.

Deposit

1 The buyer is to pay or send a deposit of 10 per cent of the purchase price no later than the date of the contract. Except on a sale by auction, payment is to be made by banker's draft or by a cheque drawn on a solicitors' clearing bank account.

2 If before completion date the seller agrees to buy another property in England and Wales for his residence, he may use all or any part of the deposit as a deposit in that transaction to be held on terms to the same effect as this condition and condition 2.2.3.

3 Any deposit or part of a deposit not being used in accordance with condition 2.2.2 is to be held by the seller's solicitor as stakeholder on terms that on completion it is paid to the seller with accrued interest.

4 If a cheque tendered in payment of all or part of the deposit is dishonoured when first presented, the seller may, within seven working days of being notified that the cheque has been dishonoured, give notice to the buyer that the contract is discharged by the buyer's breach.

Auctions

1 On a sale by auction the following conditions apply to the property and, if it is sold in lots, to each lot.

2 The sale is subject to a reserve price.

3 The seller, or a person on his behalf, may bid up to the reserve price.

4 The auctioneer may refuse any bid.

5 If there is a dispute about a bid, the auctioneer may resolve the dispute or restart the auction at the last undisputed bid.

MATTERS AFFECTING THE PROPERTY

Freedom from incumbrances

1 The seller is selling the property free from incumbrances, other than those mentioned in condition 3.1.2.

3.1.2 The incumbrances subject to which the property is sold are:

(a) those mentioned in the agreement

(b) those discoverable by inspection of the property before the contract

(c) those the seller does not and could not know about

(d) entries made before the date of the contract in any public register except those maintained by HM Land Registry or its Land Charges Department or by Companies House

(e) public requirements.

3.1.3 The buyer accepts the property in the physical state it is in at the date of the contract, unless the seller is building or converting it.

3.1.4 After the contract is made, the seller is to give the buyer written details without delay of any new public requirement and of anything in writing which he learns about concerning any incumbrances subject to which the property is sold.

3.1.5 The buyer is to bear the cost of complying with any outstanding public requirement and is to indemnify the seller against any liability resulting from a public requirement.

3.2 **Leases affecting the property**

3.2.1 The following provisions apply if the agreement states that any part of the property is sold subject to a lease

3.2.2 (a) The seller having provided the buyer with full details of each lease or copies of the documents embodying the lease terms, the buyer is treated as entering into the contract knowing and fully accepting those terms

(b) The seller is to inform the buyer without delay if the lease ends or if the seller learns of any application by the tenant in connection with the lease; the seller is then to act as the buyer reasonably directs, and the buyer is to indemnify him against all consequent loss and expense

(c) The seller is not to agree to any proposal to change the lease terms without the consent of the buyer and is to inform the buyer without delay of any change which may be proposed or agreed

(d) The buyer is to indemnify the seller against all claims arising from the lease after actual completion; this includes claims which are unenforceable against a buyer for want of registration

(e) The seller takes no responsibility for what rent is lawfully recoverable, nor for whether or how any legislation affects the lease

(f) If the let land is not wholly within the property, the seller may apportion the rent.

3.3 **Retained land**

3.3.1 The following provisions apply where after the transfer the seller will be retaining land near the property.

3.3.2 The buyer will have no right of light or air over the retained land, but otherwise the seller and the buyer will each have the rights over the land of the other which they would have had if they were two separate buyers to whom the seller had made simultaneous transfers of the property and the retained land.

3.3.3 Either party may require that the transfer contain appropriate express terms.

4. TITLE AND TRANSFER

4.1 **Timetable**

4.1.1 The following are the steps for deducing and investigating the title to the property to be taken within the following time limits:

Step	Time Limit
1. The seller is to send the buyer evidence of title in accordance with condition 4.2	Immediately after making the contract
2. The buyer may raise written requisitions	Six working days after either the date of the contract or the date of delivery of the seller's evidence of title on which the requisitions are raised whichever is the later
3. The seller is to reply in writing to any requisitions raised	Four working days after receiving the requisitions
4. The buyer may make written observations on the seller's replies	Three working days after receiving the replies

The time limit on the buyer's right to raise requisitions applies even where the seller supplies incomplete evidence of his title, but the buyer may, within six working days from delivery of any further evidence, raise further requisitions resulting from that evidence. On the expiry of the relevant time limit the buyer loses his right to raise requisitions or make observations.

4.1.2 The parties are to take the following steps to prepare and agree the transfer of the property within the following time limits:

Step	Time Limit
A. The buyer is to send the seller a draft transfer	At least twelve working days before completion date
B. The seller is to approve or revise that draft and either return it or retain it for use as the actual transfer	Four working days after delivery of the draft transfer
C. If the draft is returned the buyer is to send an engrossment to the seller	At least five working days before completion date

4.1.3 Periods of time under conditions 4.1.1 and 4.1.2 may run concurrently.

4.1.4 If the period between the date of the contract and completion date is less than 15 working days, the time limits in conditions 4.1.1 and 4.1.2 are to be reduced by the same proportion as that period bears to the period of 15 working days. Fractions of a working day are to be rounded down except that the time limit to perform any step is not to be less than one working day.

4.2 **Proof of title**

4.2.1 The evidence of registered title is office copies of the items required to be furnished by section 110(1) of the Land Registration Act 1925 and the copies, abstracts and evidence referred to in section 110(2).

4.2.2 The evidence of unregistered title is an abstract of the title, or an epitome of title with photocopies of the relevant documents.

4.2.3 Where the title to the property is unregistered, the seller is to produce to the buyer (without cost to the buyer):

(a) the original of every relevant document, or

(b) an abstract, epitome or copy with an original marking by a solicitor of examination either against the original or against an examined abstract or against an examined copy.

4.3 **Defining the property**

4.3.1 The seller need not:

(a) prove the exact boundaries of the property

(b) prove who owns fences, ditches, hedges or walls

(c) seperately identify parts of the property with different titles

further than he may be able to do from information in his possession.

4.3.2 The buyer may, if it is reasonable, require the seller to make or obtain, pay for and hand over a statutory declaration about facts relevant to the matters mentioned in condition 4.3.1. The form of the declaration is to be agreed by the buyer, who must not unreasonably withhold his agreement.

4.4 **Rents and rentcharges**

The fact that a rent or rentcharge, whether payable or receivable by the owner of the property, has been or will on completion be, informally apportioned is not to be regarded as a defect in title.

4.5 **Transfer**

4.5.1 The buyer does not prejudice his right to raise requisitions, or to require replies to any raised, by taking any steps in relation to the preparation or agreement of the transfer.

4.5.2 The seller is to transfer the property in the capacity specified in the agreement, or (if none is specified) as beneficial owner.

4.5.3 If after completion the seller will remain bound by any obligation affecting the property, but the law does not imply any covenant by the buyer to indemnify the seller against liability for future breaches of it:
(a) the buyer is to covenant in the transfer to indemnify the seller against liability for any future breach of the obligation and to perform it from then on, and
(b) if required by the seller, the buyer is to execute and deliver to the seller on completion a duplicate transfer prepared by the buyer.

4.5.4 The seller is to arrange at his expense that, in relation to every document of title which the buyer does not receive on completion, the buyer is to have the benefit of:
(a) a written acknowledgement of his right to its production, and
(b) a written undertaking for its safe custody (except while it is held by a mortgagee or by someone in a fiduciary capacity).

5. **PENDING COMPLETION**

5.1 **Responsibility for property**

5.1.1 The seller will transfer the property in the same physical state as it was at the date of the contract (except for fair wear and tear), which means that the seller retains the risk until completion.

5.1.2 If at any time before completion the physical state of the property makes it unusable for its purpose at the date of the contract:
(a) the buyer may rescind the contract
(b) the seller may rescind the contract where the property has become unusable for that purpose as a result of damage against which the seller could not reasonably have insured, or which it is not legally possible for the seller to make good.

5.1.3 The seller is under no obligation to the buyer to insure the property.

5.1.4 Section 47 of the Law of Property Act 1925 does not apply.

5.2 **Occupation by buyer**

5.2.1 If the buyer is not already lawfully in the property, and the seller agrees to let him into occupation, the buyer occupies on the following terms.

5.2.2 The buyer is a licensee and not a tenant. The terms of the licence are that the buyer:
(a) cannot transfer it
(b) may permit members of his household to occupy the property
(c) is to pay or indemnify the seller against all outgoings and other expenses in respect of the property
(d) is to pay the seller a fee calculated at the contract rate on the purchase price (less any deposit paid) for the period of the licence
(e) is entitled to any rents and profits from any part of the property which he does not occupy
(f) is to keep the property in as good a state of repair as it was in when he went into occupation (except for fair wear and tear) and is not to alter it
(g) is to insure the property in a sum which is not less than the purchase price against all risks in respect of which comparable premises are normally insured
(h) is to quit the property when the licence ends.

5.2.3 On the creation of the buyer's licence, condition 5.1 ceases to apply, which means that the buyer then assumes the risk until completion.

5.2.4 The buyer is not in occupation for the purposes of this condition if he merely exercises rights of access given solely to do work agreed by the seller.

5.2.5 The buyer's licence ends on the earliest of: completion date, rescission of the contract or when five working days' notice given by one party to the other takes effect.

5.2.6 If the buyer is in occupation of the property after his licence has come to an end and the contract is subsequently completed he is to pay the seller compensation for his continued occupation calculated at the same rate as the fee mentioned in condition 5.2.2(d).

5.2.7 The buyer's right to raise requisitions is unaffected.

6. **COMPLETION**

6.1 **Date**

6.1.1 Completion date is twenty working days after the date of the contract but time is not of the essence of the contract unless a notice to complete has been served.

6.1.2 If the money due on completion is received after 2.00pm, completion is to be treated, for the purposes only of conditions 6.3 and 7.3, as taking place on the next working day.

6.1.3 Condition 6.1.2 does not apply where the sale is with vacant possession of the property or any part and the seller has not vacated the property or that part by 2.00pm on the date of actual completion.

6.2 **Place**
Completion is to take place in England and Wales, either at the seller's solicitor's office or at some other place which the seller reasonably specifies.

6.3 **Apportionments**

6.3.1 Income and outgoings of the property are to be apportioned between the parties so far as the change of ownership on completion will affect entitlement to receive or liability to pay them.

6.3.2 If the whole property is sold with vacant possession or the seller exercises his option in condition 7.3.4, apportionment is to be made with effect from the date of actual completion; otherwise, it is to be made from completion date.

6.3.3 In apportioning any sum, it is to be assumed that the seller owns the property until the end of the day from which apportionment is made and that the sum accrues from day to day at the rate at which it is payable on that day.

6.3.4 For the purpose of apportioning income and outgoings, it is to be assumed that they accrue at an equal daily rate throughout the year.

6.3.5 When a sum to be apportioned is not known or easily ascertainable at completion, a provisional apportionment is to be made according to the best estimate available. As soon as the amount is known, a final apportionment is to be made and notified to the other party. Any resulting balance is to be paid no more than ten working days later, and if not then paid the balance is to bear interest at the contract rate from then until payment.

6.3.6 Compensation payable under condition 5.2.6 is not to be apportioned.

6.4 **Amount payable**
The amount payable by the buyer on completion is the purchase price (less any deposit already paid to the seller or his agent) adjusted to take account of:
(a) apportionments made under condition 6.3
(b) any compensation to be paid or allowed under condition 7.3.

6.5 **Title deeds**

6.5.1 The seller is not to retain the documents of title after the buyer has tendered the amount payable under condition 6.4.

6.5.2 Condition 6.5.1 does not apply to any documents of title relating to land being retained by the seller after completion.

6.6 **Rent receipts**
The buyer is to assume that whoever gave any receipt for a payment of rent or service charge which the seller produces was the person or the agent of the person then entitled to that rent or service charge.

6.7 **Means of payment**
The buyer is to pay the money due on completion in one or more of the following ways:
(a) legal tender
(b) a banker's draft
(c) a direct credit to a bank account nominated by the seller's solicitor
(d) an unconditional release of a deposit held by a stakeholder.

6.8 **Notice to complete**

6.8.1 At any time on or after completion date, a party who is ready able and complete may give the other a notice to complete.

6.8.2 A party is ready able and willing:
(a) if he could be, but for the default of the other party, and
(b) in the case of the seller, even though a mortgage remains secure property, if the amount to be paid on completion enables the prop transferred freed of all mortgages (except those to which the sale is subject)

6.8.3 The parties are to complete the contract within ten working days of notice to complete, excluding the day on which the notice is given purpose, time is of the essence of the contract.

6.8.4 On receipt of a notice to complete:
(a) if the buyer paid no deposit, he is forthwith to pay a deposit of 10
(b) if the buyer paid a deposit of less than 10 per cent, he is forthwith further deposit equal to the balance of that 10 per cent

7. **REMEDIES**

7.1 **Errors and omissions**

7.1.1 If any plan or statement in the contract, or in the negotiations leading was misleading or inaccurate due to an error or omission, the remedies are as follows.

7.1.2 When there is a material difference between the description or val property as represented and as it is, the injured party is entitled to dan

7.1.3 An error or omission only entitles the injured party to rescind the cont
(a) where it results from fraud or recklessness, or
(b) where he would be obliged, to his prejudice, to transfer or accept differing substantially (in quantity, quality or tenure) from what the omission had led him to expect.

7.2 **Rescission**
If either party rescinds the contract:
(a) unless the rescission is a result of the buyer's breach of contract th is to be repaid to the buyer with accrued interest
(b) the buyer is to return any documents he received from the seller cancel any registration of the contract.

7.3 **Late completion**

7.3.1 If there is default by either or both of the parties in performing their ob under the contract and completion is delayed, the party whose total default is the greater is to pay compensation to the other party

7.3.2 Compensation is calculated at the contract rate on the purchase price, the buyer is the paying party) the purchase price less any deposit pai period by which the paying party's default exceeds that of the receiv or, if shorter, the period between completion date and actual completi

7.3.3 Any claim for loss resulting from delayed completion is to be reduce compensation paid under this contract.

7.3.4 Where the buyer holds the property as tenant of the seller and com delayed, the seller may give notice to the buyer, before the date completion, that he intends to take the net income from the prop completion. If he does so, he cannot claim compensation under conditi as well.

7.4 **After completion**
Completion does not cancel liability to perform any outstanding obligat this contract.

7.5 **Buyer's failure to comply with notice to complete**

7.5.1 If the buyer fails to complete in accordance with a notice to comp following terms apply.

7.5.2 The seller may rescind the contract, and if he does so:
(a) he may
(i) forfeit and keep any deposit and accrued interest
(ii) resell the property
(iii) claim damages
(b) the buyer is to return any documents he received from the seller cancel any registration of the contract.

7.5.3 The seller retains his other rights and remedies.

7.6 **Seller's failure to comply with notice to complete**

7.6.1 If the seller fails to complete in accordance with a notice to complete, the terms apply.

7.6.2 The buyer may rescind the contract, and if he does so:
(a) the deposit is to be repaid to the buyer with accrued interest
(b) the buyer is to return any documents he received from the seller the seller's expense, to cancel any registration of the contract.

7.6.3 The buyer retains his other rights and remedies.

8. **LEASEHOLD PROPERTY**

8.1 **Existing leases**

8.1.1 The following provisions apply to a sale of leasehold land.

8.1.2 The seller having provided the buyer with copies of the documents en the lease terms, the buyer is treated as entering into the contract kno fully accepting those terms.

8.1.3 The seller is to comply with any lease obligations requiring the tenant the property.

8.1.4 The transfer is to record that no covenant implied by statute makes liable to the buyer for any breach of the lease terms about the conditi property. This applies even if the seller is to transfer as beneficial owne

8.2 **New leases**

8.2.1 The following provisions apply to a grant of a new lease.

8.2.2 The conditions apply so that:
"seller" means the proposed landlord
"buyer" means the proposed tenant
"purchase price" means the premium to be paid on the grant of a lease

8.2.3 The lease is to be in the form of the draft attached to the agreement.

8.2.4 If the term of the new lease will exceed 21 years, the seller is to dedu which will enable the buyer to register the lease at HM Land Registry absolute title.

8.2.5 The buyer is not entitled to transfer the benefit of the contract.

8.2.6 The seller is to engross the lease and a counterpart of it and is to counterpart to the buyer at least five working days before completion d

8.2.7 The buyer is to execute the counterpart and deliver it to the seller on co

8.3 **Landlord's consent**

8.3.1 The following provisions apply if a consent to assign or sub-let is re complete the contract.

8.3.2 (a) The seller is to apply for the consent at his expense, and to use all re efforts to obtain it
(b) The buyer is to provide all information and references reasonably re

8.3.3 The buyer is not entitled to transfer the benefit of the contract.

8.3.4 Unless he is in breach of his obligation under condition 8.3.2, either pa rescind the contract by notice to the other party if three working day completion date:
(a) the consent has not been given or
(b) the consent has been given subject to a condition to which th reasonably objects.
In that case, neither party is to be treated as in breach of contract and 7.2 applies.

9. **CHATTELS**

9.1 The following provisions apply to any chattels which are to be sold.

9.2 Whether or not a separate price is to be paid for the chattels, the contr effect as a contract for sale of goods.

9.3 Ownership of the chattels passes to the buyer on actual completion.

SPECIAL CONDITIONS

1. (a) This Agreement incorporates the Standard Conditions of Sale (Second Edition). Where there is a conflict between those Conditions and this Agreement, this Agreement prevails.

   (b) Terms used or defined in this Agreement have the same meaning when used in the Conditions.

2. The Property is sold subject to the Incumbrances on the Property and the Buyer will raise no requisitions on them.

3. The chattels on the Property and set out on any attached list are included in the sale.

4. The Property is sold with vacant possession on completion.

5. ~~The Property is sold subject to the following leases or tenancies:~~

5. The Buyer having inspected the Seller's title shall raise no objection to it or requisition on it.

Seller's Solicitors   :   Rodgers & Co

Buyer's Solicitors   :   Young & Price ·

©1992 **OYEZ** The Solicitors' Law Stationery Society Ltd.
Oyez House, 7 Spa Road, London SE16 3QQ

© 1992 **THE LAW SOCIETY**

4.92 F22381
5065046
* * * * *
2nd Edition

Standard Conditions of Sale

Appendix 4: Chapter 3, Question 4

Plan of 14 Wellington Road, Midchester

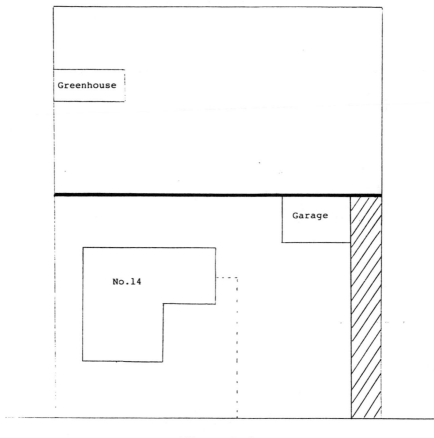

Appendix 5: Chapter 5, Question 1

Suggested Epitome of title of Tregavean, Ridgewood Close, Seatown

EPITOME OF TITLE

relating to FREEHOLD property
~~LEASEHOLD~~

known as __Tregavean Ridgewood Close Seatown__

Document Date	Number of Document	Details of Document	Parties	Indicate if Photocopy or Abstract	Indicate if Original Document to be handed over
uly 1963	1	Conveyance	(1) Richard Tyler (2) Ashley Perryman	Photocopy	Yes
iept 1974	2	Land charges search Certificate number	against names of Richard Tyler, Ashley Perryman and John Little	Photocopy	Yes
iept 1979	3	Power of Attorney	(1) Guy Budd (2) Steven Cox	Photocopy	Yes
iept 1979	4	Examined copy grant of probate of estate of Mary Ann Jessop deceased	granted to Guy Budd and Ann Budd	Photocopy	No
iov 1979	5	Land charges search Certificate number	against names of Mary Ann Jessop, Guy Budd, Ann Budd	Photocopy	Yes
iov 1979	6	Assent	(1) Guy Budd and Ann Budd (2) Philip Ross	Photocopy	Yes
Feb 1985	7	Lease	(1) Philip Ross (2) Peter Kay	Photocopy	Yes
Apr 1988	8	Deed of surrender	(1) Peter Kay (2) Philip Ross	Photocopy	Yes
June 1990	9	Land charges search Certificate number	against names of Philip Ross, Peter Kay, Christopher Browning and Jill Browning	Photocopy	Yes
June 1990	10	Conveyance	(1) Philip Ross (2) Christopher Browning and Jill Browning	Photocopy	Yes
June 1990	11	Legal Charge	(1) Christopher Browning and Jill Browning (2) Cornshire Building Society	Photocopy	Yes

1 Documents should be numbered consecutively for ease of reference.
2 List the relevant documents, for example deaths and marriages even though these will not be supplied, which show the title passing to successive owners over the last fifteen years.
3 Names of successive owners should be listed.
4 Photocopies of plans supplied should be coloured as the original.

Appendix 6: Chapter 5, Question 2

<u>ABSTRACT OF THE TITLE of Flora Nichol-</u>
<u>son to freehold property known as 'The Cor-</u>
<u>ner House' Chiltern Road Pitton in the County</u>
<u>of Cornshire</u>

7 January 1980

OFFICIAL CERTIFICATE of search in HM Land Charges Register No. 217432 against Charles Lane revealing no subsisting entries

13 January 1980
Stamp £1,000
P.D. Stamp

BY CONVEYANCE of this date made between CHARLES LANE of The Corner House Chiltern Road Pitton in the County of Cornshire (thereinafter called 'the vendor') of the one part and BENJAMIN EDWARDS of 24 Rothesay Avenue Pitton in the County of Cornshire (thereinafter called 'the purchaser') of the other part

RECITING seisin of the vendor and agreement for sale

IT WAS WITNESSED as follows:–
1. IN pursuance of the said agreement and in consideration of the sum of £50,000 paid to the vendor by the purchaser (receipt acknowledged) the vendor as beneficial owner thereby conveyed unto the purchaser ALL THAT premises fronting Chiltern Road Pitton aforesaid comprising 1.9 acres or thereabouts and delineated and described on a plan annexed to a Conveyance dated 18th January 1975 made between (1) Mark Ellins and (2) the said Charles Lane (hereinafter called 'the said Conveyance') AND ALSO ALL THAT messuage or dwellinghouse erected thereon and known as 'The Corner House' Chiltern Road Pitton aforesaid TOGETHER with the full benefit and advantage of the right of way granted by the said Conveyance over and along the road shown coloured brown on the said plan

TO HOLD unto the purchaser in fee simple SUBJECT to the covenants and the conditions contained in the said Conveyance

2. COVENANT by the purchaser with the vendor to observe and perform the said covenants and conditions and to indemnify

EXECUTED by both parties and ATTESTED

24 April 1986

OFFICIAL CERTIFICATE of search in HM Land Charges Register No. 328557 against Benjamin Edwards revealing no subsisting entries

20 June 1986

BY CONVEYANCE of this date made between the said BENJAMIN EDWARDS of 'The Corner House' Chiltern Road Pitton in the County of Cornshire (thereinafter called 'the vendor') of the one part and SHARON MUNRO of 49 Nobbs Hill Pitton in the County of Cornshire (thereinafter called 'the purchaser') of the other part

RECITING seisin of the vendor and agreement for sale

IT WAS WITNESSED as follows:-

1. IN pursuance of the said agreement and in consideration of the sum of £65,000 paid to the vendor by the purchaser (receipt acknowledged) the vendor as beneficial owner thereby conveyed unto the purchaser

ALL THAT the before abstracted premises together with the said dwellinghouse built thereon

TOGETHER with the full benefit and advantage of the before abstracted right of way

TO HOLD unto the purchaser in fee simple SUBJECT to the covenants and the conditions contained in the said Conveyance

2. COVENANT by the purchaser with the vendor to observe and perform the said covenants and conditions and to indemnify

EXECUTED by both parties and ATTESTED

20 June 1986   BY MORTGAGE of this date made between the said
                           SHARON MUNRO (thereinafter called 'the mort-
                           gagor') of the one part and BLAKEY BANK LTD of
                           10 High Street Blakey (thereinafter called 'the mort-
                           gagee') of the other part

                           After reciting seisin of Mortgagor in fee simple IT
                           WAS WITNESSED that in consideration of sum of
                           £40,000 paid by the mortgagee to the mortgagor
                           (receipt acknowledged) the mortgagor as beneficial
                           owner thereby charged unto the mortgagee

                           ALL THAT before abstracted property

                           PROVISO for cesser and other usual clauses
                           EXECUTED by mortgagor and ATTESTED

17 November 1990   WILL made on this date by the said SHARON
                           MUNRO appointing DUNCAN MUNRO and
                           SHEILA MUNRO, her parents, to be her executors

12 December 1990   Death of the said SHARON MUNRO

19 January 1991   Grant of Probate to the said will issued out of Blakey
                           District Probate Registry on this date to the said
                           DUNCAN MUNRO and SHEILA MUNRO

29 July 1991   BY ASSENT of this date the said DUNCAN MUNRO
                           and SHEILA MUNRO assented to the vesting of the
                           before abstracted property in ELIZABETH CAMP-
                           BELL

14 January 1994   BY CONVEYANCE of this date made between the
Stamp £900   said ELIZABETH CAMPBELL of The Corner
P.D. Stamp   House Chiltern Road Pitton in the County of Cornshire
                           (thereinafter called 'the vendor') of the one part
                           and   ALASTAIR   NICHOLSON   and   FLORA
                           NICHOLSON of 2 Mill Road Pitton in the County of
                           Cornshire (thereinafter called 'the purchasers') of the
                           other part

RECITING seisin of the vendor and agreement for sale

IT WAS WITNESSED as follows:–

1. IN pursuance of the said agreement and in consideration of the sum of £90,000 paid to the vendor by the purchaser (receipt acknowledged) the vendor as beneficial owner thereby conveyed unto the purchasers
ALL THAT the before abstracted premises together with the said dwellinghouse built thereon TOGETHER with the full benefit and advantage of the before abstracted right of way
TO HOLD unto the purchasers in fee simple as tenants in common in equity SUBJECT to the covenants and the conditions contained in the said Conveyance

2. COVENANT by the purchasers with the vendor to observe and perform the said covenants and conditions and to indemnify
EXECUTED by both parties and ATTESTED

14 January 1994   BY MORTGAGE of this date made between the said ALASTAIR NICHOLSON and FLORA NICHOLSON (thereinafter called 'the mortgagors') of the one part and CORNSHIRE BUILDING SOCIETY of 14 Broad Street Blakey (thereinafter called 'the mortgagee') of the other part

After reciting seisin of mortgagors in fee simple IT WAS WITNESSED that in consideration of sum of £65,000 paid by the mortgagee to the mortgagors (receipt acknowledged) the mortgagors as beneficial owners thereby charged unto the mortgagee

ALL THAT before abstracted property

PROVISO for cesser and other usual clauses
EXECUTED by mortgagors and ATTESTED

Appendix 7: Chapter 5, Question 4

Copy title entries of Flat 3, 125 Clothier Street, Kemptville

SPECIMEN

Edition date : 20 January 1995   TITLE NUMBER : CS92148

Entry No.	A. PROPERTY REGISTER
	containing the description of the registered land and the estate comprised in the Title
	Unless the contrary is indicated below any subsisting legal easements granted by the under-mentioned lease(s) for the benefit of the land in this title are included therein. The registration takes effect subject to any rights excepted and reserved by the said lease(s) so far as such rights are subsisting and affect the land in this title.
	COUNTY DISTRICT CORNSHIRE KEMPTVILLE
1.	(30 August 1960) The Leasehold land shown edged with red on the plan of the above Title filed at the Registry and being Flat 3, 125 Clothier Street, Kemptville, (KV3 8LU).

2.	Short particulars of the lease(s) (or under-lease(s)) under which the land is held:
	DATE : 17 August 1960
	TERM : 99 years from 27 July 1960
	RENT : £25
	PARTIES : 1. Marian Bell
	                   2. Margaret Elsie Logsdail and
	                     Constance Logsdail

3.	There are excepted from the effect of registration all estates, rights, interests, powers and remedies arising upon, or by reason of, any dealing made in breach of the prohibition or restriction against dealings therewith inter vivos contained in the Lease.
4.	Deed of Covenant dated 8 March 1984 made between (1) Margaret Elsie Logsdail and Constance Logsdail and (2) James Dawkins supplemental to the registered lease. NOTE:- Copy filed.

Entry No.	B. PROPRIETORSHIP REGISTER
	stating nature of the Title, name, address and description of the proprietor of the land and any entries affecting the right of disposing thereof TITLE GOOD LEASEHOLD
1.	(30 August 1960) Proprietor(s) : MARGARET ELSIE LOGSDAIL and CONSTANCE LOGSDAIL both of Flat 3, 125 Clothier Street, Kemptville, Cornshire KV3 8LU.
2.	(30 August 1960) RESTRICTION : No disposition by a sole proprietor of the land (not being a trust corporation) under which capital money arises is to be registered except under an order of the registrar or of the Court.
3.	(14 October 1994) CAUTION in favour of Stephen Longman (Finance) Ltd., care of Messrs. Parsley and Lion, Solicitors, Herb House, High Street, Kemptville, Cornshire.

Continued on the next page

SPECIMEN

Entry No.	C. CHARGES REGISTER containing charges, incumbrances etc., adversely affecting the land and registered dealings therewith
1.	(30 August 1960) REGISTERED CHARGE dated 17 August 1960 to secure the moneys including the further advances therein mentioned.
2.	(30 August 1960) Proprietor(s) : CORNSHIRE BUILDING SOCIETY of 3 Church Street, Kemptville, Cornshire.
3.	(14 June 1986) REGISTERED CHARGE dated 8 June 1986 to secure the moneys including the further advances therein mentioned.
4.	(14 June 1986) Proprietor(s) : PROVINCIAL FINANCE LIMITED of 10 High Street, Kemptville, Cornshire.
5.	(29 January 1991) REGISTERED CHARGE dated 4 January 1991 to secure the moneys including the further advances therein mentioned.
6.	(29 January 1991) Proprietor(s) : LENDALOT LIMITED of 12 Market Place, Kemptville, Cornshire.

**** END OF REGISTER ****

NOTE	: A date at the beginning of an entry is the date on which the entry was made in the Register.

Appendix 8: Chapter 7, Question 2

Suggested draft transfer of The Corner House, Chiltern Road, Pitton

HM Land Registry

Land Registration Acts 1925 to 1986

Transfer under Rule 72 Land Registration Rules 1925

County and district (or London borough): Cornshire Pitton

Property: The Corner House, Chiltern Road, Pitton

Date   19

In consideration of ninety thousand pounds (£90,000.00) receipt of which is acknowledged

I FLORA NICHOLSON of The Corner House, Chiltern Road, Pitton, Cornshire, doctor ('the Transferor') as beneficial owner transfer to:

TREVOR CLARKE (dentist) and KATHLEEN CLARKE (married woman) both of The Corner House, Chiltern Road aforesaid ('the Transferees') as beneficial joint tenants

the land fronting Chiltern Road, Pitton, Cornshire comprising 1.9 acres or thereabouts more particularly delineated and described on a plan annexed to a conveyance dated 18th January 1975 made between (1) Mark Ellins and (2) Charles Lane ('the Conveyance') TOGETHER WITH the benefit of a right of way contained in the Conveyance and SUBJECT to the covenants and conditions contained in the Conveyance

The Transferees (with the object of affording to the Transferor a full indemnity in respect of any breach but not further or otherwise) hereby jointly and severally covenant with the Transferor that the Transferees and the persons deriving title under them will at all times hereafter perform and observe the covenants and the conditions contained in the Conveyance and keep the Transferor and her estate and effects indemnified against all actions claims demands and liabilities in respect thereof so far as the same affect the land hereby transferred and are still subsisting and capable of being enforced.

The Transferees declare that the survivor of them can give a valid receipt for capital money arising on a disposition of the land hereby transferred.

Signed as a deed by
FLORA NICHOLSON

in the presence of
Name of Witness
Address
Occupation

Signed as a deed by
TREVOR CLARKE and
KATHLEEN CLARKE

in the presence of
Name of Witness
Address
Occupation

Index